THE INFORMATION ANIMAL

'A rich historical analysis and innovative framework for understanding how humans and technology shape each other through the spread of ideas. Coming at a critical time, it is an essential guide for how democratic societies can navigate the information challenges of today and the future.'

— Mariano-Florentino Cuéllar, President of the Carnegie Endowment for International Peace

'A sharp, essential guide to understanding the information environment before trying to fix it. Cutting through the noise, Wanless makes a compelling case: before we tackle disinformation or tech-driven disruption, we must first grasp how information ecosystems really work. A foundational text for anyone wanting to understand the information environment—and beyond.'

— Marie-Doha Besancenot, NATO Assistant Secretary General for Public Diplomacy (2023–5)

'Alicia Wanless does an impressive job of arguing for an entirely new way of looking at information and communication. Using a number of wonderful case studies from across the globe, throughout history, the premise of the book comes to life. Fresh, original and absorbing.'

— Claire Wardle, Associate Professor, Department of Communication, Cornell University

'Clearly, beautifully and passionately articulated, *The Information Animal* makes an important and unique argument. Rich in detail and with meticulously documented case studies, it is a compelling, substantive and engaging exploration of a critically important subject.'

— Tim Abray PhD, journalist, policy consultant and former radio presenter

'*The Information Animal* is an excellent piece of scholarship. With a compelling, original and well-supported argument, it is a very useful and important contribution to the literature.'

— David Scales, Assistant Professor of Medicine, Weill Cornell Medical College

'Using an ecological metaphor to analyse corrupting influences on good information flows, Wanless shows how the former are nucleated and strengthened, and how clean information is tainted. This book should be a foundational resource for students, scholars and practitioners working on information dysfunction.'

— Herbert Lin, Hank J. Holland Fellow in Cyber Policy and Security, Stanford University

'Smart and inventive, *The Information Animal* will make you ponder our human relationship to information—and its role in history, as well as the present. Wanless offers a holistic new way of thinking about the health and makeup of our "information ecosystems." This is a timely book.'

— Kate Grandjean, Associate Professor of History, Wellesley College, and author of *American Passage: The Communications Frontier in Early New England*

'Alicia Wanless is perhaps the world's deepest thinker on the information environment, and *The Information Animal* is a foundational text for anyone wanting to understand the informational spaces in which we live. Don't read it for quick-hit solutions—the latest faddish thing we should do about disinformation or propaganda. Wanless's core argument is that we need to know how information ecosystems work before we can understand how new technologies or human actors might be changing them. It's an argument for the development of a whole new field—one that allows us to understand the human relationship to information—so the tending of our informational gardens is based on robust understanding of how they work and what we are doing when we meddle with them.'

— Benjamin Wittes, Senior Fellow in Governance Studies, The Brookings Institution, and Editor-in-Chief, *Lawfare*

ALICIA WANLESS

The Information
Animal

*Humans, Technology and
the Competition for Reality*

HURST & COMPANY, LONDON

First published in the United Kingdom in 2025 by
C. Hurst & Co. (Publishers) Ltd.,
New Wing, Somerset House, Strand, London WC2R 1LA

Copyright © Alicia Wanless, 2025

All rights reserved.

Distributed in the United States, Canada and Latin America by Oxford University Press, 198 Madison Avenue, New York, NY 10016, United States of America.

The right Alicia Wanless to be identified as the author of this publication is asserted by her in accordance with the Copyright, Designs and Patents Act, 1988.

A Cataloguing-in-Publication data record for this book is available from the British Library.

Printed and bound in Great Britain by Bell & Bain Ltd, Glasgow

ISBN: 9781805262886

www.hurstpublishers.com

CONTENTS

Acknowledgements		vii
Introduction		1
1.	What Can Ecology Teach Us about the Information Environment?	17
2.	For Your Information	39
3.	The Information Environment	51
4.	Pulling Threads Together: Ancient Greece	71
5.	Tyrannical Ties: Charles versus the Godly	93
6.	A Tale of Two Countries: American Civil War	119
7.	Alphabets and Aliens: Vietnamese Independence	145
8.	The Ukrainian Curse of Nonexistence	175
9.	All Hail Finland?	209
10.	The Future of the Information Animal	225
Glossary of Terms		235
Notes		239
Index		293

ACKNOWLEDGEMENTS

None of us exists in a vacuum. Indeed, the people who helped along the decades that ultimately led to this book are legion and too numerous to mention by name. From the deepest past, I'll limit specific thanks to my parents, Debra and Robert Wanless, who always did their best to provide me with the space for my wilder ideas regardless of what others said. This work would also not have been possible were it not for the constant support and encouragement of my husband, Michael Berk. You are a rock, and your patience is spectacular.

Benjamin Wittes, I am indebted to you for your ongoing championing of this idea, the book and for repeatedly sharing your platform with me to spread the word. I'm honoured to call you my editor.

Likewise, it has been a blessing to publish this work with Hurst Publishers. Michael Dwyer and Alice Clarke's helpful guidance throughout the editing and publishing process brought this book to life. Falling down the rabbit hole had its charms!

The Carnegie Endowment for International Peace provided me with a home to write this book, and many colleagues supported the effort. Samantha Lai has cared for this book as if it was her own. Thank you for your edits and attention to detail in helping

ACKNOWLEDGEMENTS

this work along. Your literature review with Kamya Yadav and Iryna Adam on information ecology definitions enhanced this work, where the original was a few years old, as has our work with John Hicks on identifying factors for assessing ecosystems. I am grateful to you all. Thanks also to Carnegie's Library Director, Martha Higgins, and her team for quickly tracking down hard-to-find research whims, like Charles Dickens' letter to W. C. Macready. And a big thanks in advance for buying a copy of this book for the library. We can always count on Carnegie to support our work!

I remain eternally grateful to my doctoral supervisors at King's College, London—David Betz and Ofer Fridman. Not only did you encourage me to pursue an unorthodox thesis, but your consistent support ensured it was successfully completed.

To my friends who answered cultural questions along the way, your willingness to engage enriched this work. This includes Ioannis Petsilas answering questions about Greek words and taking us to some key sites mentioned in the book; Philip Mai doing the same on the meaning of Vietnamese words; Iryna Adam helping me choose the right quote to frame the chapter on Ukraine, and Aleksey Narinsky for giving me the soundtrack to write it (Okean Elzy). And cheers to Eli Sugarman for his Miami poolside idea of adding a pinch of fiction to this work.

Last but never least, thank you to Clément Wolf, David O'Brien, and Ryan Merkley for your unending willingness to brainstorm ideas.

INTRODUCTION

Do you feel inundated by information? Does it come in across devices? Is the news overwhelming? Is it hard to find sources you trust? Does advertising follow you everywhere? Are you having trouble making sense of things, like the rise of some politicians? Do you struggle to stay on top of all the things? Welcome to the modern information environment!

Part of the reason you might be struggling is that the information environment of 2025 is complex. There has never been more people, more technology, or more content than there is today. And every day more is added. Information is produced and shared at ever faster rates, a trend that's been continuing for the last couple of millennia.

Another reason you might be struggling is that despite all that technology and information, we humans still do not have much of a clue about how the information environment works. But this doesn't stop some people from making more of a mess of it—whether in the pursuit of power, profit, or proselytising a belief. Chances are your information ecosystem is being polluted right now with low-quality content, some spreading fear or hate. That pollution might even provoke you into taking a side. After all, in this information environment, where attention is the commodity, issues are reduced to stark terms—are you on the side of the morally just or against them? If this sounds familiar, you're likely experiencing an information competition whereby two or more communities are using all means possible to win hearts and minds—including yours—to adopt their version of reality. This plays out in the news, entertainment, among family, and on your social media feeds.

You might even feel compelled to do something, especially if your worldview feels challenged. It might be as simple as sharing that provocative online post or responding angrily in the comments. You might start investigating claims and sharing examples where you think the other side lied. Maybe you're a researcher or a journalist who wants to find a cause for the growing strife—why on earth do those people believe these claims? Be careful; here's where correlation and causation get confused. It can be tempting to tie the problem you're now noticing to something new—like the latest technology used to process information. It might be, but myriad other factors might also fuel that information competition. But, before running off with calls to control problematic content, I ask you to have a read.

I wrote this book, in part, to help anyone struggling in a cacophonous information ecosystem get better situated by taking a step back to see the forest for the trees. After watching several research-and-response cycles come and go on the problems of the day (disinformation, violent extremism, moral panics) blamed on various technologies (social media, search engines, cable news, video games), I got a sense that maybe our framing of the information environment was wrong. I wondered if we might ever only be looking at a single symptom and a probable cause, and then rushing to a solution without understanding all the possible consequences. After all, humans have done the same in other complex systems like the physical environment—for example, introducing invasive species or pesticides to deal with a pest and

INTRODUCTION

causing cascading and harmful unintended consequences. We only started to get a handle on those human-induced challenges recently, around the twentieth century, when scientists began stepping back and studying both physical ecosystems and the broader environment.

My thesis here is that it is time to look at information-related problems differently—in a sense more modestly and in a sense more ambitiously. The modesty arises from a certain caution about what we are in a position to "do" now. The urge to do something about any number of problems associated with the information environment is understandable. But trying to control the flow of information is also putting the cart before the horse—to say nothing about the unintended consequences.

And here's where the argument becomes ambitious. Before we "do" something, we need to understand what we're doing, the proverbial waters in which we are swimming. We need to move to study the ecology of the information environment, more generally. We need to build a whole new field.

This isn't to say that social media or artificial intelligence aren't posing problems. Humans are exceptionally good at finding ways to use tools for good and evil, especially as part of an information competition, when the struggle for resources or attention increases. It is more that the efforts to prove their harmful effects, not to mention the interventions to mitigate those harms, seem so futile. In part because isolating cause and effect in a system where so many variables might impact the outcome is exceptionally challenging, yet much of the research is narrowly focused on one potential problem related to an effect that many different things could cause.

Social media and, increasingly, artificial intelligence are part of the information environment. This is the space where information exists. Within it, humans use tools from alphabets to virtual reality to process information into outputs that can be shared, from the spoken word to videos and whatever comes along in the future. In so doing, we form information ecosystems through the inter-relationships between humans, the means for processing information, and the outputs created with those means, which are all shaped by conditions like the economy and education. The information environment is integral to the foundations of democracy, as this is the place where people make decisions. The very legitimacy of democracy is rooted in the ability of people to make free and informed decisions.

The challenge with doing anything in the information environment is that when it comes down to it, the most fundamental information processing happens in our heads. We might be able to see the tools and the outputs, but at some point, how that processed information is all understood comes back to cognition. The very act of intervening in the information environment, even if in the pursuit of ensuring that people can make free and informed decisions, has the potential to take this agency away from them—or, and this is equally as challenging—it can be perceived as doing so. The challenges associated with tackling disinformation highlight this problem.

The information environment did not just come into being with the internet; it has existed as long as humans have communicated with each other. Yes, the information environment is the most complex and globally interconnected it has ever been. Each new technology added changes to how information is processed, increasing the volume of outputs and speed at which they travel. But that complexity is all the more reason why we need to study the system as a whole instead of merely its parts, or worse, focusing only on whatever is most feared at the moment. When all we can see is that one big problem, we are missing the reasons why it is a problem in the first place.

Building on this thesis, I explore how fields like earth sciences and ecology emerged to make sense of the planet and ecosystems

INTRODUCTION

within it. Over a century or more, the combined knowledge generated from these and related fields helped humanity improve our material conditions and eventually begin to protect the environment. It became painfully apparent that we lack a similar way to bring the various disciplines and methods of studying aspects of the information environment together to make sense of this complex system. In other words, we need a field to explain how the information environment works. And without that, proving cause and effect will be damned-well impossible on all but the simplest of problems. This book argues why we need information ecology to fill this gap, and Chapter 1 explores how we get there by learning from physical ecology and earth sciences, while the next two chapters set theoretical foundations for reading the book.

Humans are information animals: we need information to make sense of the world. Yet the concept of information is very poorly understood. That might be one of the reasons we fixate on a problem like disinformation or a specific technology at the expense of seeing the information environment. Information is often conflated with content, but it's so much more than that. It drives us as information animals and is as much a part of our DNA as it is in the things we create to communicate with each other. Chapter 2 explores the different theories and interpretations of "information" across existing disciplines and puts forward a concept of information that facilitates greater consilience to support a more holistic understanding of the information environment.

Technology doesn't exist in a void. Humans create and use it to process and share information for myriad reasons. The interactions between humans, the means for processing information, and the outputs produced as a result create dynamic information ecosystems. The first step is to recognise they exist as a concept that can be studied. By studying information ecosystems, in turn, we might better understand why some struggle with disinformation, for example, and others do not. Chapter 3 delves into the information environment and ecosystems within it, explaining why it is necessary to understand technology in tandem with humans and the outputs generated by using it, and outlining what that might consist of, thus providing a framework for the historic case studies.

A good theory endures throughout time. That is another shortcoming in the current focus on today's challenges: an approach fixating on a specific technology used now might not apply in the future. And so, I turned to history to explore information ecosystems in different societies, starting with Ancient Greece, looking for possible trends that may offer useful lessons to us today. Hypothesising that our focus on technology leads us to miss the wider system, I chose case studies from media epochs, which scholars identified and described, usually associating them with significant technological shifts. These broad periods consisted of Orality, Print, Electricity, and Digital. Given the significance of the Industrial Revolution, I sought examples before and after steam power's introduction for the Print epoch, bringing the cases up to five. As the information environment becomes complex over time, so too did each case study as the present drew nearer, having more material to draw from.

This also means that these case studies can be detail-heavy at times, but those details are also necessary to explain those complex information ecosystems; I promise it all comes together in the end. As a student of war studies, I was especially drawn to cases that involved a known conflict, like a civil war or a regional conflict. My assumption was that studying these ecosystems over several decades that preceded each respective conflict may shed light not only on the evolving interactions, but also on societal attitudes and responses, as these communities were unknowingly nearing breaking point. Inspired by pioneering ecologists like

INTRODUCTION

Alexander von Humboldt and Charles Darwin, I set out to document aspects of those information ecosystems—the people, the tools or means of communication, and the outputs—to identify what might be studied over time using both historical works and primary sources where possible. The metaphors used draw from their ideas as well as the broader field of ecology. While this work takes from historical examples, it is not a history book in itself. It is a journey into information ecosystems of various historic periods, in homage to those early ecologists who helped people to see and understand the world around them. And, while this included considering the latest technology of the time, I also tried to expand the aperture and take an inductive approach, remaining open to what might be found instead of looking for only what I expected.

In those explorations across ages, a pattern emerged. In all the information ecosystems where two communities competed to impose their version of reality on the whole, a consistent combination of factors and conditions were observed. Yes, a new technology was introduced for processing information, but it often came along with several other related changes to how information could be processed and shared, leading to increased outputs and speed of distribution. At least one community, sometimes both, also experienced a recent increase in the number of people who could meaningfully engage with information through increased access or capacity. A new idea also emerged that challenged an existing idea, and various actors propagated it using available means and outputs, usually causing a similar reaction from those with opposing views, thus sparking an information competition. In so doing, by-products of the competition included information floods and pollution, disturbances which resemble phenomena from the physical environment. Finally, at least one side would attempt to control the flow of information, but usually with little success if measured in a favourable outcome to the conflict.

Information floods occur when there is a marked increase in a particular format of informational output conveying a repeated narrative. This increase in output can be caused deliberately, as in an entity or community intentionally flooding an information ecosystem with a repeated narrative by creating and distributing large amounts of content. Floods can also occur because of a change in the capacity to produce information, thus causing a growth in available information overall, including of a particular format. In the context of an information flood, a unit of information is defined by a particular narrative representing an idea that is being repeated at an increasingly faster rate and volume in a short period of time, such that it dominates the information ecosystem in which this occurs, drowning out other types of information. Information floods tend to follow a very rapid change in how information is processed and delivered within a given information ecosystem. A rise in the volume of content about a specific topic gives the issue prevalence, and if that idea is oppositional to another point of view held by others within that information ecosystem, it can exacerbate growing tensions between two communities. Depending on how the two sides react, flooding the information ecosystem can escalate an information competition into a conflict, as opponents attempt to gain an advantage over the other by either promoting their message or drowning the opposition. Flooding an information ecosystem with messaging on a particular topic can also create the illusion that the belief conveyed is more widely held than it might be.

Often occurring alongside information floods is information pollution, or the presence of low-quality information. Information pollution includes an array of types, ranging in scale in their degree of degradation to the information environment. On the lower end of the spectrum are irrelevant or unsolicited messages such as spam email and redundant or empty information that contributes little to knowledge, such as many forms of entertainment. At the other end of the scale are rumours, outright lies, abuse, or content spreading fear or anger to agitate a population.[1] Whereas higher quality information, to borrow from data science, would be accurate, complete, timely, unique, and coherent.[2] Of course, given that information pollution is inherently an output, classifying it comes with the usual subjective challenges discussed further in Chapter 2. That said, information pollution was one of several factors and conditions present in each case study that formed the pattern outlined above.

In Ancient Greece, before the Peloponnesian War in 431 BCE, a form of writing was the major innovation for recording and communicating information. While writing had been around for a few centuries, Socrates still worried about how it would kill the spoken word, and his student Plato thought the outputs from it, like plays, would misinform the people. But messaging from a different type of output, in building projects, was causing a stir. A new radical idea of democracy had taken hold, and Athens was enabling more and more men to participate in public decision-making, such as when to go to war. At the same time, advances in the boat construction and roads to support this democratic court system helped move information faster across the city-state and beyond, opening Athens up to the world. With a growing wealth, Athens promoted its democracy in a massive building programme aimed at demonstrating its standing in the Hellenic world after fending off the Persians—all to the dismay of Sparta, whose own information ecosystem was tightly closed and determined not to change. This sparked a rather one-sided information competition between the two Greek states, explored in depth in Chapter 4.

The information ecosystem of seventeenth-century England experienced several shifts before the outbreak of the Civil War in 1642. Sure, the printing press had existed for two centuries, but its uptake in England was heavily controlled and slow. That didn't stop people like Robert Burton from complaining in his famous 1621 medical tract, *The Anatomy of Melancholy*: "As already, we shall have a vast chaos and confusion of books, we are oppressed with them, our eyes ache with reading, our fingers with turning."[3] Print depended on an earlier innovation, paper, which was also slow to develop domestically in England. It was yet another technology people complained about because of the volume of letters its use amassed, not to mention their untrustworthiness as the reader couldn't see or hear the people sending them.[4] Letter writing created networks across Europe, spreading enlightenment and religious ideas alike, and canals and a new postal system were moving letters and the first newspapers in the form of *courantos* across England faster and cheaper than before. While King Charles worried about controlling the growing printing press and nasty rumours about his Papal ties, a new class of merchants was enriched through colonialism, emerging from a general population that had only just returned to pre-Black Death numbers. Protestantism opened public education, enabling more and more people to read, including tradespeople, who could sign their names in the growing practice of petitioning the sovereign. From these ranks came the Godly, a group of radical protestants demanding more religious reforms and changes to the governance structure with more authority in the Parliament. They were inspired by Scottish radicals, whose own information ecosystem was tied to England's with the ascension of Charles' father to the English throne. No amount of control over the production of information in England could stop its inflow from Scotland and Europe, fuelling the information competition explored in Chapter 5.

Two hundred years later, on a different continent, uneven changes rocked the American information ecosystem before the Civil War started in 1861. Steam technology moved information

INTRODUCTION

faster across oceans and along new canal and train systems, though primarily in the North. With trains came the telegraph, acclaimed by its inventor as society's nervous system, collapsing space and time, and later decried for its "vast injury. Superficial, sudden, unsifted, too fast for the truth, must be all telegraphic intelligence."[5] The telegraph enabled the creation of the Associated Press. Still, it was innovations in print that decreased the price of newspapers and advances in the postal service that made it cheaper to distribute, spurring a growing news media sector. Literacy rates in the North were high by European standards, far outstripping those in the South. With widespread education, new ideas came, including abolition. Its advocates took to earlier technology in books, using fiction as one way to rally support. Abolitionists also conducted widespread petitioning of Congress, much as the Godly had done in England. In reaction, proponents of slavery tried to control the spread of abolitionism, supporting a ban on those petitions and censoring mail about it in the South. Ultimately, they responded in kind, with their own newspapers and books pushing their side, contributing to an information flood and pollution while at it. The two sides locked into an information competition that increasingly led to violence, as explored in Chapter 6.

Chapter 7 moves into the Electric Age and the Vietnamese information ecosystem in the early twentieth century. Here again, several shifts changed how information was processed and spread. Yes, radio played a role in the fight for independence from France following Hồ Chí Minh's declaration of Vietnamese independence in 1945, itself broadcast with a makeshift system. However, its earlier use was heavily controlled by French occupiers, whose colonisation inadvertently connected the Vietnamese to a wider world of new political ideas through colonial education, exiling political activists, and advances in international travel to connect the colony with France. Ultimately, colonisation interconnected the Vietnamese and French information ecosystems, leading to disappointment in one when expectations raised in the other were not met following the First World War. The widespread educational adoption of a simplified script called *quôc nhu* sparked a rise in literacy levels, and growth in the printing sector helped a generation of nationalists formulate and spread new ideas about Vietnamese independence. Unsurprisingly, the French reached for control of the information ecosystem, made all the more difficult by the Second World War, Japanese occupation, and what seemed to be a lack of understanding about the Vietnamese. The conflation of one information competition, around Vietnamese independence, with that of another, the Cold War, interconnected a further information ecosystem in America to this conflict.

The last case study in Chapter 8 explores the Ukrainian information ecosystem before the first Russian invasion in 2014. While Russia saw the mass protests in Kyiv's Maidan Square as just another Western-backed revolution fuelled by social media, the Ukrainian information ecosystem had experienced many other shifts beyond the introduction of the new technology. This included wildly shifting levels of control over the information ecosystem, beginning with its opening to a wider information environment after the dissolution of the Soviet Union. As a new class of ultra-rich oligarchs benefited from privatisation, they captured media outlets to advance their interest and support politicians, who promised a highly educated public a lot, but seldom delivered. The quality of journalism plummeted, particularly as internet-enabled media grew, and with an astronomical rise in the advertising sector came increased paid-for content dressed up as news, locally known as *jeansa*. In this highly polluted and contested information ecosystem, a competition developed around the country's political future—would it try something new and join the European Union, or

INTRODUCTION

stick with historic alliances in Russia? At least on the surface, that's how it seemed, but mass protests had also become the one form of communication ordinary people could resort to with a corrupt elite. And so, while there was an information competition between East and West at one level, there was also just a desire for something better. Tools like social media and cell phones were used to help organise the expression of that desire, but its roots went far deeper in that information ecosystem.

This book is the story of the information animal and how it competes as part of a social group for supremacy of its ideas within its information ecosystem. As such, this is also an exploration of information ecosystems and how changing environmental conditions enable the creation, spread, and consumption of information in all its forms and, ultimately, new ideas that are the basis for information competition, as well as information disturbances that are aggravated by such competition. In other words, this is the story of a system and how humans relate to it, drawing on insights from conflicts spanning more than 2,000 years of human history.

Multiple shifts occurred across each of these information ecosystems before conflict erupted. This included changes to factors related to the people, their means, and outputs, as well as surrounding conditions. While in each case this included the introduction of a new technology, often the role it played wasn't enough for someone to declare that new tool the main or sole cause of the information competition. As we shall see throughout those explorations, various actors within each information ecosystem used many means to create a variety of outputs to achieve their own aims. These outputs, though, were an expression of ideas that were shaped by conditions, such as education, economy, and quality of life, within those information ecosystems. The relationships between these factors and conditions create a climate for information competitions, and in particular, ones that risk turning into conflict.

In all of these cases, new technology changed how information could be processed and shared, but it didn't replace what came before. Instead, it added a new level of complexity. In that way, our current information environment is directly tied to what came before. This trajectory will continue unless something significant happens that cuts us off from the past and all the information sources maintained around it. Each generation experiencing a new technology will feel that the pace of change they experience is unprecedented, but it's a sensation many have felt before when new technology was introduced to their information ecosystem. Some comfort might come from recognising this. We should expect to experience fear of new technology; that's normal, but we should also expect that this fear will lead to a desire to react. That fear will also present a convenient excuse to blame new technology for whatever problems society is currently experiencing. While there is a chance the new tools are aggravating existing issues, it's more likely the situation is far more complex than meets the eye. In a highly interconnected world, where information is produced at ever faster speeds, it will become even more critical that we are able to step back and see the bigger picture, lest we jump to intervene in ways that make the situation worse.

Information ecosystems are different. What might work to build resilience in one might backfire in another. Currently, we have little way of knowing what works and what does not because we aren't looking at the system. In the pursuit of *doing something*, we are jumping to conclusions that might be faulty. I can't tell you how many times I've heard Finland hailed as a master case in addressing disinformation. Nary a conference panel fails to praise the Finnish media literacy success story. Yet the factors and conditions present in the Finnish information ecosystem are very different from those in Canada or the United States, which

INTRODUCTION

Chapter 9 explores in more detail along with why understanding these differences matters.

This book is a call to look beyond latest threat or technology to see the information environment as a system, and in so doing find proactive, evidence-informed approaches to address problems rather than reacting in fear to a great unknown. Yes, disinformation and artificial intelligence are scary. However, jumping to a response out of fear won't get us any further in understanding how a phenomenon might change the information environment. Those answers will always elude us if we never figure out what state the information environment was in before a new threat was identified, or a novel technology was introduced. We will face this exact situation regardless of what new technology comes along in the future, as explored in Chapter 10, unless we approach the problem differently. This is why we need a new field; this is why we need information ecology.

1

WHAT CAN ECOLOGY TEACH US ABOUT THE INFORMATION ENVIRONMENT?

Using environmental metaphors to describe the human relationship with information has become mainstream. The U.S. Secretary of State, Antony J. Blinken, gave a speech in March 2024 on "building a more resilient information environment", in which he drew clear connections between rapidly evolving technologies, their impact on human behaviours, and the information space through which we all interact.[1] It is time we move beyond metaphors. Fortunately, how the physical environment came to be studied presents a roadmap for those wishing to understand information's role in society. After all, the physical environment is a complex system, but it wasn't always studied holistically. Modern fields of science, like earth sciences and ecology, emerged in the nineteenth and twentieth centuries to foster our understanding of the environment as a system consisting of many elements and relationships. In so doing, these two fields identified man-made problems within it and galvanised support to address them. For those concerned about the impact of generative artificial intelligence—or any other technology that might come along—there is much to learn from how these fields were built and how a similar approach can be applied to the information environment. What follows is a brief dive into the history of those fields, and the definitions used and borrowed from them. This foray can inform the development of information ecology, a field capable of studying the rich tapestry or web created through myriad human interactions with technology and information.

Earth sciences and ecology are related but different fields. Earth sciences study the wider environment where living and non-living things exist, comprising all the surrounding conditions and elements within it. This includes the atmosphere, hydrosphere, and lithosphere, the outer rocky layer of the planet. To name a few kinds of earth scientists, meteorologists study weather and climates, and oceanographers study the physics and geography of oceans. In contrast, geologists, seismologists, and geophysicists try to make sense of everything underneath. The environment also includes the biosphere, where, as the name suggests, life occurs. It comprises ecosystems that form through the interactions of living things with the environment around them. Ecology is the study of the biosphere, namely the interactions between organisms and their environment.[2] An ecologist draws on earth sciences to understand ecosystems. For example, the latitude of where an ecosystem is on the planet will affect the amount of heat received from the sun due to the earth's tilt and shape, and the heating of the earth's surface and atmosphere drives the circulation of the atmosphere and influences patterns of precipitation. Geological processes such as erosion, caused by water movement, move minerals into soils.[3] Together with soil, temperature and precipitation determine what types of plants can grow where.[4]

WHAT CAN ECOLOGY TEACH US?

In turn, these ecological processes impact the environment, and thus, earth scientists draw on ecology. Plants and animals eventually break down through complex food chains, contributing to the nutrients in the soil, which continue to feed the growth cycle.[5] In some cases, like in a tundra ecosystem, these processes create large reservoirs of organic carbon that, through global warming and encroaching forest fires, threaten to be released back into the atmosphere and further accelerate climate change.[6] The processes within and between ecosystems and their impact on climate change are deeply interrelated, but understanding this requires two umbrella fields and various disciplines within both. How this plays out in practice was demonstrated as the world tried to solve the acid rain problem that rose to prominence in the 1980s.

Acid rain was first identified as an issue in 1852 by the Scottish chemist Robert Angus Smith, who was worried about the polluting effects of industrialisation. It was found that burning fossil fuels releases sulphur and nitrogen into the atmosphere, which, when mixed with water and oxygen molecules, becomes sulphuric and nitric acid that then falls back to the earth in precipitation.[7] While volcanos and rotting organic matter can also introduce sulphur dioxide and hydrogen sulphide into the atmosphere, they tend to mainly alter the environment locally, meaning those natural occurrences were probably not the cause for growing rates of acid rain. Fortunately, earth scientists had set up long-running studies to measure the changes in water pH levels. One that began in 1872 returned very disconcerting results in 1963. A rain sample from the Hubbard Brook Experimental Farm in the northeastern United States was around 100 times more acidic than expected.[8]

Acid rain was also a concern north of the border. It had left lakes around Sudbury, Ontario, lifeless in the mid-1980s.[9] The long-running research of earth scientists provided a clue to the cause, while ecologists were able to study the ecosystems to understand the problem better. Thanks to another pre-existing longer-term measurement project, Ontario's Experimental Lakes Area, marine biologists could test on healthy lakes far from suspected sources of pollution. Researchers slowly increased the acidity of a healthy lake to measure the effects, and soon, nutrients and fish died off. However, after they stopped raising the pH levels, the ecosystem rebounded, suggesting that affected areas might recover if pollution stopped.

As countries like Canada and the United States implemented clean air regulations, acid rain decreased. Along with other measures, such as adding large quantities of alkaline substances to affected lakes, ecosystems began to recover regionally. To get to the bottom of the problem, long-term monitoring of air and rain quality across geographies ultimately helped isolate pollution as a significant cause of acid rain, where an existing baseline and ecological experiments determined its impact and solution.[10]

While it isn't likely that a pristine information ecosystem exists against which to make comparisons, it is possible to establish baselines and begin to understand the information environment. This begins with consistent measurements and a shared language across various disciplines studying people, technology, and outputs and the relationships between them. Environmental metaphors abound when discussing the human relationship to information and technology, but the application of terms is inconsistent or lacking in depth. Definitions are framed by who is attempting to use it, varying across disciplines. This is hardly the consistency required to unify scholarship and make sense of the system.

Analysis of scholarly literature demonstrates the scope of the problem. Early concepts of the information environment have ranged from one extreme, as all-encompassing as existence itself, to the other extreme, a limited space, like a closed computer system or a tool a researcher might use to solve a problem.[11] Many definitions of the information environment are a list of possible component parts.[12] Definitions vary across disciplines. For example, business scholars define the information environment as mainly an organisation's information system and the primary research focus is on how that might impact financial decision-making.[13] Health researchers define the information environment as a system managing health records.[14] Those in education frame it around a university's information management affecting student access to learning.[15] Often, when the information environment is mentioned, it is referenced vaguely in passing or it is conflated with one type of communication like the internet and specifically social media,[16] news media,[17] or both.[18] In 72 publications printed between 1976 and 2023, nearly two-thirds (44) using the term "information environment" did not define it.[19] Half of those publications conflated the concept of an environment with an ecosystem. In physical ecology, these two concepts are not the same, nor should they be when discussing the study of information.

The information environment is broader, the space where information exists, comprising all its myriad forms as well as the surrounding conditions affecting it. Ecosystems are more limited, consisting of information animals interacting with each other, tools, and the information environment as part of an interconnected system within that wider space. John McHale, an artist, sociologist, and futurist, was inching toward a systemic insight about the information environment in writing, "We cannot tackle one issue, one question, or one problem at a time as an isolated item. All must be viewed as being critically interactive elements in a new context of interdependence."[20] In describing the infosphere, Luciano Floridi, a philosopher of information and ethics, defined an information ecosystem as "constituted by all informational entities, their properties, interactions, processes, and mutual relations"[21] Both these scholars advanced the importance of thinking about the evolving information environment as a complex system with impacts on human endeavour. If one criticism can be offered here, it is that this is as far as they go.[22] Without an integrated approach to understanding those interrelationships and a means to study them, we aren't any closer to making sense of what the information environment is or how what happens in it affects our future. The problem is the continued lack of a theory that explains this complex system. As the biologist Edward O. Wilson wrote in his book *Consilience*, "nothing in science—nothing in life, for that matter—makes sense without theory."[23] Here is where the development of earth sciences and ecology as interdisciplinary fields can offer insights and a roadmap of how to get there with respect to the modern information environment.

As science and technology historian Ronald Doel noted, "A late nineteenth-century geologist would have been perplexed if asked to define the 'earth sciences.'" This field evolved over the twentieth century through jostling among various disciplines like seismology, oceanography, and meteorology "to develop new, synthetic theories about Earth's physical processes."[24] As a field, earth sciences emerged in the 1920s, driven mainly through funding for various academic departments such as geology or physics from philanthropists like Andrew Carnegie and prospecting firms pursuing natural resources. Similarly, new industries like aviation created a boon for meteorology. Immediately following the Second World War, government funding, especially from militaries, supported new geophysics institutes and academic departments focused on geological sciences. Maintaining modern weapon systems demanded a systemic approach integrating scientific expertise in oceanography, meteorology, and other earth sciences disciplines. For the next fifteen years, the field began to tackle more global problems and adopted computer modelling to make sense of and predict outcomes of complex issues. Then, in the 1960s, concerns over a potential nuclear war and the impact of pesticide use drove a wider acceptance of a more holistic approach to understanding the environment. For Doel, this marked a "revived interest in Humboldtian approaches to the earth sciences, stressing integrative and holistic interrelations rather than the deeply reductionist approaches that have typified major research programs of twentieth-century physics."[25] Understanding the environment required more than unlocking the mysteries of smaller parts; there also needed to be an understanding about how they all fit together and form emergent properties. Since then, earth sciences have become an established field, with institutes, academic departments, and interdisciplinary efforts emerging to study and address global challenges such as climate change.

Echoes of Alexander von Humboldt, a nineteenth-century Prussian naturalist, could also be heard in ecology, which followed a similar trajectory to earth sciences. Humboldt's explorations of the world led to discoveries of climate zones, the magnetic equator, and isotherms, the lines on maps connecting points with the same temperature. On an expedition to South America beginning in 1799, Humboldt learned from locals that colonial deforestation around Lake Valencia in Venezuela was causing the land to become barren, the water level to drop, and other vegetation to disappear. Moreover, the soil was eroded from the surrounding hills when torrential rains fell. Humboldt recognised that the trees were part of an ecosystem—the forest—helping to regulate the temperature, retain moisture and prevent soil erosion, and that removing them prevented that system from functioning as it should. To Humboldt, the ecosystem was a delicate web of which humans are a part.[26] These observations and the idea that these outcomes were all connected led Humboldt to conduct similar measurements and comparisons over time elsewhere in the world to identify ecosystems. He became the first European scientist to see the adverse effects of humans on the environment. While Humboldt's work influenced how both earth sciences and ecology would evolve, the word "ecology" would not be appear for another half-century. In 1866, German zoologist Ernst Haeckel introduced the concept but, oddly, did not become an ecologist or develop the field.[27] Ecology, as a concept, would not gain wider adoption until later that century, with definitions morphing as different disciplines championed its cause, be it botanists, zoologists, and, eventually, those concerned with ecosystems.[28] By the 1950s, ecosystems provided a framework for studying the environment by understanding interdependent relationships, energy flows, food chains, and more. Mathematical modelling was adopted, too, to study cause and effect, and as ecologist Jaboury Ghazoul noted, "these approaches helped to steer ecology from a largely descriptive to a more predictive science."[29]

Ecology really came to the fore in the 1960s. The word became more popular as the field became "an appropriate guide to the relation of humans, as well as other forms of life, to their environment."[30] This popularity arose with growing concerns over human intervention in the environment. As the use of the term increased, it also grew more muddled as seemingly everyone adopted their own definition of it. Many conflated the field of ecology with an ecosystem, mixing the study with the subject.[31] Ecology is the study of organisms and their relationship to the environment, whereas ecosystems are the emergent systems created by those living things together. The conflation, while unhelpful, is not entirely surprising. As the biologist Edward J. Kormondy noted, systems are human-made constructs that provide a frame to studying something complex. While ecosystems like ponds or forests are real physical things, the "conceptual schemes developed from knowledge" of them as systems are abstract. Yet in those constructs, scientists have identified the shared "general functional and structural attributes that are recognizable, analyzable, and predictable" across ecosystems.[32] It was that ability to understand the processes behind the system that helped scientists identify pollution as an environmental problem.

An important discovery facilitated by the burgeoning field of ecology was that dichloro-diphenyl-trichloroethane, or DDT, caused a decline in populations of birds of prey. In the early 1960s, the eggs of peregrine falcons, among others, were thinning to the point where less than one-fifth could successfully rear young, as would-be parents unwittingly crushed the too-thin eggs.[33] Fortunately, naturalists have been amassing bird egg collections for decades, providing researchers with historical samples to analyse and compare. The timeline of thinning coincided with the rise in the use of pesticides, affecting populations where it was used more. But this was a correlation, not proof of causation.

Thinking the cause was DDT, researchers fed the pesticide to falcons in lab experiments but received disappointing results. The tests assumed that exposure to DDT would be direct and cause the egg thinning. Yet that wasn't how falcons encountered it. As birds of prey, they picked up a DDT by-product later in the food chain, dichloro-diphenyl-dichloroethylene or DDE, which has been found in fish, other birds, and crustaceans, which falcons consumed.[34] For example, earthworms store metabolites acquired from breaking down leaves exposed to DDT, contaminating birds like robins who eat the worms.[35] As DDE spread through the food chain, apex predators like falcons are exposed differently through bioaccumulation, whereby more toxins build up over time. Spraying DDT is the catalyst for problems in an ecosystem, but it comes to the falcon through a series of interconnected processes in the food chain.

Ultimately, it was the proof of the connection between DDE and egg thinning using multiple methods that would lead to the United States' ban on DDT in 1972. Lab experiments alone weren't enough, though; researchers needed historical collections of eggs to compare as well as an understanding of how the ecosystem worked in the form of food chains (to name a few things) to deduce how falcons experience DDT.[36] To understand a complex system, in addition to experiments, one needs consistent measurements of the same factors over time, structured field observations, analysis of processes, and systematisation of research covering a variety of methods to bring it all together. In other words, a consistent convergence of methodological approaches across several relevant disciplines was required, and thus, ecology as a field of study was developed. If humans want to understand the impact of technology on the relationship between humans and information, a similar interdisciplinary field is needed.

At present, research on the human relationship with information is much like the situation with earth sciences and ecology at the turn of the twentieth century, before systems thinking stitched various disciplines together. There are many different disciplines studying parts, but there is a lack of overarching theory that brings them all together to understand the broader system. Each field brings its terminology and methods to bear on research questions that interest them. The media studies scholar looks at media ownership or how social media changes news consumption patterns. The democracy researcher cares about the impact of censorship or media freedom on elections. The political scientist wants to know why one candidate's campaign wins over another or how information flows affect decision-making that ultimately leads a government to enter a disastrous war. Computational social scientists want to use social media data to understand how polarisation happens in a society or the effectiveness of a particular countermeasure to hate speech. The psychologist wants to know why people are susceptible to disinformation. A legal scholar wonders about regulation's impact on information communications technology use. The list goes on, and the disconnected studies not only contribute to a definitional mess but sometimes contradict each other. This, in turn, leaves policy decision-makers to rely on the "loudest in a crowd" rather than the best available evidence. As the world finds itself in what some observers call a "polycrisis", this situation can hardly be deemed acceptable.

A first step towards consilience is getting out of the definitional soup. Much like the confusing use of the phrase "information environment" by various disciplines described earlier, definitions of information ecology are also disparate. Terms like information ecology have been adopted across many fields but with little consistency in their use. One of the earliest uses dates from the 1970s, but the wider adoption of information ecology began in the 1990s. In one meta study looking at 138 papers published between 1993 and 2013 using the term "information ecology", the majority (78 per cent) came from fields within earth sciences and ecology, with the rest from computer science, information science, and business.[37] As time passed, the term began to be used more by researchers in information science. In exploring 41 papers using the term, published between 1997 and 2023, our team at the Information Environment Project found that twenty-three came from information science. However, ten other fields have also used the term, including sociology, business, and media studies, to name a few. Nearly half (nineteen) of those papers conflated the concept of information ecology with information environment or ecosystem.[38] As a recurring trend across eleven papers, the concept of ecology, an *entire interdisciplinary field of study* with many methods, was simplified to one individual method of inquiry or singular framework.[39] A couple of papers conflated ecology with a philosophy or worldview about information framed in ethics.[40]

By and large, the use of the term "information ecology" presently is, at best, a metaphor, losing the powerful sense of meaning for the borrowed term. Moreover, as Norris and Suomela pointed out, such metaphors often neglect the role of the natural environment in the human relationship to information yet also have the potential to "green-wash" the technologies used to process and share information by creating an illusion that man-made systems are natural.[41] However, notwithstanding the above, a few uses of information ecology showed promise. A concept emerging from ecological anthropology, which studies the relationships between humans and the environment, defined information ecology as the study of the relationships between information, including that derived from the physical environment and individual decision-making.[42] Some biologists framed information ecology as the "study of how organisms acquire and use information in decision-making and its significance for populations, communities, landscapes and ecosystems."[43] Indeed, Bergman and Beehner wrote about an organism's "information foraging strategy—the time and energy dedicated to gathering information at the expense of other biological processes".[44] A couple more papers defined information ecology as a science but differed in focus, with one emphasising the influence of information on "bio-systems" and the other on the "information environment, including the entities within it and their relation to each other and the wider system."[45] While this more systems-oriented approach to ecology is promising, it is still only applied in relation to more basic biological organisms, not human societies. Far more work must be done to develop a unifying field for studying the information environment, and ecosystems within it, in relation to human activity in rapidly changing contexts. This is particularly the case if the intent is to foster a scientific field capable of proving causation in a complex system. But right now, research about the information environment is not structured to lead to such results.

There are currently many disciplines studying parts of the information environment. However, that research is rarely connected in a way to help understand how information ecosystems work. Research is conducted across disciplinary silos, with little systematisation that might help piece together an understanding of the whole system and its functions. In other words, we lack a picture of the bigger system that is the information environment.

If we want to know how a technology changes an information ecosystem, we first need to know what the ecosystem consists of and how it functions. To measure change, one needs a baseline against which the new state can be compared. But that requires looking at all the component parts together, not just the phenomenon or technology that has the attention of the day. For example, there are ample case studies on various phenomena, like disinformation, at a given place in time, but they tend not to be longitudinal or repeated, which makes it hard to track changes over time. It's a little like focusing on counting instances of egg thinning, or other negative effects that might be caused by DDT, without first having baselines for comparisons to know what the ecosystem was like before it was introduced. Understanding how an information ecosystem changes requires taking a longer-term view of decades and centuries, rather than weeks or months. And given the complexity of information ecosystems, it will also require systematising longitudinal research across subjects and disciplines to build a whole picture. With that picture, we might be able to understand the processes that drive information ecosystems, and how interventions impact them.

Without an understanding of how the system works, experiments to prove causation in an information ecosystem are like the lab approach of directly feeding falcons DDT. For example, to test if fact-checking works to counter disinformation, small groups of volunteers are run through experiments to see if they can spot problematic content after exposure to so-called corrective information. While the approach is promising in these limited studies, it's hard to say if it works at scale, out in the wild, or has a long-term impact—or, indeed, if other variables might have led some people to be more responsive to fact-checking as an intervention.[46] Similarly, correlation is often mistaken for causation. Correlations, such as a perceived increase in polarisation occurring after social media is widely adopted, led to experiments to prove one caused the other. Much like the example on DDT, experiments are designed with the assumption that engagement with content on social media directly causes the polarisation of users. Some studies find causation, and others refute it.[47] Among the many challenges to building consensus on causation is an ongoing replicability crisis whereby researchers struggle to repeat experiments conducted by others. This is a problem in three fields prevalent in studying aspects of the information environment, namely psychology,[48] social science,[49] and communications.[50] The reasons for the crisis are manifold, including a lack of availability of raw data, protocol, and analysis scripts.[51] A similar pattern repeats in research on artificial intelligence, where studies are dominated by those in the private sector, where the use of proprietary technology is used as an excuse not to share raw data.[52] Beyond the replicability issue, these experiments represent limited sample sizes and time frames, and are often conducted in isolation from the wider system where they occur—the information environment.

These challenges in proving causation open the door to doubt, which some actors use to their benefit, usually the culprit accused of causing the problem. This has been the infamous tactic of tobacco and oil companies, and, as some have alleged, big tech firms when accused of causing harm or faced with regulation that will impede their operations.[53] In this approach, if scientific consensus indicates that a harm is stemming from a specific cause, any studies that might suggest otherwise are exploited to erode faith in the consensus. Indeed, while working on this chapter, I came across persistent claims by conservative and libertarian initiatives that DDT was not killing birds and should be reintroduced.[54] Often, the evidence for these claims pointed to laboratory studies that failed to replicate the egg-thinning results identified in the field. This underscores an important issue for consideration as we explore how to approach the information environment, both in terms of research and in guiding management of it.

In any complex system, be it the physical or information environment, a variety of agents will have interests in how that space is used and managed, and sometimes these interests will come into conflict with each other. When those interests collide, agents on both sides will engage in information competition to ensure their point of view is the dominant one. In the case of complex systems, this competition will inevitably involve research to support and refute claims. It is inevitable that each side will make arguments in their own favour, selecting evidence to support these claims while refuting, ignoring, or suppressing evidence to the contrary. This raises questions about how such debates should be had in the public interest. Such competitions invariably target the public, and indirectly through them, the media and politicians, to encourage policymaking moves in the agent's favour. How they are conducted could affect the outcomes of policy decisions, which in turn affect everyone in a society. It is possible that DDT could be both effective pest control and harmful to the environment. Who gets to decide where the balance falls, and how that decision can be trusted if agents selectively choose evidence to support their position while working to undermine that of their opponent? Is it possible to create rules around such competition—demanding agents be transparent about funding or ties?[55] How can we account for an imbalance in power and means whereby wealthy companies can throw disproportionate resources to argue their side? These are all issues that rest firmly within the information environment, but they also have a serious impact on the physical environment, making the two inextricably linked. Answering these questions and developing means that can remain independent from powerful actors requires shared values in a society and some sense of a common reality that can let people agree on some fundamental principles. Finding answers or bringing some current information competitions to a conclusion is becoming increasingly challenging, in part because the conditions have been set to discourage a science-based approach.

This is the information environment we now find ourselves in, one where doubts have been sown about science-driven policy and attacks on researchers are rampant, be it on climate change, the COVID-19 pandemic response, or disinformation in general.[56] This is why it is so important that research on the information environment is systematised. In its current fragmented approach, research about the information environment is too easily dismissed—it's study versus study, at this point, with few of those studies put in the context of historical data about the information ecosystem where they occur.

We can learn from how the study of the physical environment has evolved. The process started by researchers seeing it as a system. Indeed, in all the environmental issues outlined above—acid rain, Lake Valencia, and DDT—finding answers required first recognising that the environment is a complex, interconnected system. Identifying and understanding the challenges faced in it required measurements of the same factors over time, using different types of methods. To achieve this, different fields like oology (the study of birds' eggs), meteorology, toxicology, history, and more had to be brought together in a way that was mutually intelligible. In other words, there was a consilience across fields. To establish baselines and observe variations, the collection of long-term historical data on a variety of factors was a prerequisite. Understanding acid rain involved historic samplings of water and air quality and an example of a healthy ecosystem to test and compare. Uncovering DDT as a problem in the environment needed historic egg collections and surveys of bird populations. Finding causation in all these cases required ruling out other variables and identifying the one with the most evidence to support it out of all the possible options. This is the only way to build consensus on issues, which is very important on easily politicised topics. Results must be defensible, and how researchers came to those results needs to be presented in an accessible and transparent manner for others to assess their quality and replicate them. It is not enough to point to a study and say, "Here is proof". Articulating the process or story behind those results is critical to making this work more accessible to laypeople.

Consensus about the evidence based on numerous long-term measurements is how so many scientists have concluded that climate change is happening. They determined that the cause is anthropogenic by ruling out other causes and identifying the one with the most evidence to support it. Researchers studying the information environment might learn from this approach. For example, institutes like the United States' Environmental Protection Agency have developed approaches that move beyond reducing complex problems down to simple situations to help researchers conduct causal assessments of ecosystems. This approach looks at multiple potential causes to determine which cause of many is best supported by evidence, which it finds by drawing on a variety of sources like "site observations, regional monitoring studies, environmental manipulations, laboratory experiments, and general scientific knowledge" and mixed methods, including "interpretation of reported observations, summary statistics, and statistical and mathematical modelling." Indeed, as the EPA noted, "no single method can accommodate the range and diversity of evidence often available."[57] Understanding how a complex system works, much less a singular problem within it, requires multiple points of inquiry brought together in a systematised effort to make sense of the greater whole.

The current situation is a nightmare for policymakers who hope to have evidence-informed policymaking related to the information environment. Understandably, they are expected to act in a meaningful way now. Under the current research model, they are left to identify best practices by analysing what studies they know of, or worse, basing policy on a handful, or fewer, reports. In the context of democracies, this situation should be very alarming. The information environment is the space where citizens make decisions, and democracy's very legitimacy is based on them doing so freely and fairly. Not understanding the information environment or lacking the means to study it as a system makes it very difficult to determine what the impact of policy measures on it is. Likewise, it makes it difficult to know how much pollution there is within the information environment or how manipulation erodes the agency of people to make free decisions. This renders it difficult for policymakers to set rules to ensure that citizens' ability to make informed decisions is protected, or indeed, what those measures would even entail. In fact, introducing rules might erode that ability further. What happens to the information ecosystem when one type of content is removed? What happens when a new technology is added? For all of this, there needs to be a systematisation of existing literature, consistent types of measurements conducted over time, and an approach to studying the information environment that fosters consilience between fields. No single study is going to unlock the mysteries of a complex system. We need to understand what the equivalent measurements of things like temperature, air quality, currents, and climate distribution are in the information environment and start documentation. Many case studies offer evidence of disinformation existing—so what? Is it changing over time? Is it a significant occurrence or really small in comparison to all the other information available on a related topic? Is it always there, or does it get introduced and dissipate? How does the information ecosystem change with its presence? How are information animals accessing and using it? How does disinformation interact with different types of information ecosystems? These phenomena need to be put into the context of the information ecosystem to make sense.

Information ecology provides a framing for building this field. If ecology is the study of the environment and the relation of living things to them, then information ecology is the study of the information environment and the relation of information animals to it, including with outputs, the means for processing information, and our attempts to govern and intervene in this space. Information ecology is the study of the infosphere, connecting multiple disciplines to develop an understanding of the information environment across ecosystems.

To have information ecology, we first need to accept that we are studying an environment, an interconnected web of myriad relations formed between its component parts. As information animals become more dependent on technology, we must adopt the view that the health of national information ecosystems is as vital to our existence as clean water and air. If one hopes to continue reaping the benefits of an ecosystem, then one must understand that the cascading effects of deforestation outweigh the short-term benefits of clear-cutting trees for farming. Humans tend to solve the immediate problem before them; we miss the unintended and lasting consequences of our actions. It's quite likely that we are making similar missteps in the information environment, but those mistakes will continue to be made until we understand the information environment as a system.

Information ecology also requires a schema for connecting different disciplines, which could draw on that of physical ecology. For example, population ecology, which is concerned with studying populations of organisms, their organisations and dynamics, is readily adaptable for studying the information environment. This could include analysing factors such as population size, density, and changes in numbers and drawing from disciplines such as history, ethnography, and linguistics. Similar parallels can be drawn both from evolutionary ecology, which explores how competition and parasitism affect changes within organisms over time, and behavioural ecology, which deals with the interactions between organisms within an ecosystem. These readily apparent equivalents in information ecology include mapping agent behaviours and tactics over time vis-à-vis two or more actors engaged in an information competition to understand better how such activity escalates conflict or how entities change approaches and adapt tactics over time in relation to others. Similarly, models taken from behavioural ecology could be deployed to study how information animals engage with each other, technology, and information regularly.

Another more direct approach drawing on physical ecology takes a page straight from Humboldt: observing and documenting conditions and factors within various spaces, across times and geographies, to identify what kinds of information ecosystems exist and what happens within them. As mentioned earlier, information ecosystems are composed of the information animals living within them, the outputs they produce, along with the means used to do so. As with the physical environment, these must be assessed together not only to understand how that system works but also to classify and define information biomes and ecosystems and identify what patterns of activity occur within each type. Then, the question becomes one of what *can* be measured consistently over time. Apart from the methodological issues involved, this question is also important due to various inherent ethical, political, privacy, and human rights considerations.

This baselining of information ecosystems can be used in several ways. At the most basic level, it will identify unknown gaps in the current understanding of national information ecosystems. Identifying these gaps, either in missing data or limited research on specific communication mediums, can inform future priorities for supporting research aiming to furnish policymakers with the required evidence. In comparing different national information ecosystems, decisionmakers can identify patterns and categorise ecosystems to inform the development of best practices, measure progress or decline, justify budget allocations, or tweak regulations. Moreover, patterns could provide advanced indications regarding possible fluctuations before an information disturbance occurs. Better pattern analysis explains why some societies are more resilient to information pollution and offers insights for countering threats like disinformation or determining what might reasonably work from one ecosystem to another. But more importantly, taking an ecosystems approach can provide an objective means of analysing the information environment, which is much needed in a highly-polarised world.

Before democracies can talk about governing the information environment, it must first be understood. And that begins with consilience on the fundamental driver of that system—information.

2

FOR YOUR INFORMATION

You're walking down a busy street and notice a person facing you. The stranger deliberately catches your eye and abruptly points upwards. What do you do? Odds are you look to the sky to understand what they are trying to convey. You might register the act of pointing and the intended message in searching for what they are pointing at, but you aren't likely to think to yourself, "Now, that's information!" That is the problem with information; humans tend to notice it for the message it contains or, worse, the absence of it, for example, in a crisis. Indeed, we are more interested in the interpretative meaning that could explain a situation to us. In this regard, information is a lot like energy. In the physical environment, humans are more likely to recognise energy as it manifests in movement, heat, light, or photosynthesis, where solar energy transforms carbon dioxide and water into food for plants. The utilitarian lenses we deploy tend to emphasise tangible outputs and processes rather than the inherent potential contained in the ability to cause change. Similarly, information is recognised as outputs like content, often through a lens of the tools used to produce it rather than the ability to inform. Like energy in the physical world, information is constantly flowing through and around us, and where energy is necessary for all physical life, information is necessary for all understanding and, in particular, for one that is shared with others. To understand information, its attributes, and impact to the level that science currently enables an understanding of energy, we need to study it not only for its qualities and role but also as a constituent component of a complex information environment. This means content and meaning, not just what is produced from it, but also how it flows, is harnessed and shaped, and ultimately binds humans together or tears them apart.

As philosopher Fred Dretske aptly noted, "In the beginning, there was information. The word came later."[1] As with so many words, information means many things to many people. Much of the problem with defining information stems from its interchangeability of outputs, moving easily between forms while often meaning something slightly different to each field of study or practice that encounters it, be it physics, computer science, or communications.[2] Information determines almost everything about our existence, from the risk of developing diseases such as Alzheimer's to concepts for telling the time or forecasting the weather.[3] As a result, information comes in many forms. It can present as an utterance, a word, or a sentence, but information can also be a scene, an output, an experience, or a string of code.[4] The most common ideas of what information is are likely in the outputs produced from it, such as documents, books, songs, and images. At its broadest, then, information is anything processed to provide meaning. At its most muddled, information is a contested concept that is much debated, still lacking a clear consensus for a core definition that can be consistently applied across disciplines.[5]

Some philosophers break information out into parts like meaningful data and documents, which puts the emphasis on an output's ability to inform.[6] Others think information defies neat categorisation and ideas like data, information, and knowledge are something more of a continuum.[7] In this thinking, raw data is somehow analysed and coded into a structured form that is then aggregated to generate knowledge.[8] But this notion, that humans are always rational creatures seeking out raw data to churn into information in some structured manner that leads to wisdom, seems more like a technology-inspired dream of robot-like humans than how we often function. It's a pervasive idea, though. Technological language around mental information processing has crept into neuroscience descriptions of how humans think, becoming a dominant metaphor, albeit one some neuroscientists are pushing back on.[9] But is the human mind like a computer, or did humans build computers to function like our minds? It's an interesting conundrum, though I can't help but wonder if it isn't also stemming from a need to set humans apart from the rest of the animal kingdom.

Yes, humans can be rational and draw on experience, and we have a natural tendency to think in hierarchical categories. But we are also still animals.[10] Is a newborn baby's "startle response" to a sudden movement or loud noise based on data they've acquired in their short life? That's unlikely, but there is *something* coded in the biological makeup of that child that causes this response, and I would argue that this something (like the fight, flight, or freeze response) is information. Indeed, renowned evolutionary biologist John Maynard Smith noted that information is a central concept in contemporary biology and that "developmental biology can be seen as the study of how information in the genome is translated into the adult structure, and evolutionary biology of how the information came to be there in the first place."[11] Some information processing happens without humans even knowing, and not all of it results in direct knowledge for the human. The fact that genes are already coded renders the data-information-knowledge continuum insufficient as a definitional concept to explain information in the context of the information environment.

In continuing this utilitarian approach, some researchers view information through the prism of veracity, maintaining that false or faulty information invalidates its key purpose—to inform.[12] Others, particularly drawing from computer science, view any sort of data as information, regardless of its accuracy, for something need not necessarily be true to hold meaning.[13] While this perceived difference may be useful in technological domains where information is either statically stored or used in a purposefully defined logical chain, the situation becomes more complex with humans. The fact is that the ability to inform happens a lot faster than the truth is often established. In some ways, humans are informed unconsciously, mooting the idea that information must inherently be truthful. When we feel cold, we need not verify the accuracy of the sensation with a thermometer before grabbing a sweater. (Although my father might if I ask him to turn up the thermostat instead.) The feeling informs our response. If someone comes at us with a knife, we don't need to know that the person wants to harm us before the situation has informed an automatic response to danger in our brain. For people who didn't know what an earthquake was, experiencing one would be terrifying. If they believed in deities of any sort, an obvious conclusion was that the gods were mad. This thinking would inform their response to placate the gods through sacrifices or some other behavioural change. The act of informing is not dependent on the truth. Information and truth are two separate concepts, confused with each other in that truths are an informational output, something humans create through processing information. Truth is inherently dependent on information, but not the other way around.

Truth can be based on social norms that take time to develop. In this sense, Nietzsche was not far off when he described truths as "illusions of which one has forgotten that they *are* illusions."[14] It's much easier to forget that something is an illusion if others share it, reaffirming its validity through a multitude of echoes. Moreover, truth is often much slower to arrive than information. And sometimes, when truth arrives, prejudices prevent its acceptance. The truth is pineapple is delicious on pizza. The addition of pineapple to pizza by Sam Panopolous in Canada in 1962 informed some people how tasty the dish could be, while it informed others how dear their pre-existing idea of pizza was to them.[15] On one side, you have those who love it; on the other, those who see it as an aberration, including many Italian friends who regularly send me jokes about my poor taste. That's the funny thing about our relationship with "truth"; our need to have it validated by others compels us to share it. In addition to being information animals, humans are inherently social creatures, and we seem to have a deep-seated need for the beliefs we've formed from information to be confirmed by others in our society.

In some cases, being presented with the truth fails to inform an audience as intended. As the philosopher Jürgen Habermas noted, "the concept of truth is interwoven with that of fallible knowledge" and can be based merely on the better argument.[16] The subjectivity of determining truth is complicated by human perception, with people processing information based on how they already understand the world, not necessarily corresponding to facts.[17] For example, people who felt the process for testing and approving COVID-19 vaccines was simply too quick to be trusted based this thinking on information such as how long it had taken other drugs to get through this process under normal circumstances. It can take years for drugs to go through testing and approval processes, but that doesn't mean it isn't possible to do so quickly and safely. How a person might process this information to inform their choice about taking COVID-19 vaccinations will be based on their prior knowledge and trust in the system overseeing the drug approval process. If a person used the data of past processes to inform their thinking that COVID-19 vaccines can't be trusted, is that not the act of informing, even if it is a faulty conclusion?

Increasingly, much of the information we process over a lifetime is not based on first-hand experience but comes from our interaction with society and the wider knowledge base it has accumulated.[18] As evolutionary biologist Richard Dawkins noted, "Man is dominated by culture, by influences learned and handed down."[19] A growing interdependence on shared information is a hallmark of an information society.[20] According to philosophers Cailin O'Connor and James Owen:

> the ability to share information and influence one another's beliefs is part of what makes humans special. It allows for science and art—indeed, culture of any sort. But it leads to a conundrum. How do we know whether to trust what people tell us?[21]

This dependency on shared information has consequences, not in the least in terms of the relationship between information and the development of beliefs and, ultimately, knowledge. Given that we cannot possibly experience all information first-hand, we are reliant on others to fill in the gaps, blurring the distinction between that which we believe we know and actual knowledge.[22] Perhaps we ought to take the twentieth-century political commentator Walter Lippmann's words on the topic as wisdom and warning: "The only feeling that anyone can have about an event he does not experience is the feeling aroused by his mental image of that event. That is why until we know what others think they know, we cannot truly understand their acts."[23] Truth can be a very difficult thing to pin down. Much of what can inform, such as other people's experiences or interpretations of them, suggests that truth is not an inherent component of information.

However, truth often plays a role in how democracies attempt to govern engagement with information. Many democracies claim their attempts to influence audiences through strategic communications, information operations, public affairs, or public diplomacy are truth-based, versus adversarial propaganda which is not.[24] Truth has also been used in community standards on social networks and an increasing body of legislation addressing the use of information to influence target audiences.[25] In this way, truth is factored in more deliberatively, as a means for setting rules and boundaries and can only be done *a priori*. However, policymakers should take care in using truth as the singular line across which we shouldn't step, given how slippery, subjective, and, most importantly, evolving the concept can be. Indeed, these attempts to euphemise communications and regulate content along lines of truth from fiction do not work so well in practice, because one person's truth might not be another's.

The point is that truth can be subjective depending on how it is derived. Truth based on social norms and beliefs is more subjective than truth based on rigorous scientific evidence, especially if it is developed based on many studies over time. Regardless of origins, truth is not guaranteed to inform people, at least not always insofar as the person sharing it might intend. The ability to inform is contingent not on the truth but on other factors, such as biology in our automatic stress response, our preconceived notions that affect information processing, and our ability to make sense of information. This means that information, the potential ability to inform, cannot be understood in isolation but as part of an everlasting process that combines the totalities of interactions between individuals and is impacted by the conditions in which it occurs.

In this holistic approach, information like energy can be seen as potential. The ability to inform, like the ability to cause change, is unharnessed and unformed. An early idea of this can be seen in Plato's description of "the colorless, formless, intangible essence, visible only to mind, the pilot of the soul."[26] More recently, the authors of one meta-study on definitions of information concluded that "information can be thought of as a lot like air or the 'ether' of the Middle Ages."[27] Just as energy is bound into organic matter through photosynthesis, for example, so too does information require a process to manifest into something more. In the case of plants, this process requires factors including sunlight, heat, and precipitation. In the information environment, this process requires conditions such as the ability to process, share, and understand information. In other words, it needs someone or something to process that potential into a form that is intelligible to other information animals. Where energy becomes plants, information becomes content, codes, and messaging, a diverse array of informational flora shaped by its environment. This means that understanding what information really is also requires understanding the beings that process it and the context in which it occurs.

Like with outputs, the tangible means used to process information have often been the focus of study. But, as with outputs, while focusing on technology itself may be warranted for specific utilitarian purposes, many of these missed or avoided discussing the essence of what information really is. Throughout the ages, the apparent necessity to improve one's tools to survive and excel may have led to the interpretation of human experience with information through a technological lens, leaning the discourse toward concepts and technologies used to process and disseminate information.[28] Take Claude Shannon's theory of information, for example, which drew on mathematics and focused on the act of quantifying, storing, and communicating information, rather than on the nature of information itself.[29] Similarly, in the Soviet Union, Andrei Nikolaevich Kolmogorov developed mathematical models related to information transfer, which is considered today as a foundation for modern complexity theory.[30] While both applied approaches are integral to explaining how information transmission over a variety of carriers works, their narrower focus did not address what information is more holistically.[31] It's sort of like having just one theory of energy that focuses only on power generation and grids, neglecting the role of energy in the wider environment.

Many processes enable the ability to inform, such as codes that connect a combination of letters with spoken sounds to translate alphabets into language.[32] Taking a pen to paper is a form of processing information, just as thinking can be.[33] Changes in technology often influence how information is shaped and presented to wider audiences, such as through mass media, but each is essentially just the introduction of a new means for transforming and transmitting information.[34] Approaching the idea of information through a narrow lens, such as one means of processing it, misses the forest for the trees and can have dire consequences for policymakers.

Focusing on one piece of technology used to process information can be a distraction and attempts to govern its use can create an illusion of control. As is covered in more detail in Chapter 5, the first King Charles of England learned this the hard way. Like many leaders today, he fretted about a rise in disinformation, leading him to try to control the newly introduced printing presses and ban all rumours and slander about him, particularly those about returning England to the Catholic papacy.[35] Despite Charles' attempts, controlling who could print material in England didn't stop the flow of propaganda from abroad or domestic politicians from using such content for their own gain. Charles focused on the weeds, missing the wider forest where he operated. He failed to see the changing conditions in his information ecosystem—the rise in literacy and the growing engagement of the public in politics, or the increased speeds information was moving via the newly founded post and advances in waterway travel. He didn't see how interconnected the English information ecosystem was with the wider information environment in Scotland, Ireland, or Europe. By the time he understood he was in an information competition with political actors demanding change and increased democracy, it was too late. Despite his attempt to control the information environment, Charles still lost his throne. And his head.

Similar patterns are being repeated among modern policymakers today. In assessing challenges arising in the information environment, such as disinformation, the emphasis is placed on the content or the means of processing and distributing it. Perhaps instinctively, to protect ourselves from what we consider unwanted, we reach for blunt tools like content moderation and regulation in a bid to control its spread. Often, this does not achieve the desired effect of removing the offending disinformation, nor, more importantly, the beliefs it spawned in society. Yesterday, we worried about social media; today, it is artificial intelligence.[36] While studying technology is important, we must look beyond single tools and studies that use limited audience samples to show the impact they might be causing and study the system. Understanding what makes an information ecosystem resilient starts with an appreciation for the true nature of information.

As alluded to earlier, information starts as potential and, as such, is an abstract quality: it is the ability to inform. This ability manifests in automatic responses informed by biology and it teaches us to mimic others and learn. The ability to inform also manifests in new ideas that spread, leading to outputs once information has been processed into a form that can be shared among humans. Often, this is done by some process or means of communication, which can be as simple as pointing and as complex as the wireless transmission of a message through the ether. The processing of this information will be shaped by the experiences and understanding of the people making sense of it. In this sense, both the sender and receiver of information are important. To understand information, then, we must first recognise that it is fundamentally potential, shaped by all who process it, before moving on to studying who is doing that, under what conditions, and using which means to produce what types of outputs. It is the relationship between these elements that must be analysed to understand information's role in the information environment. As ecologist and complexity scientist Eric Barlow told a TED audience, "The more you step back, embrace complexity, the better chance you have of finding simple answers, and it's often different than the simple answer that you started with."[37]

3

THE INFORMATION ENVIRONMENT

You find yourself in a busy train station, tickets to a destination in one hand and, in the other, a folded map of the metro you used to get here. All around, people are moving about in different directions; some are talking, and you pick up bits of conversation as they pass. A sizable group has formed in front of a screen showing details about train departures, stops, and platforms for boarding. On either side of the digital ticker are television screens playing a loop of commercials for restaurants, clothing, electronics, and more. Overhead, a repetitive voice calls out the same details on the ticker but intersperses this with warnings about security threats and travel rules. You think about the book you just picked up for the trip and glance around at the signs for platform locations to get ready for your train's announcement. Your phone vibrates, so you look at it; it's a notification from an app about severe weather in the area. Looking up at the digital ticker again, you can see the sky has darkened considerably in the windows above. A storm is coming. Something catches your eye to the left; pushed halfway into the train station wall is a cart of luggage. You recognise it from the Harry Potter films and take a photo, posting it on social media. All of this unfolds almost at once, in the same area, involving the same you. You are an information animal, and this is your modern habitat: the information environment.

Even right now, you are reading this book. It might be words on a paper, maybe a screen, or someone's voice narrating it, but you are processing information by weaving together various threads in your head. So long as a human is alive, they are processing information. Information is all around us; it is part of us, and it is what drives us. We are as much a part of the information environment as it is a part of us. The two things are inextricable. We might have fooled ourselves into believing that we are something separate from nature, but our relationship with information is impossible to sever. Even if you can stop your brain from thinking thoughts through meditation, the cells in your body are still busy processing information.

The information environment might be more easily thought of as an often-unseen layer within the physical world that sometimes manifests itself in material outputs, mostly produced by humans, although some are outsourcing that role to human-created tools such as artificial intelligence. In this regard, the information animal is an agent of change, processing information to make sense of the world and sharing it with others. They are a catalyst through which the ability to inform *becomes* its potential to inform. These human agents are one of three basic and interconnected aspects of the information environment that, when combined, create ecosystems. Unlike the other two, outputs and means, without information animals, the information environment and ecosystems within it cannot come into being. In other words, human consciousness is required to create outputs, means, and the information environment. The information environment is as much inside our head as it is in the outputs we produce, like chatter, directions, timetables, characters, and weather forecasts, or the means we develop to share them, like language, signs, digital tickers, printing presses, and mobile applications. These outputs and means are the basis for processes that move information through the information environment between information animals, creating complex and dynamic ecosystems. All three of these aspects—the agents, their outputs, and means—must be conceptualised and analysed together, for collectively, through their relationships, they form information ecosystems. Think of it as a web or a tapestry consisting of numerous threads of different sizes and colours. While it is possible to investigate each aspect (or thread) in isolation, doing so misses some crucial element of what makes the information environment a system and, moreover, why it is so important to a social group and humanity overall.

Agents

Information animals, as agents, are the one fundamental aspect of the information environment that must be understood to make sense of ecosystems. As the catalyst, it is necessary to understand the context in which agents process information, including what factors might have preconditioned them prior to, or influenced them during, the act of processing information such that it might be distorted or changed. Through their agency, the information animal processes information into outputs that can be shared with others, who in turn process that information anew. This is the basic process by which information flows through the ecosystems. This act of processing information into something shareable for other agents to then process again creates something akin to the food chain in the physical world, except information rather than energy is transferred through the ecosystem. As an agent, I wrote this book: an output based on the works of others I could process, limited by my means such as language skills, and framed by my education in Canada and England, the fields of Russian and War Studies, as well as my work experience. Now you, as an agent, are processing what I've written based on your circumstances, and if you choose to tell someone else what you've read, it will be from your perspective. We are two links in an information chain. This information chain builds more like a cyclical loop over time than in a direct linear fashion, and the longer it is unbroken, the greater the likelihood that the information ecosystem in which it is forming will become more complex. At the same time, the longer it is unbroken, the stronger the information chain between generations or groups becomes, just like brain neurons forming a strong pattern when they activate together over time. Because so much of the processing that happens in the information environment happens in the minds of agents, the circumstances that influence the cognition of information animals are the basis for contextually understanding how an information ecosystem develops. Understanding what happens in the minds of humans is difficult, but thanks to various fields, including branches of psychology and neurology, we are learning more, especially about some populations of today's information animals. It is, of course, more challenging to really understand agents who are no more, as the outputs they produced are often the only thing left behind that offer clues. However, we can't truly understand the outputs produced by agents if we do not understand the context in which those information animals processed them.

Take Sumerian proverbs, for example. Thanks to the likes of Edmund I. Gordon, some Mesopotamian proverbs have been translated into English. Sumerian is one of the oldest inscribed languages in the world. It was spoken for a thousand years before it fell into obscurity for more than another millennium. Working from cuneiforms, linguists began attempting to decipher their meaning in the nineteenth century. These tablets are covered in tiny symbols representing syllables, etched in neat rows in the clay around 3,500 years ago. Some of these cuneiforms were used in Mesopotamian schools, posing riddles to students, for example:

> A house based on a foundation like the skies
> A house one has covered with a veil like a secret box
> A house set on a base like a goose
> One enters it blind,
> Leaves it seeing[1]

More often than not, when someone quotes this Sumerian riddle, they leave out the first three lines. Something clearly doesn't make it through the translation. The introduction must have meant something to teachers in Mesopotamia, but without that context, it is hard for someone today in, say, Canada to follow. However, the last two lines still resonate. What might a person figuratively enter unseeing and exit from with sight? The answer is a school. Yet even there, one would need to have some sense of what a school is and, moreover, believe wisdom was acquired in it to deduce the answer. Having the means to make sense of an output, such as having linguists with the language skills to translate cuneiforms, isn't enough. A shared cultural reference is also required.

Outputs

Information ecosystems are built on a shared cultural understanding, which adds an important social element to the information animal. Information moves through ecosystems via communication, and that process requires agents to be able to understand each other. The ability to communicate emerged from a need to cooperate with others, beginning with pointing and gestures that eventually developed into languages.[2] This process might have grown out of a demand to hunt large animals or herds collectively or for another evolutionary reason.[3] That need certainly influenced early paintings, another means of communication producing an output in the form of an image. In one such painting found along the La Valltorta ravine in Spain, someone depicted a group of hunters attacking a herd of deer with bows and arrows some 7,000 years ago.[4] But long before that, humans were painting figurative images like the one five times older in Sulawesi, Indonesia, depicting a babirusa or pig-deer in the wild accompanied by a series of silhouetted hands against red paint elsewhere in the caves.[5] Unfortunately, all we have remaining is the output of these communications, the rock art, and today we can only guess at the original meaning and the agents behind them. The information environment has been around for a very long time, but our ability to make sense of what occurs within it is not an unbroken line. An agent must have the means to understand communication, like knowing what a gesture represents or what a picture is trying to say.[6] Is that cave painting instructional, explaining to others how to hunt together? Are those hand outlines the equivalent of today's sign outside a house telling passers-by that the Jones family lives here? The point isn't always in the message or output so much as it is in knowing the context in which the agent processed that information and why. Being able to unlock the message is key, a process that is as much about decoding the communications as it is about understanding the context in which it was formed.

Decoded outputs can help provide context about information animals. For example, in 2013, Pierre Tallet discovered the oldest papyri in the world, "written by men who participated in the building of the Great Pyramid, the tomb of the Pharaoh Khufu, the first and largest of the three colossal pyramids at Giza just outside modern Cairo."[7] These documents shed light on the people and circumstances around the construction of these massive structures, which required a significant farming, mining, and shipping economy to achieve. Similarly, we know that the Parthenon in Athens was meant to be a testament to the then-growing importance and hoped-for dominance of democracy in ancient Greece as part of the Periclean building programme, thanks to other outputs like written histories, plays, and decrees.[8] Contemporary memoirs like those written by Edward Hyde, Earl of Clarendon and a supporter of King Charles I of England, shed light on how opponents reacted to the regent's actions.[9] Whereas collections of pamphlets like the Thomason Tract at the British Library and the Library of Thomas Marshall at Lincoln College at Oxford University provide insights into what people at the time of the civil war were reading and, sometimes, who was printing it. Outputs can help us better understand the context in which agents were operating and, thus, the situation in an information ecosystem at the time. Some outputs are more permanent than others. The spoken word is fleeting if no further outputs are created to document what was said. Paper can disintegrate over time or be burned. Even pyramids, some representing the pathway for a pharaoh to the afterlife and thus their importance, can be destroyed. Yet outputs can long outlast the agents who make them.

Outputs tend to be the most widely studied aspect of the information environment, in large part because they are the most accessible and tangible element to study. It's far easier to study propaganda posters that have been plastered in public as part of a campaign, than it is to analyse the organisation that might have created them or the reasons why people might be receptive to them, if at all. The same goes today with public social media posts. Studying a phenomenon like Donald Trump's tweets only tells us what he posts and who might be engaging with that content, but it doesn't shed much light on the former president's relationship with the wider information ecosystem. Influencers like Trump have a symbiotic relationship with traditional media. Coverage of his antics on social media helps drive more traffic to his posts, but he also responds to media coverage to elicit reactions from his followers. In turn, Trump's sensationalism attracts eyeballs to news coverage, helping raise media profits. What Trump posts on social media is only part of the story, which is also reflected in whatever he is responding to, including what happens in person, through his online comments and moves through his followers on to different platforms and into media coverage where it reaches further audiences. In this sense, information ecosystems are dynamic, and with the addition of social media, mass communications have become more participatory, enabling almost anyone to get involved.[10] Trump's social media posts don't exist in isolation. Indeed, they acquire additional meaning beyond content based on how they are responded to and used by other agents within an information ecosystem.

It can be easy to forget that context matters in trying to understand the modern information environment from today's vantage point. Chances are, if we are investigating our own information ecosystem, the shared cultural knowledge needed to do that is readily available—we live in it. This makes outputs seem like the easiest way to conceptualise the information environment (and perhaps this is why censorship of content is a common response to unwanted outputs). Today's movies, memes, news coverage, and books are all things that we can engage with, but they are just one component of the overall information environment at a specific point in time. Indeed, with a little bit of distance, what might be readily understood today could be gobbledygook in a decade, century, or millennium. (Or even from one generation to another, what is gigachad rizz anyway?) Moreover, given our proximity to the context in which these outputs are made, we might be deluding ourselves into thinking we understand the system in which this occurs without a systematised framing around which to situate these case studies. Knowing that an output exists is not the same as knowing what its existence means in relation to the wider information environment. This understanding is especially critical in policymaking where putting emphasis in the wrong place (e.g. limiting distribution of outputs or countering unwanted content in low-trust settings) will lead to responses that, at best, are ineffective and, at worst, detrimental to the integrity of the overall information environment.

When a society fails to take a systemic approach to problems in a complex environmental system, a single well-intended intervention can have disastrous outcomes. Unfortunately, human history is filled with such stories. For example, the introduction of the South American cane toad to address pests in Australian sugar plantations continues to wreak havoc nearly a century later, killing its prey and predators alike. Australian droughts made establishing sugarcane challenging enough, but a domestic pest that became known as the cane beetle was a bigger challenge, eating the roots of the crop. So, upon learning that a toad had been successful elsewhere in the world, officials from the Bureau of Sugar Experiment Stations captured a sample and brought 102 of them back to Australia to breed, releasing 2,400 in 1935.[11] As of 2019, an estimated 200 million cane toads were on the continent. That's more than an 8 million per cent increase in eighty-eight years. Cane toads lay between 8,000 to 30,000 eggs twice a year. They eat almost anything and yet cannot be eaten by anything in Australia. And sadly, the introduction of the toads did little to nothing to address the beetle problem.[12] Some politicians in Australia have called for programmes to pay kids to kill the pests, but the toads breed so quickly that experts say the pursuit would be futile.[13] The moral of this story? What might work to solve a problem in one ecosystem can have disastrous consequences in another, but you'd have to study the ecosystems to know that.

Current approaches to counter foreign influence operations are similar. We see a problem like disinformation on social media through singular posts and think banning users from spreading it will be the answer. Far from eradicating a lie or silencing a liar, blunt tools like de-platforming and content moderation are poorly understood, and some research indicates that affected users simply migrate to new platforms with less oversight.[14] The main problem is the way democratic societies are attempting to understand the information environment through its component parts or problems within it. This piecemeal approach means missing the forest not for the trees—but for the weeds. Misinformation and disinformation are just that: weeds that, if unrooted, will pop up somewhere else. Policymakers in democracies are trying to eradicate a noxious and prevalent pest that has grown alongside humans forever. It might not even be possible to remove it entirely. And yet that's just what many democracies are attempting to do: spraying disinformation with content moderation to make it go away.

Means

The means of communication is the third basic aspect of the information environment and relates to how information is processed into a format that can be shared. That can include things we recognise as tools, like pen and paper, radio, or the telephone, but it can also be things we take more for granted and don't see as tools, like non-verbal behaviour, language, or alphabets. The continued evolution of tools, from the printing press to social media and now artificial intelligence, and the buzz generated about them by those profiting from or fearing them, often eclipses other aspects of the information environment. In this way, common understanding about the information environment at any given time is framed through the narrow lens of what new means has captured the popular imagination. This isn't surprising, given what is known about which emotions drive people to share information. Jonah Berger, a marketing professor at the Wharton School at the University of Pennsylvania, found that among the arousing emotions that lead to information going viral is the feeling of awe.[15] Information animals are inspired by innovation, but that emotional hit we get in learning about it might cause us to over-emphasise the latest technology. This has led some philosophers to think in terms of media epochs built around what they believe to be key game-changing inventions, with ideas that the written word ended the age of orality and Gutenberg ushered in an age of print.[16] In this line of thinking, the new technology constitutes some revolutionary shift, fundamentally changing the nature of the information environment.

However, most new technologies don't emerge from an absolute void but build on each other. Ancient Egyptian hieroglyphs inspired cuneiforms, which in turn stimulated the alphabet in a process known as stimulus diffusion.[17] Photographic cameras were inspired by earlier technology like the camera obscura, which helped artists to make projections of scenes from the physical world on to flat surfaces, which itself draws on the use of shadows and silhouettes to create images that date to the first cave paintings of a person's hand.[18] Paper and letter-writing had just as much to contribute to the Renaissance as the printing press, possibly more, but if we focus on one innovation, we lose sight of the role of the other.[19] All these innovations built over time into what we perceive today as our current information environment. While it is true that new technologies shape how information is processed, the impact of a new processing method may be more technical than far-reaching and systemic. Certainly, the telegraph led to forms of shorthand codes due to length constraints and cost, thus presenting information differently from how it might have been written in a letter that could provide more word space.[20] Text messaging on mobile phones has led to a pantheon of acronyms and initialisms replacing phrases. However, neither the shorthand nor the text lingo has supplanted modern language, not yet anyway. Gestures didn't lose their meaning or utility because language evolved. How would you tell someone to be quiet without making a sound? In many parts of the world, an index finger to the mouth will do it. Humans still paint, and some of it is in public spaces and walls, conveying nuanced political commentary, as is the case with the work of Banksy. The philosopher Marshall McLuhan believed electronics created a global network that was an extension of the "central nervous system" that would see humans "translated more and more into the form of information, moving toward the technological extension of consciousness."[21] In a way, McLuhan was right, but it wasn't technology making us information animals; we had been so since communication in its most basic form developed. Technology merely changes how we process and share information.

As our means become more complex, so too does the underlying infrastructure needed to make it work. Therefore, the understanding of the role and impact any means have in a society must also include an analysis of all the infrastructure required to make use of any given means, including cyber and electricity, which, in turn, must consider investments into communication systems and dependencies in the provision of hardware. The role of infrastructure to facilitate communications is not new to the current era either. In ancient Athens, the governance system was structured in a networked manner, with demes (a sort of suburb) and trittyes (groups of demes) connected via a sixth-century BCE road system that helped move information through the city-state.[22] The United States Postal Service was seen as a means for fostering national unity in the mid-nineteenth century, and new legislation in the United States in 1845 and 1851 helped decrease the costs of postage, offering favourable rates for distributing newspapers and periodicals.[23] The means are things we create to make information shareable, including both the tools we use to produce outputs as well as the channels to facilitate the flow of information through information ecosystems. While the means and the outputs they help produce can influence information animals, these are things agents can control and destroy—yes, even artificial intelligence. The means and outputs are nothing without humans; for both to work and have a purpose, information animals are still required to make use of them. The question is really *how* we use them and here there are patterns that span time.

The means beget more means, but they don't do that on their own; agents do. Humans continue to develop their means and outputs—they build on each other over time. So long as an information chain remains intact, this process of creating new tools that change how we communicate is likely to continue unless there is a cataclysmic break that wipes out current means and outputs down to the most fundamental, like language. Even then, the nature of the cataclysm would impact what follows. For example, an environmental disaster that destroys most of civilisation and leaves a few people to pick up the pieces from output fragments and a shared language could be a massive setback. However, history shows that humans have persisted in building information chains anew. A society that decides to break the information chain and control future developments deliberately, much like the Taliban in Afghanistan, might persist for a time in an isolated space. This would become increasingly challenging for some societies depending on how interconnected that information ecosystem is to the wider information environment.

Knowing all of this, we can look past outputs and means alone to study what the reactions of agents have been to the introduction of innovations and seek to understand what their impact has been on the overall information environment throughout history. This comparative analysis may assist with uncovering patterns that might help policymakers prepare for the changes that the next innovation will inevitably bring about. Likewise, we must also seek to understand what happens when an information chain is broken to identify what constitutes resilience to help society recover. This might seem like a distant concern, but as more and more information becomes digital, our ability to store and retrieve it over time will be limited by our changing means, which is cutting us off from recently made outputs. In a very short span of time, information has been stored on floppy discs, CD-ROMs, flash drives, and now the cloud. As computers change, some of these storage methods are becoming inaccessible, to say nothing of how long the technology will endure physically or the questions that arise regarding accessibility to and control of information. In a nightmare scenario, the loss of the power grid and the internet would be enough to destroy all that we have saved in the cloud, like photos, documents, and communications. The mass number of outputs we produce today might be voluminous, but their ability to last, like Mesopotamia cuneiforms, is unlikely. The key question here, of course, is the preservation of knowledge in the information chain.

Information Ecosystems

The state of an information ecosystem is not permanent; it changes just like the physical environment. Understanding the processes that connect agents, means, and outputs, along with the factors that embody information ecosystems and the surrounding conditions that influence them, is equally important.

Here, processes are the actions that move information through ecosystems, whereas factors are aspects of ecosystems that can be quantifiably measured to indicate the state of an ecosystem at any given time. These factors are surrounded by conditions, such as the economy and state of education, that also influence the overall ecosystem. For example, Athens' proximity to water and its economic interests (two conditions) influenced the development of its navy, helping move information farther and faster (a means) that connected the city-state to the outside world, opening the information ecosystem, which spawned new ideas, such as democracy (an output).[24] Factors that make for a more open information ecosystem similarly brought new ideas to Vietnam, as will be explored in Chapter 7. The Vietnamese information ecosystem became increasingly more interconnected to the international information environment with the introduction of ocean steam liners, the Suez Canal, transoceanic communication cables, and wireless telegraphy (means). These changes, coupled with a French policy of exiling Vietnamese dissenters (agents) in a rather physical process of "de-platforming" to other parts of the empire, helped expose a generation of reformers to political ideas (outputs) that would spur an independence movement. From this movement emerged the likes of Hồ Chí Minh, whose declaration of independence in 1945 preceded decades of conflict, first with the French and later with the Americans.[25] The opening of an information ecosystem is one factor that might affect the information environment.

Information ecosystems contain different archetypes of information animals, the presence of which could help categorise various kinds of ecosystems. *Political agents* engage within information ecosystems to seek power over public decision-making processes and often try to control the means of information and outputs to their benefit. Those efforts, in turn, might impact the factor of how open an information ecosystem remains. *Proselytisers* are information animals who are motivated by the spread and adoption of their beliefs or ideas by others. *Profiteers* are agents who have the means to process, produce and distribute information and do so for financial gain, much like Mark Zuckerberg does with Meta. These archetypes will feature as recurring characters throughout this book. The agents use the means and outputs available in an information ecosystem to meet their aim, engaging with other information animals who are often swept up in the information competition that ensues. Sometimes, this leads to overt cooperation, but it can also result in other relationships between agents like mutualism, commensalism, and parasitism.[26]

Just like among species in the physical world, information competition leads to evolution, what Charles Darwin described as a process of struggle and adaption.[27] Instead of producing species, however, information animals are producing ideas and beliefs that they need to have shared by others to develop a consensus reality. These beliefs do not have to be the best explanations for the world, much like the way nature produces species "'just good enough' to reproduce", to quote marine biologist, Rafe Sagarin[28] The surviving outputs simply must be enduring enough to stay in the game, passing from one generation to the next or, in the case of information, from person to person.[29] The evolutionary struggle can also be conceptualised as an escalation, whereby prey and predator continuously adapt in juxtaposition with each other.[30] Such thinking is similar to Carl von Clausewitz's ideas on war, which others have described as using opposites to trace the "dynamic links that connect all elements of war into a state of permanent interaction."[31] Through this struggle to survive and the adaptation of traits leading to successful procreation, species become, according to zoologist Charles S. Elton, "more or less specialised for life in a narrow range of environmental conditions, for by being so specialised they can be more efficient."[32] When this happens, species that share similar specialisations begin to compete for resources if they attempt to live in the same niche.[33] This point will become clearer in the following chapters when we dive into historical accounts discussing dynamics that led to civil conflicts. For now, suffice it to say that all information animals share the same specialisation, which dictates the need to maintain a sufficiently organised and stable pattern of interwoven information threads that form a complex tapestry of our consensus reality. This is a complex process that happens constantly in a society, informed by myriad circumstances and social interactions. As this tapestry of reality forms in one's head, the need grows to confirm that the picture woven is accurate. Societies develop around these shared realities, enabling cooperation and co-existence. If two communities of humans develop different realities but attempt to live within the same niche or information ecosystem, they will begin to compete for resources, or in other words, the hearts and minds of those around them to ensure that their worldview is the one adopted by all.

Understanding these mental tapestries is key to unlocking the information environment. In assessing a formed tapestry, one needs to look at the various threads woven into it—they might be very, very old and consist of stories told over time. They might be new and reflect more immediate circumstances. The stitching might vary or be uneven. Some might have been added through education or indoctrination or the arrival of newcomers carrying different threads that changed the weaving process abruptly. Perhaps a thread or ability to connect them was lost partway through. Maybe one thread is so crucial, pulling it threatens to unravel the whole tapestry. In an information tapestry, the colours may inform when it might have been woven. They might also reflect the means available to create a reality, the tools and the outputs, which in part are impacted by available resources (recall the infrastructure reference above). The component parts of a tapestry form a whole, a picture of reality. Often, the accompanying interpretative narrative which explains that tapestry is what is most analysed in research about the information environment. While it is important (putting aside its often-subjective nature), it is just as, if not more, important to understand how the tapestry was constructed. Both the reality and its construction must be looked at in tandem to fully make sense of it and unlock the forecasting potential hidden behind identifiable patterns found across tapestries. Tapestries are created on frames, much like reality is woven in our heads. Social norms and experiences will frame worldviews in ways that inform how a tapestry develops. Shifts in that frame will alter the picture. All these parts are interrelated and must be assessed in tandem. This makes analysing the information environment exceptionally challenging. It can often be easier to construct histories in a chronological fashion, but it's important to remember that events in time are but one thread along with which many others are interwoven, like ideas, education, communications, and economy, each with their own past and complexity that must be considered in tandem. Assessing the tapestry of an information ecosystem can be discombobulating as the threads intersect, and their origins need to be unpacked.

The information environment is the space where information exists, comprising all its myriad forms and the surrounding conditions which affect it, such as the economy, geography, climate, and more. Information ecosystems within it are communities of information animals interacting with each other and the information environment around them as part of an interconnected system. The three aspects—agents, means, and outputs—must be understood together to understand the information environment: take away agents, and the context is lost; take away the means, and the outputs might not be produced; take away the outputs, and the context around the agents might be lost. As information is processed into outputs that build a shared understanding among information animals, that information ecosystem becomes more complex. In this way, humans shape the information environment, but they are also shaped by it. The information environment isn't a modern invention built solely of mass media or digital technology, but something that evolved far more organically of which humans are a part. It existed in some distant human past when our ancestors first began gesturing in a bid to organise themselves. It is safe to say that it will exist long after we've added generative artificial intelligence and whatever else we dream up in the future. The good news in seeing the information environment this way is that it enables the identification of patterns. If we know that there will always be new developments in the means of communication, and there will always be agents who seek to use those (and existing) means for similar ends—could there be ways to study those patterns and the conditions in which they occur, much like we study the physical environment? The answer is yes. Let's explore what they are in some information ecosystems of the past.

4

PULLING THREADS TOGETHER

ANCIENT GREECE

Much like the physical world, the information environment can be thought of as an intricate web of threads. These threads represent historical events, myths, cultural beliefs, and other ideas that connect a group of information animals through shared meaning and relevance. Interwoven in this complex tapestry are the means for sharing these ideas in common alphabets, languages, and other methods of expression. In this web, these interlaced threads begin to form patterns and pictures that emerge as something more tangible, like a book or a sculpture, only to knit back into the fabric that is the information environment. These threads can fray or snap, rendering the link and what came before less obvious to those who come later. But these threads can also be long, spanning millennia and geographies, becoming part of new tapestries along the way. In this constant state of interweaving change, sometimes two separate information ecosystems emerge, similar in their nature but quite different in their character. Such was the case with Athens and Sparta in Ancient Greece.

The changing factors and conditions within the Athenian information ecosystem created a climate in which a focus on democracy led to its mass promotion to the annoyance of their Greek neighbour. At this time, a growing number of men could engage in politics, and the information ecosystem opened to the world with the help of naval advancements, spreading people and information. Means such as a writing system and imported papyrus supported the growth of outputs like theatrical plays, among other arts that boomed. Economic conditions enabled major building projects promoting the real Athenian preoccupation at the time—its new sense of self as a leader of Greece and spreader of democracy—which might have come with little thought of their neighbours or even an understanding of them given Sparta's closed information ecosystem. But these two very different information ecosystems had something in common that fuelled tensions between them—a shared thread about the idea of honour.

Before the ancient periods that produced the lifelike sculptures, plays, and architecture which many moderns recognise as classically Hellenic, there was another older Greek civilisation, that of the Mycenaeans. These mainland Greeks, living during the Bronze Age, developed an advanced society that engaged in trade across the Mediterranean and organised resources to build large-scale infrastructure around palatial states. The Mycenaeans produced metalwork, pottery, figurines, and frescoes. They also developed a system of writing known as Linear B, which was borrowed from the earlier system of Minoan Linear A. Then, some 3,000 years ago, in the eleventh century BCE, the Mycenaeans, along with several other Bronze Age civilisations, collapsed, ushering in the Greek Dark Ages. And yet, a few threads from the Mycenaeans to those that followed held fast.

It took a couple of hundred years after the Linear B script was lost, but in the eighth century BCE the Greeks developed an alphabet building on that of the Phoenicians. Someone used this writing system to transcribe an epic poem called *The Iliad*, usually attributed to a mysterious blind poet, Homer, who may or may not have existed. The poem centres around the end of a ten-year siege by the Mycenaeans of Troy, featuring the hero Achilles, who is still remembered today. Writing in the second half of the fifth century BCE, Herodotus estimated that the "wars of Troy" happened 800 years before him, in the thirteenth century BCE, leaving a few hundred years between the event and its literary documentation. Over those centuries, the story was kept alive in the oral retelling of an epic poem. While the ancient Greeks certainly believed the war happened and the Romans later convinced themselves they were the descendants of Troy, moderns long thought both the event and place to be non-historical. That was until archaeologist Heinrich Schliemann uncovered the location of Troy in 1870 at Hissarlik, Turkey. Excavations at Troy have since uncovered arrowheads and a destructive fire, which some historians believe to be proof of war. It's not conclusive evidence to prove the Homerian epic true, but it's clear that no matter how many *means* are lost, so long as humans can communicate, information will continue to be shared. Troy was one thread connecting the Greeks to a tenuous past before the Dark Age. It was threads like this that both Sparta and Athens tugged for their origin stories.

A shared evolution stemming from the Homeric tradition bound Sparta and Athens. It can be easy to see the differences between the two city-states, but culturally they were connected. They were both Greek. They followed the same traditions and shared the same pantheon of gods.[1] Athens and Sparta shared similar concepts of honour, shaping their interpretations of and strong reactions to each other's actions. In some ways, it might have been the *nature* of their similarities from a shared tradition coupled with their *character* differences developed within their city-states that led to the rising friction and, ultimately, the outbreak of two wars between them. After all, as the novelist Hermann Hesse remarked, "If you hate a person, you hate something in him that is part of yourself."[2] Speculation on causes for the wars aside, these differences in character shaped the information ecosystems of Sparta and Athens, influencing their respective relationships to information. Despite shared traditions and ethnicity, the two communities told separate origin stories, and from there, the two information ecosystems began to diverge.

The Spartans claimed their kings were descendants of the divine Greek hero, Heracles. They were also viewed by Athenians and others to be invaders from the north, speaking the Dorian dialect of Greek. Wherever they came from, archaeology suggests that after the collapse of the Mycenaeans, settlements began to appear around what became Sparta, placing someone in the region from about the tenth century BCE.[3] Within a hundred years or so, the Spartans began facing internal instability, which Lycurgus was accredited with solving. His gift of law and order around the ninth century set the wheel spinning to create a yarn that endures to this day. Lycurgus's order was framed around three core principles: equality among citizens, military fitness, and austerity—or, in other words, everything for which the Spartans became famous. What resulted was an oligarchic system, where the power rested with a wealthy elite and, peculiarly, two kings as rulers. In practice, a small council made the decisions before bringing them to an assembly for a vote.[4] This reverence for equality, military, and rigour became the basis for the Spartan character and, in turn, shaped their relationship with information.

The information ecosystem of Sparta was a closed one. Indeed, little is known about Sparta, given Spartan control of access to the city by outsiders.[5] This information void about

Sparta perhaps facilitated the spread of misinformation about the city-state. Thucydides, an Athenian and the father of political realism, bemoaned how readily people accepted any story about the Spartans.[6] The city-state of Sparta was inland, and its coastal port of Gythio lies roughly forty-two kilometres away, which, at the time of writing this book, would take nine and half hours to reach by foot. This distance might have discouraged Spartan city-dwellers from being more outward-facing and enabled greater control over their information ecosystem.[7] What comes down to the present day is a carefully crafted image of what Spartans most likely wanted to be projected about them: an image of an extremely rigid and regimented society where Spartan male citizens dedicated their lives to the state and military.[8] The Spartan emphasis on military training overshadowed other pursuits, such as the arts, which were deemed less necessary to their society, although the city did have a rich history of poetry before this martial culture took deep hold. To this day, however, what is remembered about Spartan culture is its lack of art for art's sake. Even the way Spartans spoke was renowned, preferring a simple style of speech used sparingly and referred to by Greeks as laconic, named after the name of their region, Laconia.[9] These cultural quirks were a source of amusement in Athenian plays. In his eponymous piece, Aristophanes had the Athenian lead Lysistrata comment on the Spartan woman Lampito's looks: "Such clear skin, and that firm body—why, you could strangle a bull," to which she replies in a simplified dialect "By Castor and Pollux, that I could. It's the work I do in the gym, buddy, jump-kicking and bumping my tail."[10] Despite providing both boys and girls access to public education, Sparta put fewer resources into the means of information production, leaving little behind in records.[11] Indeed, Thucydides remarked how future generations might miss the greatness of Sparta given how little material they'd leave behind as a marker.[12]

This strict way of life was made possible because of another Spartan peculiarity in their social structure. In the eighth century BCE, the Spartans waged war on neighbouring Messenia, subjugating the people to the status of semi-slaves or serfs that they called Helots, whose labours ultimately enabled the Spartan mandatory lifetime dedication to military service. Along with the Helots, a loose grouping of second-class people called *perioikoi* also supported the system, although little is known about them today, other than that they were free but not citizens of Sparta, and their name meant "dwellers round about".[13] As Spartans were banned from engaging in trade and manual labour, they relied on Helots and *perioikoi* to sustain their way of life. In fact, Spartan citizenship was predicated on maintaining the strict military training programme, the *agoge*, which also required the financial means to be able to support the mess or *syssition* to which a man belonged and where he would take his meals with fellow soldiers. Failure to do so would result in a reduction of citizenship to an inferior status.[14] That was a dishonour any self-respecting Spartan would do all they could to avoid. Conquering and subjugating the Helots made this possible. It also helped Sparta build its reputation. This subjugation of neighbouring peoples, followed in the sixth century by annexing territory from rivals like Argos, helped Sparta build a reputation for military acumen. This reputation, in turn, made them the presumed military leader of the Greeks, first as the head of the Peloponnesian League from around 550 BCE comprised mainly of Dorian allies, and for a brief period as the head of the Hellenic alliance against the Persians. All allies in the Peloponnesian League were autonomous, except that they subordinated their foreign policy to Sparta. These threads, to the local people forced to support them and to the allies to whom they were reciprocally pledged, connected the Spartans to various other information animals beyond their fellow citizens. This web would impact how Spartans processed information to make sense of the world around them and to make the decisions to act.[15]

The Spartan domination of and dependence on the Helots made their society more insular and created a need to control the information ecosystem. Also needing to keep the Helots down, Spartans avoided lengthy foreign military campaigns. A ban on trade led to fewer Spartan economic ties abroad compared to Athens. This lack of exposure was conducive to suspicion and paranoia. Fearful of a Helot uprising, outsiders were suspected as potential allies to this oppressed people, who outnumbered the Spartans sevenfold.[16] This included the Athenians, who, despite having been a recent ally, were turned away from Sparta after offering help to quell a Helot uprising following a massive earthquake in 465 BCE.[17] For the Spartans, their information ecosystem had to be controlled, lest ideas of freedom permeate and take root with an already restive population of enslaved people. This fear shaped the character of the Spartan information ecosystem.

Sparta was a conservative society resistant to change. Spartans were bound by their traditions even more than they were by their desire for military superiority. They preferred clear orders and would celebrate traditional festivals when they were supposed to happen, even if this meant a military disadvantage.[18] The historian Kenneth W. Harl quipped that adversaries must have had a Spartan calendar of festivals to pick appropriate dates for attacking Hellas when the Spartans would otherwise be engaged.[19] Spartan commitment to observing the holidays would, on more than one occasion, delay them in fighting a battle. This is why the Spartans failed to show up on time to the Battle of Marathon, leaving Athens to miraculously defeat Persia in 490 BCE without the famed warriors' help, which in turn started to inform a changing Athenian sense of self that it too was a leader of Hellas. Encroachment from Persia was the catalyst that sparked the change in thought.

As the Greeks were emerging from their Dark Age, a massive empire formed to their east. The Persian Empire was the biggest to that date, spanning 5.5 million square kilometres.[20] Pushing its borders west in 547 BCE, the Persians conquered Ionia, inhabited by Greeks. Their rule wasn't an easy one, and the Ionians, sometimes aided by mainland Greeks, rebelled. In revenge, Darius the Great launched an invasion of Greece in 492 BCE, which ended badly for the Persians at Marathon. As the threat of reprisals loomed, the Greek city-states met in Corinth in 481 BCE, resulting in a Hellenic alliance to fight off future attacks from Persia. Sure enough, Darius's son Xerxes returned in 480 BCE, leading to a disastrous defeat of the Greeks led by the Spartans at Thermopylae. As the Greeks retreated, evacuating Athens, the Peloponnesian Allies led by Sparta built a defensive line to protect Corinth, destroying the road to Megara and effectively cutting the Athenians off to be left to invading Persians.[21] Things would turn around again in favour of the Greeks at the naval battle of Salamis in 480, led by the Athenian politician and general Themistocles. The Hellenic alliance would continue to push the Persians back under the Spartan leadership of Pausanias until the sacking of Byzantium in 478 BCE.

Thucydides recounted that the other Greeks were not big fans of Pausanias' behaviour at the siege. Rather vaguely, he speaks of his violence being "disagreeable to the Hellenes, particularly to the Ionians and the newly liberated populations."[22] Apparently, the Spartans had a rather intolerable habit of treating other free Greeks like Helots.[23] The Spartans were then asked to step down as leaders of the Hellenes, and the Athenians were invited to take their place. With this, the Spartans left the alliance, possibly because they felt the war was won and they needed to return to keep the Helots down, and the Delian League emerged with Athens as its head. Events and actions are a form of communication, open to interpretation by the information animals both sparking or experiencing them. Seen in the light of Greek honour, this change in leadership conveyed a dangerous message that became more problematic later. None of these information ecosystems existed in isolation from the other. The reaction to a neighbouring information animal's invasion, shaped by the confines of the Spartan information ecosystem, had a cascading and lasting effect in Athens, which, in turn, started an information competition between the two.

These details are more than an account of events that preceded the outbreak of the Peloponnesian wars; they shaped the perspectives of those who experienced them. In a way, the Athenians formed their worldview in juxtaposition to Sparta. In contrast to the Spartan origin story as northern invaders, Athenians fostered a shared identity of being "autochthonous or indigenous" to the region, speaking the Ionian form of Greek.[24] There is archaeological evidence to support this, with a settlement at Athens dating back 5,000 years which includes an important Mycenaean centre. As Athens emerged from the Greek Dark Ages, they too experienced social unrest and sought reforms. These started in the seventh century BCE with Draco's code, which aimed to stop the aristocracy's unfair manipulation of the Athenian oral law by enshrining a written constitution.[25] The Draconian code introduced new concepts like the Council and Assembly, enabling citizen-soldiers known as hoplites to participate in political life. As the name might suggest, the experiment didn't end well. Solon followed Draco in the early sixth century BCE, and his reforms laid the foundation for what would eventually become Athenian democracy, which enabled the poorest classes to vote but not hold office. Democracy emerged as a means to prevent tyranny, a government controlled by one person that generated considerable Athenian fear and was generally regarded negatively.[26]

It would be a rocky road with setbacks by would-be dictators until reforms in the mid-fifth century implemented by Ephialtes redistributed power from the Areopagus to the courts composed of common Athenians.[27] Ultimately, the Assembly would become both a legislature and supreme court, open to all citizens, meaning free-born males to Athenian fathers. Radical democrats like Pericles continued to expand citizen engagement, paying jurors, workers on public construction projects, and the rowers in their navy.[28] This type of political system increased the number of men who could participate in public decision-making, helping foster a more open information ecosystem in contrast to the more closed one in Sparta. The openness of an information ecosystem does not necessarily mean freedom for all. Athens was free for a few, even if those few were a lot more than before or in Sparta. Athenians still owned slaves. Women had no status. They couldn't own property, they were expected not to leave the house, and the only men they could encounter were relatives.

Athenian democracy was not perfect nor loved by all. Some wealthy Athenians felt the direct taxation imposed by the city-state was just a form of tyranny of the people or demos.[29] Only the rich could afford to educate their children, resulting in just a basic literacy level among male citizens.[30] The situation worried the likes of Aristophanes and Thucydides, who came from wealthy families and thought democracy required educated people to lead it. This raised questions about the legitimacy of a system that was effectively based on persuading the largely uneducated masses to agree on something. Athenian citizens voted on many things, including who would be a general in the army, what laws would be passed, and which politicians should be ostracised or sent into temporary exile. To learn how to convince the masses, politicians hired teachers, known as Sophists, who instructed on the art of persuasion. Less scrupulous politicians pandered to the masses, plucking emotions and playing on prejudices.

Aristophanes derided these demagogues and Sophists alike. In *Acharnians*, the protagonist accuses another character of being interested in democracy for the pay, implying that those who fight wars do it for the gains.[31] In *Knights*, Aristophanes attacks a real politician, Cleon, who represents for the playwright all that is wrong in democracy: a selfishly ambitious populist who deceives the public into a disastrous war for his own gain.[32] And in *Clouds*, the playwright takes aim at contemporary philosophy, criticising those teaching politicians for smooth-talking. The fact that Aristophanes could produce these plays and win awards for some of them says something about the openness of the information ecosystem in Athens at the time.

Athens was far more open to the world than Sparta. By the fifth century BCE, the port of Piraeus, just nine kilometres from Athens (a two-hour walk today), was an important trading centre exporting Greek goods and importing products from Egypt, the Black Sea, Macedonia, and Thrace. Indeed, Attica was dependent on grain imports to feed its population. This outward-focused trade, coupled with Athens' role as the head of the Delian League, opened the information ecosystem of Athens to a wider world. The proximity to Persia and its encroachment on lands where other Greeks lived, including other Ionian speakers, perhaps forced the Athenians to be more aware of the other populations beyond the Hellenic world. In fact, although Herodotus migrated to Athens, he was born in the Greek city of Halicarnassus, then under Persian rule. And Athens did perceive itself as a place of refuge.[33] Foreign trade, as well as threats, tied Athens to distant information ecosystems, adding different elements, like a more porous ecosystem, to its tapestry.

Through its far-flung economic ties, Athenians sourced papyrus from Egypt. Made from the stems of the eponymous plant, papyrus was a thick paper-like material for writing, perfect for capturing plays and histories, which were emerging as a new form of output. The first recorded Western histories included that of Herodotus, who narrated a colourful account of the Greco-Persian wars with a sprawling cast of characters, including foreigners, women, and slaves in *The Histories*, which situated Greece in the context of a wider and diverse world around it. Whereas his contemporary and critic Thucydides strove to provide just facts in his work, but in so doing neglected the roles of women, slaves, and was sometimes derisive of non-Athenians. That is to say that every output created by information animals is open to the biases of its producer, whether related to accuracy or exclusion, and all outputs are a product of their time. This newer form of writing did not supplant older means of communication. The oral tradition remained central to Athenian life, and young men continued to compete in retelling epics. Athenians also continued to publish political decrees in stone and post them in public. Stone featured heavily in many Athenian visual outputs, like statues, reliefs, and buildings. The sculptures of this period became much more realistic and were used in public monuments like the Parthenon. Statues depicted Greek history and myths and marked the passing of a person, much like headstones do in some modern cemeteries. There were many other forms of visual outputs too, like paintings, figurines, pottery, and metalwork. Along with plays came masks used in performances for dramatic effect and the creation of backdrops. In short, especially when compared to Sparta, the Athenian information ecosystem was vibrant, with various types of outputs well recognised to this day.

One type of output, architecture, left an indelible mark, as much for the volume of its production as the mixed messages, intended and otherwise, that the buildings conveyed. Pericles started a massive building programme that included the reconstruction of the Acropolis and Parthenon and the construction of the Temple of Athena Nike, among others. Such a huge programme was an effective form of network building, given how much of society must have been mobilised to achieve it. This included the Athenian elites and the citizens raising funds, organising labour and materials, ensuring the proper delivery of supplies, and creating more jobs. Such an effort exemplified the growing sophistication of Athens' organisational capacity (culminating in the erection of the said buildings), helping to reinforce the message that democracy as a governance model was superior to oligarchy. Engaging a populace in a collective effort is a vast production, including communities beyond Athens, in hiring labourers or sourcing materials, establishing bonds and networks that bind people across lands together. These networks, in essence, can be seen as a contemporary (non-technological) means of information exchange, as this is how the message of democracy's superiority was spread across Attica and its allies. This growing interdependency aided in promoting Athens and democracy but also was perceived as a threat to others who were not happy to see this growth, such as Sparta.

This massive construction project was, in effect, an information flood, evidenced by the noticeable increase of grand buildings erected over a relatively short period of time following the Persian invasion. These informational outputs promoted the city-state's radical new form of governance in democracy, symbolised Athens' might, and projected Athenian heroism and glory abroad. Along with this building programme, Pericles doubled the western walls to the port of Piraeus, arguably needed given the recent memory of Athens' sacking by the Persians when the Spartan-led Hellenic alliance retreated. Yet the fortifications signalled other messages, including that Sparta was a threat.[34] The speed and scale of the Periclean building programme sent unmistakable messages to friends and foes alike. In the context of such rapidly changing surroundings, one can see how disruptive such activity would be for the contemporary information ecosystem, especially those concerned about Athenian ascendancy.

While Athens intended to promote democracy, this message did not resonate with some audiences. One issue was how the building programme was funded. Athens had grown rich thanks to trade and its nearby silver mines, but it had also garnered tribute funds from some 200 allies in the Delian League. Joining this voluntary league was a lot like going to the Hotel California, you could enter, but you could never leave. For allies like Mytilene, who had opted into a military alliance under Athens to fight off the Persians decades before, the tributary status it then found itself in was far from free, rendering the democratic messaging in grand Athenian buildings ironic.[35] The fact that Athens began to use the tribute funds for more than collective defence purposes probably didn't help.[36] This architectural extravaganza also played a role in the information competition that ensued with Sparta.[37] In promoting Athens as a leader, and spreading democracy and freedom, the building programme was a reminder to Sparta that its hegemony in the Hellenic world was threatened, especially by those defensive walls. Why would Athens need them if Persia was thwarted? From whom did Athens need to protect itself? The building programme sent unintended messages. Less a promotion of freedom and democracy, the use of tributary funds signalled to those sceptical of Athenian intentions that the city-state was, in fact, subjugating its allies instead of freeing them from oligarchy.

The Athenian promotion of democracy started an information competition with oligarchic Sparta, with the former advocating that other city-states adopt their form of governance. This competition between the two powers also played out along economic lines and territorial expansion. Athens asserted its sovereignty around a radical new form of governance, which it actively encouraged other city-states to adopt, which could not co-exist with Sparta's views on governance. Indeed, the transformations emanating from Athens did not sit well with the traditionalist Spartans, whose tolerance level for change would probably not have been high. The historian Victor Davis Hanson interpreted Athenian democracy as providing incentives to the poor and lower classes at the expense of the rich, which threatened Sparta's oligarchic model.[38] And thus, Sparta sought to support city-states under a similar type of rule and, as the classicist Geoffrey de Ste Croix noted, to "enlist the enthusiastic cooperation of the propertied classes in whose hands power would in this way be permanently retained."[39] In response to Athenian proselytisation around democracy, the Spartans doubled down on oligarchy as their preferred form of government. The two concepts, particularly when pushed to other city-states, could not co-exist for long. The rapid growth and spread of democratic ideas, as an overarching ideational narrative underpinning the Athenian notion of shared purpose and identity, led to an increasing information competition between Athens and Sparta. From here, the road led to a struggle for hegemony over the Hellenic world, just as between niche species in a confined space.

Moreover, while claiming Hellenic hegemony, both sides' constant appeal to an existing concept of honour fuelled the information competition.[40] Honour was a long-standing notion marked by beliefs about where each city stood in relation to the other in the Hellenic hierarchy.[41] The importance of position, according to the historian Donald Kagan, tied Sparta to its Peloponnesian allies and their interests out of the need to keep the League intact, as it was critical to their defence strategy. Sparta saw itself as the leader of Hellas and defender of liberty, and couched its subsequent war under a campaign of "freedom for the Greeks".[42] Yet, Athens was unwilling to subject itself to Sparta and pointed to their own successes in fighting off the invading Persians as justification for their position.[43] The idea of honour was at the heart of problems between Sparta and Athens when Athenians refused to tear down their long defensive walls to Piraeus, and the Spartans rebuffed Athenian support to help quell a revolt of the Helots.[44] Honour also bound both Athens and Sparta to their respective League members, presenting another Greek city-state, Corinth, with an opportunity to persuade the two into war with each other, in the hopes it would help regain her wayward colony, Corcyra.[45] This thread of honour was woven so tightly into the fabric of both city-states that any snag tore violently at the fundamental belief both Athens and Sparta held about themselves. A mere threat to this pattern appeared sufficient to produce bad decision-making.

As the head of the Peloponnesian League, Sparta was the only member who could call for a League Congress, rendering the city-state the central node in the alliance network.[46] The members of the League tended to be oligarchies. While Sparta did not intervene in the day-to-day governance of allies, it did take measures to ensure that allies maintained the form of governance they had when first joining the alliance.[47] The League provided its members with security, including support for Sparta against any possible Helot revolts.[48] However, continued Athenian expansion threatened the Peloponnesian alliance, particularly should Sparta fail to protect its allies from Athens.[49] As the conflict between League member Corinth and the newly Athenian-aligned Corcyra intensified and Athens besieged the Delian tribute of Potidaea, a colony of Corinth, Sparta called a congress of Peloponnesian allies.[50]

At this congress, Corinth painted Athens as a tyrant city, a serious and expanding danger vis-à-vis Spartan stagnation and inaction, effectively questioning the utility of the Peloponnesian League. The Corinthian delegation explained:

> You, Lacedaemonians, of all the Hellenes are alone inactive, and defend yourselves not by doing anything but by looking as if you would do; you alone wait till the power of an enemy

is becoming twice its original size, instead of crushing it in its infancy.[51]

The Corinthian delegates berated the Spartans for taking too long to convene the allies, for failing to stop Athens from building defensive long walls, and described Athens provocatively as:

> Addicted to innovation, and their designs are characterised by swiftness alike in conception and execution; you [Sparta] have a genius for keeping what you have got, accompanied by a total want of invention, and when forced to act you never go far enough.[52]

Sparta had failed to convene a congress in a timely manner, and her allies were frustrated by this and the lack of a Spartan response to limit Athens. In this example, the lack of action by Sparta was interpreted by its allies as its uninterest and unwillingness to defend them against Athens. Perhaps, had Sparta convened more regular League congresses, its leaders might have better understood the growing discontent among the League. With their leadership position threatened and their honour at stake, most Spartans voted for war with Athens, despite concerns raised by one of the city-state's two kings, Archidamus.[53]

Much like crises create information voids in modern ecosystems, the start of war opened a chasm into which Athenians poured pollution. This included inventing answers to explain the origins of a horrible plague. The war drove Athenians to seek refuge within the city's defensive walls which led to overcrowding and illness. Within a couple of years, a quarter of the population was dead, and most citizens had been infected, including Thucydides, who survived the disease and left an account. Knowing little about the origins of diseases, a rumour spread among Athenians that the Spartans had caused the outbreak by poisoning the city's wells.[54] For as long as humans have sought answers, they have filled information voids with pollution. In the face of such tragedy, other information pollution developed around political figures such as Pericles. Given the status of women, a particularly insulting line of attack focused on Pericles' relationship with his lover Aspasia. Playwrights like Aristophanes drew on rumours that Pericles' partner Aspasia ran a brothel, suggesting in *Acharnians* that the cause of the war was the abduction of two of her prostitutes.[55] Even his triumphs were belittled. At the end of the first year of conflict, Pericles delivered his famous funeral oration, one of history's most celebrated speeches, exalting democracy and freedom and the willingness of men to die for these ideals. This commemoration, Socrates suggested, was written by Aspasia, if we are to believe Plato's account in *Menexenus*. Information pollution, or the presence of low-quality information, has been around for a long time. This is a challenge leaders have faced throughout history.

While Athens and Sparta were different information ecosystems, a disturbance in one (such as an information flood in Athens to promote democracy) had reverberations in the other; after all, they existed in a shared space, the Hellenic information biome, wherein the commonalities of a language and shared cultural and religious beliefs tied populations together.[56] However, the structure of their information ecosystems, shaped by geography, trade, political, and social structures, made each markedly different. Also within this Hellenic information biome were other political agents, such as Corinth and Corycra, among many other city-states. Just beyond the Hellenic biome, and sometimes overlapping, causing friction, were other information biomes, such as those of Persia, affecting the beliefs of information animals in Athens. These biomes are like a patchwork of smaller tapestries consisting of their own threads that are, in turn, stitched together in a much larger pattern that is the global information environment, with information ecosystems and communities within. The Hellenic biome was made of many smaller information ecosystems, like Sparta and Athens, each controlling or shaping how information was processed within their city-states, some of which we know more about than others. Within an ecosystem, these communities produced, shared, and consumed mutually intelligible outputs in conjunction with the means used to produce them, all interacting as a system. An essential factor of an information ecosystem is that agents within it can communicate intelligibly with each other. Communities within an ecosystem, in turn, are defined by shared traits and interests. All these layers in the information environment's hierarchy are interconnected and bound through different relationships; they are, in essence, an interwoven fabric.

Within these information ecosystems are information animals, who, as agents, perform different roles. Some seek to win or maintain political power, like Spartan hawks, who couldn't accept Athenian competition and called for war, or Pericles, who was unwilling to cow down to Spartan demands. Among these politically motivated agents, we can also identify proselytisers advocating for their causes, be it the adoption of democracy for Athenians or the meddling Corinth, which agitated for war between Sparta and Athens in pursuit of its own agenda. There were still other agents, like the Sophists, who profited from helping politicians persuade audiences. All these agents were interconnected through a never-ending cycle of processing and sharing information, both factual and some not so much, which generated the outputs delivered through plays, monuments, trade exchanges, and more to shape the Greek information biome.

The exploration of this historically distant information biome reveals that, just like today, the means for processing information beget more means. Following the collapse of the Mycenaean culture, Greeks were again reliant on the spoken word, using it to hold the thread of a history that threatened to disappear.

However, as new Hellenic communities evolved, and with them more elaborate forms of processing and passing on information, we see an increase in means for processing information built on the foundations of pre-existing ones. Thucydides' lengthy written account of the Peloponnesian War highlights the importance of speeches in diplomacy and public decision-making. The act of writing did not replace speaking. Rather, it became a new way to process and document what was said.

And, just like today, the concern over the impact of new tools for processing information is far from new. All did not welcome the alphabet and writing. Socrates, who lived (and served) during the Peloponnesian War between Sparta and Athens, left no written works behind. For him, ideas were best engaged via spoken dialogue. In accounts of his former teacher, Plato suggested that Socrates felt the written word was somehow dead or less alive than spoken words and that writing would impair memory.[57] For Plato, though, the means for processing information were not as concerning as the outputs derived from it. As the religious studies professor Charles Mathewes noted, for Plato, "the cultural context in which we live shaped our sense of what is right and wrong", and in that, poetry and theatre play a dangerous role in potentially misleading people about how the world works.[58] The human relationship with technological change and information has long been fraught with worry.

Information moves through an ecosystem through various means, taking different forms and potentially changing its meaning as it does. The more means for processing information, the more forms information might take within an information ecosystem, appearing in speeches, theatrical plays, sculptures, or histories. In this process, fact and fiction can blur, but both will still inform information animals. Athenians and Spartans used myths to explain their origins, some of which might have been based on some grain of truth. While taking very different approaches to it, both Herodotus and Thucydides tackled the challenges of writing history from the accounts of others, or indeed, from his memory. But in the accounts both left, they are dependent on information animals to inform it, be it themselves or others. An information ecosystem consists as much of the processes behind information production as it does the outputs and people within it.

Things like geography, trade, culture, and social structure all shape the character of an information ecosystem. Sparta's closed, inland geography imposed physical barriers on trade and information exchanges while likely contributing to an insular social structure dominated by a rigid military culture dependent on the Helots and ultimately driving a need to control information. Whereas Athens embraced the sea around it and fostered a navy to engage heavily in trade, developing an open culture where more and more men were invited to participate in public decision-making over time and information could move quickly. However, as Aristophanes warns, this open culture ruled by the demos provided no guarantees for the best decisions, just the most popular or financially rewarding. Each system of governance, with corresponding political, economic, and social relations, shapes the information ecosystem where it is imposed, influencing how decisions are made, and is, in turn, shaped by emerging means and outputs in a constant loop. Just as governments of all kinds struggle with it today, cities in ancient Greece also dealt with challenges related to information quality and control. That isn't the only thread that knits this distant past to other societies in time, as we shall see.

If there is one key takeaway from the exploration of Ancient Greece, it is that information ecosystems are not islands. They do not exist in voids apart from one another. What happens in one can impact the beliefs that form, and decisions taken, in another. Moreover, it isn't just the actions of others that shape beliefs and decisions, but culture and history. Awareness of one's own information ecosystem, and how the factors and conditions within it might shape understanding is key to good leadership. Equally as important is understanding those information ecosystems around you, not just those that are similar, but also those that are different or adversarial, and how factors and conditions there might influence reactions to your actions.

5

TYRANNICAL TIES

CHARLES VERSUS THE GODLY

That Tuesday in late January was bitterly cold. Feeling the chill in his bones, the condemned man asked for a thicker shirt to avoid shaking from the winter weather, lest onlookers think he was afraid of his fate. It had been a long hard path towards finally caring about how others perceived him, but here he was. On a short walk to the gallows, he passed under the ceiling he'd had painted glorifying his father's rule and the divine right of monarchy, a depiction his Godly detractors no doubt viewed as idolatrous art. Exiting through a window on to a specially constructed scaffolding, he greeted the crowd assembled in the freezing air. Among his last words, he uttered, "I go from a corruptible to an incorruptible crown," a biblical reference evoking a belief in his own self-denial and perseverance. For some (no doubt himself), Charles I, King of England, Scotland, and Ireland, was a martyr. For others, he was a tyrant and condemned as such at his trial.[1] Regardless of perspectives, his life came to an end on that cold day in 1649. Charles was unlucky in that his reign followed a series of significant shifts in the English information ecosystem, but perhaps his greatest misfortune was that his own beliefs prevented him from adapting in response to unfolding events shaped by these changes. Some of these changing factors and conditions within the English information ecosystem included the gradual adoption of paper, print, and later a postal system, helping increase the volume of outputs and distribution of them. At the same time, ever more people were gaining agency, with a rise in education spurred by religious reforms, increasing the number of people engaging in politics. Yet Charles couldn't seem to see this changing information ecosystem for the pollution in it. He might be forgiven in that many of these changes began long before him, but they shaped the information ecosystem of his time.

Since the beginning of human settlement in the British Isles over 12,000 years ago, the land has seen numerous waves of new people coming to its shores, often by force.[2] Bringing their culture, language and customs, Romans, Anglo-Saxons, Vikings, and their Norman descendants all shaped how administration, education, and law evolved over time.[3] Following the Norman invasion, the English language as we know it only became more commonly used by 1422 during the reign of Henry VI when the Chancery clerks who prepared documents for the King began to use it.[4] This revival as a literary language ensured that the information ecosystem of Charles' time would, in fact, be English, and the people within England would be able to understand each other across the country. This increased use of English probably also stemmed from a renewed engagement of the non-Norman elite in legal matters. The traumatic aftermath of the Black Death resulted in increased legal disputes over inheritance. When the disease came to England in 1348, the population was an estimated 4.81 million, but within a decade the country had lost nearly half of its people, dropping to 2.58

million in 1358.⁵ The population continued to decline for most of the next century, only beginning to grow again in 1450, which, by then, sat at around 1.90 million. This colossal loss of life had a profound impact on the economy, eroding the feudal system, freeing serfs and increasing mobility, giving rise to a growing entrepreneurial class that was able to start acquiring land and begin to contest the ancient feudal aristocracy.⁶

Before the development of a Chancery Standard, written English was improvised and varied from place to place.⁷ What was written in the north of the country might not be intelligible to someone in the south. In one account, William Caxton wrote of a merchant traveller in another part of England in the late fifteenth century asking a local woman for some "eggys", to which she responded, "that she coude speke no frenshe." The merchant wasn't impressed because he also didn't speak French. A passer-by catching the exchange explained that the merchant wanted "eyren", which the woman finally understood as eggs.⁸ As people began to move into London, many from the East Midlands, a dialect drawing more from the middle of the country, began to develop and become popular, which influenced the Chancery Standard as well as the writing of Geoffrey Chaucer.⁹ Standardisation of English was also helped by another development within the English information ecosystem—Caxton's introduction of the printing press.

The invention of the printing press by Johann Gutenberg in the mid-fifteenth century increased the capacity to present information to large audiences.¹⁰ Gutenberg developed his invention in Strasbourg, then an Imperial Free City in the Holy Roman Empire, before launching the first commercial printing press in Mainz. While the German diaspora widely introduced the printing press across Europe, the technology was first brought to England by the Kent-born Caxton.¹¹ After watching a printing press in Cologne, Caxton set up his own in Bruges.

There he printed the first book in English, *The Recuyell of the Historyes of Troye,* around 1474, a translation of a French novel about mythological Greek heroes (so important to Athens and Sparta in the previous chapter) set as medieval knights.[12] In 1476, Claxton set up a printing press in London.[13] As printing presses were commercial interests, they behoved their proprietors to create products that as many people as possible could consume, which, after all, the innovation enabled. So, a standard of English understood by the largest audiences was adopted. Thus, the standardisation of English owes as much to its official use as it does to printing and commerce.

The success of the printing press depended on the earlier invention of paper. Like printing, paper was first developed in ancient China.[14] It was introduced to Europe around the eleventh century. Paper enabled the rise of letter writing in Early Modern Europe, connecting philosophers, merchants, and bureaucrats, forming networks of interest and supporting the spread of the Renaissance.[15] The leading Humanist scholar, Erasmus, built up an extensive network of correspondents across Europe and England, which historian Diarmaid MacCulloch described as "a salon of the imagination, which embraced the entire continent in a constant flow of letters to hundreds of correspondents, some of whom he never met face to face."[16] Paperwork increased, as Paul M. Dover outlined, with some functionaries like the Jesuits' founder Ignatius Loyola receiving upwards of 250 letters in a matter of days by 1542.[17] The sixteenth-century Archbishop of Milan, Charles Borromeo, left behind 30,000 letters.[18] The importance of letters in connecting people across countries should not be underestimated in the face of other printing innovations at the time, and letters continued to be a common means of sharing information in Charles' England, where a weekly postal service introduced in 1635 helped distribution.[19] Other outputs such as hand-copied books increased across Western Europe, growing on average 89 per cent each century from 769,000 in the twelfth century to nearly 5 million in the fifteenth. Printed materials only added to the growth. Print books vastly outstripped this production by 151 per cent for the second half of the fifteenth century alone, with 12.56 million created. By the sixteenth century, around 216 million print books had been produced.[20] For literate people living through this period, this increase in outputs must have felt like a flood, from letters to print.

As with cuneiforms and alphabets before, paper development in Europe coincided with economic needs and interests, with paper mills expanding in the thirteenth century. England would be slightly behind this curve, with paper production following the introduction of the printing press. Publishing was controlled by an organised group of merchants or a guild created in 1403. It was only natural that the Worshipful Company of Stationers also oversaw the printing industry once it was introduced to England.[21] Paper production also fell under the Stationers Company, and by the 1490s, John Tate was operating the first commercial paper mill in England, which supplied Caxton.[22] Neither papermaking nor printing were cheap endeavours. Paper was expensive and often produced outside of England, even in Charles' time. Moreover, the printing process was labour-intensive and involved a network of actors to produce and distribute content.[23] By 1500, there were just five printers in London, and all of them were foreigners. They dominated the book trade in England until Henry VIII began imposing restrictions in 1523 on who could engage in the business out of fears over religious content coming into England from Europe.[24] An influx of foreigners from the Low Countries twenty-five years later would be a boon to the nascent English publishing market, bringing much-needed expertise and an increase of cheap material on changing religious ideas.[25] Later decrees would limit the number of printers allowed overall. In 1582, when there were twenty-two printing houses in

London, a member of parliament complained that eight or ten would suffice.[26] There were also limits on the volume of editions that could be printed.[27] These restrictions around publishing were deliberate attempts to control the information ecosystem, particularly the flow of changing religious ideas coming in from the continent, which, as we shall see, did little to stop the tide.

Henry VIII might have been right to worry about Protestantism. After all, long before Martin Luther, there were those preaching similar ideas in England. John Wycliffe, an Oxford Don, was among the first to challenge the centralisation of power by the Catholic Church and attacked the power and wealth that the bishops and the Pope had amassed.[28] More than a century before Luther, a German priest, translated the bible into his vernacular, Wycliffe did so into Middle English by 1384. Wycliffe believed that the church's practices should be tested against the Bible, and to do that, the scripture needed to be accessible. Until this point, the Bible was written in Latin, and the Church jealously guarded instruction on it. Such ideas became more popular after Luther published his *Ninety-Five Theses* in October 1517 in Wittenberg, railing against the Catholic church's practice of selling indulgences.

Luther wasn't alone. Other reformers were also calling for change, including Heinrich Bullinger and John Calvin, whose eventual Academy in Geneva attracted students from Britain.[29] Along with the centralisation of papal power, which effectively turned the Church into an alternative empire complete with its own legal system, Protestants also attacked the service of the Eucharist. Commonly called Mass in English, the practice had morphed into what MacCulloch described as "an intricate industry of prayer", selling people reduced time in purgatory, a place between heaven and hell which Western Christians had fabricated in the twelfth century.[30] This was coming at a time when Western Christians began fearing that the prophesied

Last Days or End Times were upon them, and the encroaching Muslim Turks were a sign. A belief that the Church had been corrupted and the Pope was at the centre of the conspiracy took root, with some believing he was the antichrist.

For some in northern Europe, Luther's rant hit a nerve. Incensed clergy used their pulpits to proselytise to the masses. Print helped spread the word further. Luther would later claim that the reprints of his *Theses* spread across Germany in two weeks. They reached England via Thomas More on 5 March 1518.[31] According to MacCulloch, in 1523, 390 editions of Luther's works were published in Germany, and some 3 million copies of related pamphlets by 1525, causing Wittenberg's otherwise small economy to boom as a printing powerhouse. Much of this proselytisation was happening in German. Across the Holy Roman Empire, particularly in German-speaking towns with enough autonomy to make religious decisions like many Imperial Free Cities, some started turning Protestant.[32] Cities like Strasbourg became beacons for religious reformers, and there they congregated from across northern European countries, including Britain.[33] Indeed, critics at the University of Cambridge referred to a group of reformers there as "Little Germany."[34] The ability to access the Bible directly, and not only through the rigid control of the Church, engaged lay people in religion, a process that spread into England and Scotland and would soon shape access to education and political ideas. Several threads related to religion, such as questioning Mass, indulgences, and fearing the end times, became woven into the English information ecosystem and central to a growing information competition.

Inspired by Luther's Bible translation, William Tyndale began a new translation into vernacular Modern English in the 1520s in Europe after being prevented by the Church authorities in England. He completed the New Testament in 1525.[35] Copies of Tyndale's Bible were smuggled into England by other Protestant followers and merchants, sometimes inside bales of cloth.[36] Upwards of 16,000 copies of his Bible made it to England by the time of Tyndale's execution for heresy in 1536. At the time, the country had a population of around 2.71 million people and a yet undeveloped print market.[37] Until the tides turned in favour of some form of Protestantism in England, people read Tyndale's translation in secret, which provided them with direct access to the Bible at a time when preachers had been banned.[38] Beyond a translation into vernacular English, people also had to be able to read, which itself was increased given a few interconnected societal shifts.

Henry VIII warmed to the idea of Protestantism in the 1530s when he wanted to divorce his first wife, Catherine of Aragon. In pursuit of this, he made himself the head of the Church of England, becoming the first European regent to break with Rome. The ongoing Protestant Reformation in Europe presented a convenient cover for the separation. Henry's chief advisor, Thomas Cromwell, was a Protestant, and the king chose the diplomat and Oxford don, Thomas Cranmer, for his next Archbishop of Canterbury. Cranmer had come to see the merits of Protestantism while serving in Nuremburg, yet another Imperial Free City that had reformed early. These men led church reforms that stopped short of what either Luther or Calvin called for, and instead took a confused middling approach that became contested between a growing group of Godly and traditionalists. Henry's son Edward VI would implement more Protestant reforms to the liturgy, only to have his half-sister Queen Mary reverse them during her short but bloody reign. Her persecution of Protestants left followers with a choice to convert back to Catholicism, flee, or die, killing nearly 300 people in less than four years, including Cranmer whose public burning was a spectacular propaganda disaster as he recanted his forced reconversion dramatically.[39] This led to so-called Marian exiles who took refuge in those Protestant-friendly cities like Strasbourg and Geneva, as well as the territory of East Friesland. It also spawned a book that was still widely read in Charles' day, commonly called *The Book of Martyrs* by John Foxe, which documented in detail the burning of Protestants.[40]

With the ascension of Elizabeth I in 1558, England would be returned to Protestantism. For the next few years, Elizabeth and her advisors worked out a Religious Settlement, which reintroduced a new version of her brother Edward's *Book of Common Prayer*. This attempt followed a third way whereby Reformed doctrine was adopted but Catholic trappings remained, like cathedrals, choirs, priestly clothes, and a bishopric rule. In many ways, it left the Church of England neither here nor there, and contributed to fears among more hardcore Protestants that the papacy was always lingering behind a thin veneer of reform, ready to seize the chance and return. Elizabeth attempted to export this new church to her other kingdom of Ireland, where she'd initiated colonisation through a plantation scheme, to little success. The religious imposition was half-hearted and was seen as the invader introduction that it was. As tensions around religion increased in Europe, more than information flowed into England. Periodic waves of Protestant refugees sought refuge in England, beginning in the 1550s and then again following the St. Bartholomew's Day Massacre of the French Huguenots in Paris in 1572. This isolation on one hand, and deepening connections via Protestantism on the other, helped create the conditions for an echo chamber in England, whereby some Protestants believed the country was "part of a global struggle of Christ and Antichrist, a struggle of good and evil, with the pope, to coin a phrase, as the axis of evil."[41] Meanwhile, north of the border, Scotland was undergoing a very different reformation.

In 1560, the Scottish parliament legislated the creation of the "Kirk." This followed the first successful armed rebellion against Catholicism in Europe the year before and took on a

Calvinist or Reformed strain of Protestantism, rather than Lutheran. The Scottish reformation was unique in that it was not initiated by a monarch or prince, but grew out of support from lower Scottish nobility and the people. The Kirk adopted democratic organisational structures, such as electing church elders or presbytery rather than having bishops appointed by Rome, drawing on the ideas of the still exiled John Knox. The following year marked the start of the brief and disastrous reign of Mary, Queen of Scots, full of poor choices. Her rule exacerbated already high tensions in Scottish society, culminating in a civil war which was won by fervent Protestants, who then ruled on behalf of Mary's infant son, James VI.[42] The Protestant caretaking left its imprint on James Stewart, helping him later to present his religious reform credentials to an English audience as he published pamphlets on vanquishing the devil in *Newes from Scotland* in 1591 and then his book on witch hunting in 1597.[43] In the end, the Scots achieved a legally enshrined Kirk and a passionate desire to maintain it, and woe betide any ruler seeking to impose changes. The Scottish model also offered inspiration to a growing group of malcontents in England who wanted to see similar Church reforms in their country, leading them to be derisively called the Godly. To their detractors, the Godly were puritanical fundamentalists. The ideas that had taken hold in one information ecosystem were spilling over into another.

Debates about further church reform played out in print, presaging what would become the public sphere. Pamphlets were less expensive and easier to produce than books, consisting of no more than a dozen sheets. Wading into political opinion, pamphlets were iterative and responsive, drawing on and attacking past publications of opponents to convey a message. The Martin Marprelate tracts by anonymous Godly authors starting in 1588 attacked the episcopacy, or rule of bishops, in the Church of England.[44] Meanwhile, Catholic Church defenders began responding in their own tracts, engaging in an information competition, which was mirrored in sermons on both sides in attempts to inculcate the masses.[45] A subset of these short and often satirical printed outputs were play pamphlets, which tackled issues in the form of dialogue, enabling the projection of a voice into an opponent to mock or attack them.[46] Whereas another genre of pamphlets, the libels, slandered public figures. These anonymous papers could also target groups of people like the Godly, attacking their character or lack of charity for the poor. Some pamphlets called *courantos* were the precursor of newspapers, sharing updates on current events. The quality of content contained in these pamphlets was often questionable. Other pamphlets were pure entertainment, telling tales of human deformity and other monstrosities.[47] Most printers were driven by profits, not always motivated by politics or religion, and publishing sensationalist material or content espousing both sides of an information competition led to larger revenues.[48] These pamphlets would emerge quickly and in great quantity, in many ways reminiscent of social media today. As the modern historian Joad Raymond explained: "Pamphlets, and their meanings, were ephemeral because they carried the impression of their moment, transient political, rhetorical and generic conjunctions."[49] Pamphlets played an important role in the English information ecosystem under Charles, in a large part because of the new and growing audience they targeted.

Without an heir, on her deathbed, Elizabeth named her Scottish cousin as her successor, making him also King James I of England.[50] With the ascension of James to the throne, Scotland was tied to the English information ecosystem from 1603. James also expanded the Irish plantation scheme in Ulster by adding Scottish colonisers to the English and greatly increasing the number of settlers in a predominantly Catholic society. This binding of the three kingdoms led to a largely unconstrained flow of information between them, whereby any existing conflicts in one disturbed another. James also reconnected the English information ecosystem with the European biome, which had been cut off with the break from the Vatican almost seventy years earlier. The ending of the war with Spain resulted in an exodus of aristocrats to the continent for the first time in generations. London became increasingly connected to the outside world through immigration and trade.[51] Foreign artisans streamed into England as the elite invested in paintings, architecture, statues, tapestries, and more. While the transition in style from Elizabethan to Jacobean art was subtle, towards the end of James's reign the classical style of architecture emerged under Inigo Jones, which evoked Ancient Greece, as well as now Papal Rome. For those few who might have seen it, this sort of pomp probably didn't sit well with the purposefully plain Godly. Information flowing into London was carried across England by traders and travellers, their movement facilitated by expanding access to waterways and improving transportation.[52] By the early 1600s, London became part of a Protestant information network with Glasgow, Edinburgh, Leiden, and Amsterdam, which, in addition to strengthening views favourable to the new religion, also served, perhaps unsurprisingly, to spread fears about the threat of Catholicism returning.[53] For those fervent believers who thought the antichrist ruled the Vatican, peace with a Catholic country like Spain did little to quell fears of the end times. In fact, any thawed relations with the Pope or regents within his dominion only increased the risk of returning to his fold and, with it, eternal damnation. These fears spurred the Godly.

The Godly had a history of petitioning the monarch to make religious reforms. They sought changes that would make the Church of England, in their minds, less Catholic. This was an organised effort, which, in many ways, resembles modern public relations campaigns. Pamphlets like *Advice Tending to Reformation* counselled followers to push for reforms by submitting variations on the same petitions to the King and rousing people to action through sermons. James would make some concessions at the Hampton Court Conference in early 1604.[54] The chief change emerging from the conference was that the bible was translated into English heavily based on Tyndale's words, along with more minor shifts away from the trappings of Catholicism, such as replacing the term "absolution" with "remission of sins", and "confirmation" with "laying on of hands."[55] These were a far cry from the bigger desires of doing away with the *Book of Common Prayer* or restructuring the church governance to a Presbyterian model. The Godly did not just want changes; they wanted to save the church from papal influence for good. For them, the threat of reversing the course, a possibility constantly reinforced by events targeting Protestants across Europe, was pressing and very real. The uncovering of the Gunpowder Plot, a Catholic-led conspiracy to blow up Parliament and the King with it on 5 November 1605, only helped stoke those fears, and the memory of Bloody Mary's return to Catholicism remained ever-present.

The English Reformation brought with it social change intertwined with longer-standing shifts in demographics, both of which had implications for the Godly. Besides a divorce for Henry VIII, breaking with Rome came with the additional benefit of confiscating all the wealth from the Catholic monasteries in England, which in turn had consequences for education in the country. The dissolution of the monasteries closed one of the main avenues of education for English students. At the same time, the population was consistently growing again. However over the sixteenth century, this gap was filled by a growing number of lower-level schools of three levels: petty, apprenticeship, and grammar.[56] Petty schools taught young children basic literacy levels and were increasingly endowed to educate the poor, including girls. Children destined for the trades went to schools which would prepare them for apprenticeships, where they learned maths, English grammar, and writing, as entry into many guilds required literacy.[57] The third type was grammar schools, which prepared students for higher education or the Inns of Court, which taught law. Greater access to education meant that literacy rates rose. Some estimates put the percentage of literate people in England at a quarter of the total population by Charles' reign.[58] In some of the public protestations against him, a third could sign their name, and two-thirds could make a mark.[59] Moreover, nearly half of the convicts sentenced to death in the counties surrounding London between 1612 and 1614 demonstrated a level of literacy to successfully plead benefit of the clergy and have their punishment reduced.[60] One thing is certain: England was setting itself apart from many other European countries at the time. As the historian Lawrence Stone noted:

> What made this society different was that basic literacy was common even among the poor, and that cultural activity was appreciated and practised by the whole of the rural and urban propertied classes, not merely by a tiny elite of noblemen and higher clergy.[61]

While all levels of society were becoming more literate, one group was doing well—the Godly. Literacy was particularly important given the need to experience the Bible directly, but education went beyond those basics. The last Parliament Charles faced was one of the most educated until the nineteenth century. At least half of the members attended university, and 55 per cent attended an Inn of the Court.[62]

Many Godly were educated and active in trade, increasing their wealth and connecting them to protestant communities abroad. James further enabled their enrichment with the creation of the Virginia Company and colonisation in North America, which connected some Godly to a group of political actors known as the Parliamentarians. Together, they drew support from prominent nobility who espoused a militant Puritanism that combined hostility to Spain with colonial ambitions for England.[63] With London as the ascending centre for this Atlantic trade community, these gentlemen first raised excess capital by trading grain to the city, then ventured into colonial investments, forming a new network of port towns connected by waterways and coasts in the southern and eastern counties.[64] What emerged was a protestant business class driven by capitalist ethics increasingly in opposition to "a traditional mediaeval catholic economic morality."[65] For modern historian Christopher Hill, Puritanism offered this community "a body of ideas which would emphasise the dignity of labour for its own sake; which would be critical at once of the careless and extravagant rich and of the idle and irresponsible poor."[66] These changes led to a further expansion of the English information ecosystem as well as the growth of a community based on shared business and political interests that would come to challenge James' son, Charles.[67] This taking of territory and movement of people marked the beginning of an Anglo information biome that exists to this day.

    Where James seemed to have a knack for maintaining a balance between traditionalists who felt the church had sufficiently reformed and the Godly who wanted more, his son Charles excelled at making matters worse. Charles had been a sickly child bullied by his father, the combination rendering his adult-self pathetic, irritable, indecisive, stubborn, uncompromising, and unable to take criticism well.[68] He did not believe a sovereign owed any explanation for his actions to the people, particularly on foreign policy decisions.[69] Charles made changes at Court that cut him off from the people, disrupting what was effectively the decision-making centre of a complex system, blocking the flow of information up from the counties and countryside to the monarch.[70] According to historian Kevin Sharpe, the king was expected to "rise above court factions, selecting advisors who would act in the interest of the country and king" and serve as a linchpin in a vital communication chain binding all threads of government.[71] However, once George Villiers, the Duke of Buckingham, was installed as favourite, his subsequent manoeuvres to control future patronage destabilised this balance of power.[72] For example, Villiers would bypass the Privy Council should it not agree with him and go straight to Charles, diminishing the power of the principal executive body.[73] This shifted influence at the Court from the traditional aristocracy, "those with vast estates, patronage and local influence, the king turned first for assistance with the execution of royal commands throughout the country," towards "court acolytes entirely dependent for their fortunes upon his [Duke of Buckingham's] favour".[74]

Moreover, for those aristocrats and gentry Charles was most dependent on, the king insisted they reside not in London but on their estates year-round, further challenging regular flow of information between the countryside and the King. The other newly risen men had few links to the localities, leading to a break in the chain connecting King and the people.[75] Lacking access to the king, many "turned to parliament in order to serve their localities and represent their interests."[76] As a result, a growing body of apprentices and tradespeople who would previously petition the King were now turned into a dissatisfied public engaged in politics.[77] This criticism, in turn, led Charles to dissolve Parliament more than once, including in 1626 to avoid the Duke of Buckingham's impeachment and in 1629 when he decided to rule alone, not calling another sitting until 1640.[78] As Hyde noted, "the course of exempting men from prosecution by dissolving of parliaments made the power of parliaments much more formidable, as conceived to be without limit".[79] In other words, denying people parliaments only made them want such representation even more, an example of the scarcity heuristic, a cognitive bias whereby people desire more that which they cannot have.[80]

In the face of fears about a return to the papacy, Charles embarked on some curious choices. He married the sister of the French King, Henrietta Maria, whose marriage contract ensured she could have consistent and permanent access to Catholic worship, and with her came a thousand of her closest Catholic friends and priests. Once in England, Henrietta Maria openly flaunted her faith in London and hosted demonstrable services. Centred around and protected by the Queen were a community of Court Catholics whose visibility was disproportionate to their representation in the broader populace.[81] As if the return of Catholics to Court was not alarming enough, Charles embarked on religious reforms under the leadership of Archbishop William Laud, which in part exalted the altar and to the Godly smacked of a return to Catholicism.[82] What's more, as MacCulloch noted, between Charles and Laud, "they showed no awareness that they might need to inspire popular enthusiasm for the innovations in religion that they now foisted on a horrified Church of England."[83] Indeed, Charles waited eight years to hold his coronation as king of Scotland and was only just dissuaded from forcing religious changes on that country then.[84] Going further, Charles took the *Book of Common Prayer* his father had published, which had not been all that well received by the Godly in England, and imposed it on Scotland in 1637, causing a riot at St. Giles Cathedral in Edinburgh. Attempts under Charles to reform aspects of the Anglican Church and the Scottish Kirk provoked both the Godly and the Scottish Presbyterians, the latter, in response to these reforms, signing a *National Covenant* in 1638, forming a religious and political movement known as the Covenantors, and sparked the Bishop's Wars between Scotland and England, after the Scots expelled the bishops from the Kirk.[85]

The Covenantors initiated an intense and sustained anti-Catholic propaganda campaign aimed at winning English protestants to their side, which often positioned religious changes as a papist plot.[86] Despite restrictions on the number of presses allowed in England, Scotland was a separate kingdom and not beholden to such laws, resulting in an influx of printed material from the north.[87] Just like today, controlling the information flow across borders appears impossible, especially if this concerns organised networks already spanning across ecosystems.

Meanwhile, on international issues of import, Charles often seemed ambiguous in his stance. Religious conflicts ravaging Europe at the time were viewed by some Protestants in England as part of a bigger international struggle between good and evil.[88] With the Thirty Years' War (1618–1648) raging in Central Europe, a strain of popish fears spread through English communities, manifesting in rumours, news, propaganda, and accusations against the King and his advisors who were perceived to be secret Catholics.[89] Despite having many means at his disposal to influence his subjects, including through the pulpit, Charles seemed to do little until it was too late. His royal declarations were rare and tended to be reactive.[90] The poetry written by his supporters, who came to call themselves Cavaliers, was decadent, sexualised, and about living for the day, everything the Godly was not.

Charles I is a prime example of how deeds communicate, and how those actions often relay unintended messages. For Charles, Parliament's principal function was to raise funds for his absolutist needs, and with it dissolved, he sought other means to make money, including "selling the crown-lands, creating peers" and reviving an archaic law to collect Ship Money, which only added to his unpopularity.[91] He derived considerable revenue from customs, which was made possible due to England's neutrality in the Thirty Years' War, and in protecting Spanish traffic through the English Channel—both of which also helped feed papist fears.[92] In addition to these activities, which were perceived by opponents as unjust, Charles attempted to exert more control over the information ecosystem. He used the Star Chamber, a closed court of hand-selected Privy Counsellors and judges that became synonymous with the arbitrary use of power, under his personal rule from 1629 to 1640, to impose "a series of highly controversial and draconian punishments upon leading critics of royal policy."[93] Carrying seditious letters and publicly criticising the king and queen was criminalised.[94] And in October 1632, Charles banned the publishing of *courantos* because the Spanish Ambassador complained about how some portrayed him, an act which must have done little to quell fears of popish plots given that Spain was a Catholic country and a long-standing enemy of Protestant England.[95] Yet around half of all publications at the time were anonymously authored, making enforcement challenging.[96]

Despite Charles' attempt to self-finance the fight against the Covenantors, he was finally convinced to recall the Parliament to seek funds in 1640. After eleven years, the so-called Short Parliament endured for only three weeks before Charles could no longer bear the grievances the members aired. John Pym became a leader among them, calling for royal abuses to be addressed before any support was approved to assist in the Bishop's Wars. Charles was forced to recall another Parliament later that year, where things really went awry. The concept of sovereignty sat at the core of much debate during this period. Greater mobility and flow of information contributed to growing awareness in society, leading those aspiring for change to question existing processes around legislation, taxation, appointing magistrates, war declaration and allegiances, creating money, religious governance, and property rights.[97] These issues were often intertwined with each other, particularly with religion.[98] Fears of popish plots and most things foreign only aggravated the questioning of sovereignty, with the Godly leaning towards the millenarian view or that an apocalypse was coming in the form of a reinstated Papacy in England, and the King and his supporters viewing such debates as treason.[99] Judging by their speeches, Parliamentarians like Pym and William Strode were driven by such a religious mission.[100] Pym had been in contact with the Covenanters, and through their influence, he came to view bishops, who were given seats in the House of Lords and considered a remnant of Popery, as the main threat to the Church and politics.[101] In the first year of the Long Parliament, the Commons initiated several investigations to uncover papist plots, including the role of Catholics in armies raised to repel the Scots and at court. As Caroline M. Hibbard noted, anything could be viewed as part of a papist conspiracy to destroy Protestant England—from Ship Money to the Bishops' Wars to the raising of armies.[102]

The Long Parliament drew up lists of Catholics deemed dangerous to the country.[103] Those who disagreed with the Godly Parliamentarians' intent on change were decried publicly to be attacked by mobs.[104] The Godly courted the support of trades apprentices, who were becoming more engaged in highly politicised information exchanges as consumers, developing a sense of political agency as a result. Some pamphlets and plays directly targeted them as an audience.[105] After the 1550s, a person might not enter a guild before twenty-four years of age and would be unable to marry until then. With growing literacy rates, and swayed by preachers, these youths found a channel for their frustration in the Reformation and took to heckling London clergy and Catholic clerics.[106] Along with young servants, the apprentices were also part of a communication network and were sent to gather news on behalf of their masters.[107] As historian Diane Purkiss explained, apprentices also reacted to rumours and events with protests and riots, as in May 1640 when a group of 500 descended on the London home of the Archbishop, Lambeth Palace, and broke prisons open. The following year, at Christmas, 30,000 signed "a petition presented in the violent demonstrations".[108] Those who voted against the Godly bills faced public attacks, their names posted outside the House of Commons as traitors to foment public outrage. Pym and his colleagues seemed to understand that they were part of an interconnected information ecosystem, working and responding to public sentiments. They used petitions to channel public support, gaining tens of thousands of signatures at a time.[109]

Restrictions on printing were also eased with the Long Parliament. The English book market boomed. Printed books nearly doubled year after year, from 848 in 1640 to 2,042 the next year and 4,038 in 1642, increasing the volume of information outputs.[110] An information flood, however, was manifested in a spike in printed pamphlets conveying anti-Catholicism and outlining popish plots, which had started just after the Short Parliament failed.[111] Dozens of Catholic conspiracies were covered in the press in late 1641 and early 1642.[112] Hibbard explored several of these in her work. For example, John Browne testified at a House of Commons committee in 1641 about a detailed popish plot that involved the Jesuits, courtiers, the archbishop, and Catholic emigrants from England. In another, a French fleet raised a panic, leading to a plot whereby Charles' wife was planning to overthrow the King with financing from the Pope. In November 1641, the tailor Thomas Beale claimed to overhear plotters planning to kill Parliamentarians in advance of a general Catholic uprising.[113] While the printing press created the conditions for a new type of information flood, consisting of mass printed material, such floods tended to also occur in responses to events including: the introduction of the *Book of Common Prayer* in Scotland; the dissolution of the Short Parliament; and the Irish Rebellion.[114] Like today, scandals, plots and impending doom attracted readership in an information ecosystem where instability and concerns for the future were clearly present.

In the wake of the Irish Rebellion in November 1641, atrocity stories stoked anti-Catholic fears in England, alleging that the rebels were acting with the King's approval.[115] These brutal tales would sometimes be accompanied by fabricated letters from papists acknowledging this regal support. Published as pamphlets, atrocity stories struck a chord with readers who entertained the idea that the Irish Rebellion was a culmination of a series of Catholic plots from the Spanish Armada and the Gunpowder Plot to Charles' disastrous marital match with the Spanish Infanta Maria Anna of Spain and ultimate marriage to Henrietta Maria. In response, Charles I issued denials, trying to debunk rumours and "shift the ground of debate away from popery and toward 'order.'"[116] Given draconian laws preventing dissent about Charles, one approach by supporters of the Parliament was to attack Lord Strafford, one of the king's closest advisors and Lord Deputy of Ireland, and "the propaganda campaign against Strafford that preceded his trial linked him with an intricate web of Catholic conspiracy in Ireland, Wales, and England."[117] Parliamentarians gained 20,000 signatures in London alone against Strafford.[118] Charles would eventually sign Strafford's death warrant.

Charles became increasingly afraid that Parliament would impeach the Queen and tried to stoke fears to encourage Parliament to side with him.[119] He accused the Parliamentarians of conspiring with the Covenantors to invade England.[120] He sought evidence of foreign interference, which he found when a letter was discovered from the Scottish Covenantors to the French King requesting that he mediate between the two sides, which was never sent. As historian Oliver Thomson noted, "Charles now used the letter to France as a major propaganda tool to demonstrate the treachery of the Scots and encouraged his English subjects to supply men and money to stop this 'trampling of our crown under their feet'."[121] It didn't work. Ultimately, Charles made the foolish move of attempting to arrest five members of Parliament, Pym, Hampden, Strode, along with Arthur Haselrig and Denzil Holles, in early 1642. Charles Stewart overstepped his royal privileges with this action, and favour fell away from him. A brutish civil war ensured, which he lost.

Several interrelated factors stand out as essential points of analysis to understand the English information ecosystem in the years preceding the early Stewart dynasty. Innovations like print enabled faster production of information outputs. Still, their use often depended on other means, like paper, to produce outputs, and postal systems and trade networks to disseminate them. Their development and sustainability, in turn, were often tied to a business model that depended on reaching the biggest markets possible. Not only does this impact what sorts of information outputs are created, but it can also shape language development and lead to further connections between wider audiences. Yet innovation alone isn't always the sole catalyst of changes such as language standardisation, which are also influenced by shifting demographics and social order. The standardisation of the language into Modern English arose from its growing use in administration, born out of major socio-economic shifts arising from the Black Death, as well as in print. Meanwhile, the consumption of these informational outputs depends on an audience capable of processing it, which, in the case of growing literacy rates, arose from changes in education and new ideas around religion. This means that our ability to comprehend possible factors and conditions for studying information ecosystems, their emerging interrelationships, and their impacts on a society must draw on disciplines like economy, sociology, and history, as well as the study of technology, among other disciplines.

THE INFORMATION ANIMAL

The qualitative change in the British information ecosystem brought about by new means of information production and distribution also raises important questions regarding the extent to which information ecosystems can be controlled. Limiting who could own a press and how much they could print didn't end the published fearmongering that Catholicism would return to England. Nor did exiling those who disagreed with religious changes. In fact, banning Protestants from England and denying their sense of identity might have helped strengthen a community of reformers across Europe connected by shared ideas and letter writing. The fluidity with which information passes in an information chain through physical outputs, or as ideas transmitted from agent to agent, makes it hard to control. While regulation is an oft reached-for tool in attempts to govern an information ecosystem, its use might provide more of an illusion of control rather than achieving it. Charles' expectation that his decrees would produce the desired effect in a society no longer bound by the norms of an absolutist monarchy was clearly misplaced and led to his downfall. One lesson, which we will see repeating in later cases, is that ways of measuring the impact of laws, intended and otherwise, must be developed in the context of the information environment to make sense of their application and utility.

Here again, information ecosystems are not islands. England was tied to many ecosystems to varying degrees, each influencing the other. It is also clear that information ecosystems expand and change. The introduction of information animals from one ecosystem to another can change the languages spoken there, and tie information ecosystems together, whereby ideas and events in one influence information animals in another. The information environment is dynamic, and agents within it are not operating in a void. Their actions cause reactions, which in turn cause further rejoinders. In the English information ecosystem, mirroring developments of a dynamic society with high stakes, different types of agents competed and cooperated to gain an advantage. The proselytising Scottish Covenantors, for example, were co-ordinated in their influence efforts and targeted an English audience to win sympathy among the proselytising Godly, who continued to push their cause into 1640. The Irish rebellion stoked anti-Catholic fears in England to increase tensions. Various political agents used events or resources in one kingdom to influence outcomes in another, including the Parliamentarian John Pym and Charles I. Increasingly literate consumers, such as apprentices, grew more politically conscious and began supporting the Godly, signing petitions and protesting. And so on. In turn, the King's own detachment from the rapidly changing realities on the ground, with corresponding effects in the information ecosystem, precipitated poor decision-making. Charles' attempts to control the information ecosystem and his disastrous intervention in Parliament in 1642 to arrest five Godly Parliamentarians led to his flight with his family and his decision to launch an influence campaign, thus escalating the information competition into conflict and eventually war. Case studies that look at the activity of only one type of information animal risk drawing faulty conclusions about the importance of an event or phenomenon. The dynamic interplay between agents expressed through physical behaviour and associated communications causes and escalates information competition. If the aim is to prevent such competition from escalating into open conflict, understanding those dynamics is key.

Charles worried about controlling the means and outputs in his information ecosystem, missing that the agents within it were becoming more literate and thus increasing their capacity to participate in the public sphere. Instead of cutting himself off further from the existing elite in the landed aristocracy and the emerging leaders in Parliament who were channelling this growing body politic, Charles should have set his ego aside and found ways to engage in their concerns constructively. In short, he might have sought to democratise and incorporate an increasingly educated population into a changing system. Charles' folly is a lesson in adaptation and the need for it. Leaders are not separate or independent from the information ecosystem in which they rule; they are as much a part and dependent on that ecosystem for survival as anyone else within it. One must read the situation—if it demands change, there might be a need to adapt accordingly. Feedback between the governed and the governor must be maintained to understand those shifts.

6

A TALE OF TWO COUNTRIES

AMERICAN CIVIL WAR

The government was on the verge of shutting down, lacking the funds needed for it to operate. Unworthy to represent the people who elected them, politicians had paralysed Congress with their partisan contests. Shootings and stabbings abounded. The United States was eating itself alive.[1] Meanwhile, the media profited from attacking public figures, discouraging anyone of quality from entering politics.[2] While all of this could be said about the United States of 2024, this paraphrased account came from Charles Dickens in 1842 after a trip to America. Within the country, two communities had locked into an information competition over worldviews incompatible with each other concerning the lives of a people often excluded from the very debates about their future. As the competition escalated, a fringe minority of abolitionists gained influence in the North's public sphere, to which supporters of the South's slavery stubbornly resisted, with both sides reacting to a sequence of events that cascaded into open conflict. Despite being in the American information ecosystem, the North and

South developed differently. With mass education, the North was experiencing a flourishing of radical ideas that challenged the *status quo*, abolitionism among them. In contrast, the South was clinging to past ideas of itself and resisting change, much like Athens and Sparta before them.

The country that ultimately fought itself, the United States, was mainly born from English and later British colonisation. By the time of Dickens' visit, many Americans in the North and South shared this cultural and historical past, even though they were otherwise diverging on several social and economic issues. Politically, the twenty-six states were tied by a shared Constitution, legal system, and a dedication to republican institutions. As a society, Americans in this period tended towards fierce independence and self-reliance while generally distrusting government, perhaps a long-lasting hangover from their colonial past.[3] On the whole, this was a homogenous population of people with a lineage mainly from the British Isles and following some form of Protestantism, particularly among the governing elite.[4] German and Irish immigrants came in growing numbers, but they were marginalised from collective decision-making, as were, to a greater degree, Indigenous and African American populations.[5] Overall, the population in the first half of the nineteenth century was booming in the United States, jumping from 3,929,214 in 1790 to 17,069,453 in 1840, at an average growth rate per decade of 34 per cent.[6]

A vast and still growing country, different settlement patterns emerged across the North and South, divided by views of slavery. When writing about this period of American history, the twenty-first-century journalist Colin Woodward identified different "nations" grouped by distinct views on religion, community norms, and questions of political governance.[7] In the North was the Yankeedom of the radical Godly (a thread pulled from the seventeenth-century English information ecosystem described in the last chapter), emphasising community, political control, and education. Dickens quipped that in Connecticut, "any citizen who could be proved to have kissed his wife on Sunday, was punishable, I believe, with the stocks. Too much of the old Puritan spirit exists in these parts to the present hour."[8] Nearby in the Midlands were the English Quakers who prized tolerance, along with the religiously persecuted German protestants sceptical of hierarchical authority. In the slavery-supporting South were three more nations: the Tidewater of old Virginia fancying itself a continued aristocracy of Cavaliers harkening back to Charles I, the frontier Greater Appalachia of Scots–Irish (descendants of James I plantation scheme), Scots and northern English, and the Deep South remade in the image of despotic Barbadian slavers.[9]

Another significant community comprised a diverse group of African Americans. Despite their centrality to the competition in the American information ecosystem at the time, they were often treated as secondary in the written histories used to explore this space, frequently reduced to names and numbers in ledger books.[10] It's little wonder that the American abolitionist and grandchild of enslaved West Africans, Martin Delany, would state "we are a nation within a nation."[11] Even when free, African Americans were given no citizenship rights and faced immense racism.[12] Yet, in 1840, African Americans accounted for 17 per cent of the total American population and double that in enslaving states.[13] Adding insult to injury, a clause in the Constitution afforded slavers increased representation in Congress by counting three-fifths of enslaved people "as part of the population on which representation in the House was based."[14] The adjustment gave the South disproportionate power in the House, Senate, and ultimately in presidential elections as well. It's clear that others used African Americans for profit and power. Yet, given how segregated, oppressed, and distinct the African American population was during this period, this community constitutes a smaller information ecosystem within a larger American one that merits study in its own right, but that is beyond the scope of this chapter.

In general, inconsistencies in how people were counted over time, racism, and gender discrimination can make finding exact figures about various conditions, such as education, in the first half of the nineteenth century challenging. However, historians tend to agree that for free people in the United States, education rates were relatively high for the period. By Dickens' visit, enrolment in elementary school had outstripped Germany and other European counterparts.[15] A decade later, the literacy rates of Americans, including enslaved people, outstripped those in Britain and northwest Europe by around a quarter. However, the approach to schooling differed between North and South. In New England, public education was widespread, with almost 95 per cent adult literacy. On average, three-quarters of the children between ages five and nineteen attended school half the year,[16] whereas in the South, just under half the population was literate.[17] Of course, those numbers increase when just counting European Americans in the South (80 per cent), but it still trailed the North by 15 per cent, and only one-third of their children attended school on an "average of three months a year."[18] In addition to the amount of time and number of children in school, the emphasis on education also differed between the two regions, with the North focusing on applied subjects and the South on the classics and a liberal education.[19] And yet, despite these differences, the South depended on the North for education. Many Southerners went to universities in the North, and colleges in the South hired Northern professionals to run and staff their institutions.[20] That dependency, however, did not necessarily translate into fondness.

As education became more widespread, the movement of information through the ecosystem in America also accelerated through improved means. New legislation in 1845 and 1851 decreased postage costs, including more favourable rates for distributing newspapers and periodicals.[21] Steamships moved people farther and faster across waterways, including the Atlantic Ocean, than ever before. These boats also moved outputs between information ecosystems more quickly. Contemporary author James Fenimore Cooper complained that journals printed in England were used in America "in support of the pretensions of politicians, writers, artists, and all others, who are liable to the decisions of their fellow citizens for the estimation in which they are held."[22] It took Dickens just eighteen days to travel from Liverpool to Boston.[23] He was received like a rock star by an American audience who had delighted in his earlier works, demonstrating how quickly information moved at distances and was consumed across ecosystems.[24] Links made during the trip endured, producing long-lasting outputs. Dickens hosted the American poet Henry Wadsworth Longfellow in London a few months after his journey to the United States. There, the poet read Dickens' draft account of his voyage, which sparked Longfellow to share his observations with Charles Sumner, who urged him to write anti-slavery poetry inspired by the travelogue, which he did later that same year.[25] Even the ocean was no barrier to information transfer, with steamships connecting the United States to Europe. Railways were also developing, and in the 1840s, the telegraph came with it, significantly increasing the speed at which information could travel.[26] Much like claims about the internet in the late twentieth century, the telegraph inventor touted it as society's nervous system, collapsing space and time.[27] In turn, the railways would be followed by a canal system, further increasing the movement of people, and with them, information.

Changing means had an impact on outputs. The telegraph, coupled with changes in making paper and printing, heightened the importance of newspapers in the United States, dropping the price of a newspaper by two-thirds.[28] Indeed, newspapers were the most popular form of literature in antebellum America.[29] The very concept of the freshness of news was changing with how quickly it could now travel.[30] Circulation rates were increasing manifold. The creation of the Associated Press in 1848 by a consortium of news outlets increased the distribution of syndicated stories, which meant more people were exposed to the same information.[31] By the late 1850s, "virtually every family in New York was buying a daily paper."[32] However, as had happened before in the information ecosystems of Ancient Greece and Britain, quantity did not equate to quality. Most newspapers were political, both in the North (74 per cent) and the South (83 per cent), conveying all sorts of information from rumours to political calls and selling so much more.[33] For Dickens, news media in the United States was sub-standard and could not be compensated with all the education in the world:

> Year by year, the tone of public feeling must sink lower down; year by year, the Congress and the Senate must become of less account before all decent men; and year by year, the memory of the Great Fathers of the Revolution must be outraged more and more.[34]

Cheaper printing costs promoted more book publishing. In addition to the likes of Cooper and Longfellow, the North was producing authors like Nathaniel Hawthorne, Ralph Waldo Emerson, and Henry David Thoreau, whose recognition spread widely.[35] However, little control over literary intellectual property rights meant that cheaply made reprints abounded that undercut the official books.[36] This practice helped a book to become widespread, much like digital platforms would do for ideas in the twenty-first century.

Other means of content production existed beyond print, including pamphlets, lithographs, and broadsides, through which various information sources often intersected. Political debates were common.[37] Conventions were organised around women's rights, trade, slavery, and abolition.[38] Churches remained a vital institution where people congregated regularly, and politics often encroached. The circuit court system acted as a road map for orators of all persuasions, as part of a public lecture culture that was an essential form of mass media.[39] Events, lectures, and political speeches were picked up by news media. Political speeches were publicised and reprinted by sympathetic newspapers to increase distribution.[40] As with education, though, more of this activity was happening in the North than the South.

Moving information through the South was not as easy, and a lack of infrastructure development did not make it any easier. In fact, there seemed to be a lack of development in general. From Washington, DC, Dickens forayed into the south to Richmond, Virginia. The distance between the two places is 175 kilometres, and as of this writing if the traffic is miraculously clear, it should take less than two hours to drive. For Dickens, however, the journey required an overnight steamer ferry and a coach ride down a barely passable sixteen-kilometre road that took two and half hours to traverse, "breaking no bones, though bruising a great many; and in short getting through the distance, 'like a fiddle.'"[41] This got Dickens and his wife to Fredericksburg (just over ninety kilometres from the capital), where a train connected them to Richmond. The author presented a grim picture of the landscape between the two towns, of the acreage that had once been productive and was then reduced to "a sandy desert overgrown with trees", the soil exhausted, forcing crops with enslaved labour, whereas "the same decay and gloom that overhang the way by which it is approached, hover above the town of Richmond."[42]

Roads, railways and canals just were not developing in the same way in the South as they were in the North. According to historian John Hope Franklin:

> the center of power, the basis of the entire economic structure, rested on the land and on the people who owned the land. Where towns emerged, they were for the purpose of serving the peculiar and relatively simple needs of the agricultural interests.[43]

In his recounts from the period, the author Frederick Douglass, who had been enslaved, described how some planters maintained large sloops to move their products on the river to Baltimore, which rendered canals and railways less necessary for development in parts of the South.[44] Indeed, most of the canal system (86 per cent) ran through Free States.[45] And as railways developed, the South's portion of the system dropped from 44 per cent of the national total in 1840 to 26 per cent a decade later.[46] Even Southern centres weren't developed, lacked paving, and, in the case of New Orleans, closed sewers up to 1857.[47]

Beyond infrastructure, the South seemed to lack the same degree of entertainment and access to information that the North enjoyed. Southern towns were by and large bereft of public amusements like libraries, lecture halls, gardens, or art galleries.[48] They just did not seem to be making the same cultural investments as the North. As noted above, the South was also dependent on the North not just in some aspects of education but also in printing, with most of the presses producing material even by Southern authors located in the Northern Free States.[49]

While the South resisted change, the North brimmed with ideas. Dickens was impressed by the massive accumulation of patents and inventions that seemed to blossom with the North's focus on practical education and commerce.[50] This time was also marked by the emergence of numerous radical movements in the North, including those focused on abolition, free sex, women's rights, temperance, and religious revival.⁵¹ Some of these movements built communes with schools to try and foster a new society. In *American Radicals* (2019), Holly Jackson credits abolitionism and the rights movement for pushing boundaries on all other issues, including diet, clothing, sex, kinship, government, work, animal rights, and medicine, effectively snapping Americans from their apathy of accepting previously established patterns of sociopolitical behaviour.⁵²

From a fringe minority grew the abolitionist movement, a key group of agents in this information ecosystem. The earlier part of the nineteenth century had experienced a Protestant revival, one of a series of so-called Awakenings, out of which came questions about slavery.⁵³ Abolitionism counted among its supporters other Protestant sects, like the Quakers, who also encouraged women to participate with the right to speak at public meetings. Indeed, many drivers of abolitionism were women, some of whom also led the women's rights movement.⁵⁴ Abolitionists viewed themselves as agitators trying to influence public opinion against slavery, which they considered a sin.⁵⁵ To that end, in 1831, Lloyd Garrison opened the *Liberator*, a newspaper promoting abolition, following it with the creation of the American Anti-Slavery Society in 1833. Garrison attacked not just slaveholders but also what he viewed as Northern white complicity.⁵⁶ What set the paper apart from prior abolitionist works was "both the emotional pitch and the high ambition of the *Liberator*." The *Liberator* also featured work by African Americans, including Frederick Douglass, until he later opened *The North Star*. These exchanges, according to modern historian Elizabeth R. Varon, could be interpreted as a chain of mutually respectful conversations between the editor and his correspondents, which aimed to engage his audience in the dialogue.⁵⁷ Douglass acclaimed the paper, writing that:

> Its sympathy for my brethren in bonds—its scathing denunciations of slaveholders—its faithful exposures of slavery—and its powerful attacks upon the upholders of the institution—sent a thrill of joy through my soul, such as I had never felt before![58]

Garrison pursued immediate abolition, though through peaceful means, a view that was still very much in the minority even among abolitionists.[59] In the South, newspaper editors blamed Garrison and his paper for causing slave rebellions, leading to a ban on the *Liberator*.[60] Although, banning was a light response compared to some. Garrison would have a bounty put on his head, an effigy of him burned, and be attacked by a mob that put a noose around his neck all in the course of his career, but he survived the Civil War.[61] In 1837, another newspaper editor was not so lucky. Elijah Lovejoy was killed by an anti-abolition mob in Alton, Illinois.[62] The competition between worldviews was on the rise, and the American information ecosystem was already producing signs of heating up.

As new ideas of women's rights and abolitionism took root in the North, sectionalism and a reactionary sense of honour flowered in the South. Along with it came a myth about Southern origins. As historian John McCardell noted, the idea of a plantation myth emerged in the 1830s, promoting an "image of a genteel, non-competitive way of life, where old families ruled, old values were retained, loyal slaves performed their happy tasks, and culture and chivalry abounded."[63] The notion that this culture was somehow separate and distinct from the North was fertilised by the Nullification Crisis of 1832–33, whereby the state of South Carolina invalidated a federal tariff that supported Northern manufacturing. The tariff had taxed low-priced imports, which were undercutting the economy there but hurt the South, which was predominantly agricultural and a high importer of goods. In response to the high import taxes, foreign markets blocked the sale of American cotton, primarily produced in the South. To say the predominately agricultural South was unhappy with the tax is an understatement. The incident sparked a movement of Nullifiers and Southern Nationalists, who increasingly believed that the Union did not have the South's best economic interests at heart and that the South needed to become more separate to survive, including in preserving slavery, which they saw as essential to cotton production and their way of life.[64]

New publications opened in the South. For example, the Virginian *Southern Literary Messenger* launched in 1834 and aimed "to show our Northern brethren that Southern learning can think for itself."[65] It became a leading periodical in the South. The *Messenger* also endured longer than other periodicals, making it what McCardell called "an accurate barometer of changing feelings in the South toward the Union."[66] Generally, the number of newspapers fluctuated in the South, with partisan outlets popping up before elections only to disappear after.[67] Overall, though, it was a less developed and less stable media market compared to the North.

The idea of a culturally separate South was nurtured by novels like *Cavaliers of Virginia* by William Alexander Caruthers in 1834. The book romanticised an archetype of an American aristocratic hero, drawing on myths that the South was settled by Royalist supporters during the English Civil War.[68] This would develop into a belief that the Southerners descended from the Norman conquerors of 1066, while the Northern forebears were subjugated Saxons.[69] Slavery was positioned as the foundation for this aristocratic society on the basis that European Americans were elevated in having African Americans do menial work.[70]

Along with these ideas of honour and lineage, Southerners also relished the notion that they were quicker to fight and prone to violence.[71] Dickens hinted at this perception in his recounting of why he and his wife chose to visit Richmond instead of farther-flung Charleston, "my companion being threatened with more perils, dangers, and discomforts, than I can remember or would catalogue if I could; but of which it will be sufficient to remark that blowings-up in steamboats and breakings-down in coaches were among the least."[72] It wasn't all hyperbole. The practice of duelling was alive and well in the South, and sociologist Randolph Roth observed, "they murdered one another over insults, slights, or revelations of embarrassing truths."[73] This propensity for violence in the South spanned all classes and races, especially among public figures who cared most about their reputations.[74] It was this very well-nourished sense of honour, historian Bertram Wyatt-Brown posited, that prevented Southerners from ever displaying the contrition abolitionists demanded of them regarding slavery. Quite the contrary.[75]

As abolitionists pushed for an end to slavery, and Southerners reacted with growing outrage, a tit-for-tat information competition escalated in Congress. The American Anti-Slavery Society launched a petition campaign calling for the end of slavery, resulting in 130,000 appeals received by Congress in one legislative season.[76] This effort was met with a ban pushed by Southern politicians on discussion about such petitions. Abolitionists then used this gag rule to stage debate about free speech, increasing their spread of antislavery material in the South, to which leaders there then censored mail delivery.[77] Far from controlling the flow of information, the Southern efforts to block discussion about abolition in Congress only helped amplify the cause, providing it with a stage. Such drama created audiences for books like *American Slavery As It Is*, published by the American Anti-Slavery Society in 1839, which also inspired Dickens' *American Notes*.[78] The established practice of republishing unlicensed copies ensured the American information ecosystem was flooded with such material.[79] All in all, by 1845, abolitionists had sufficient political power to have the "gag rule" on bringing petitions about slavery to Congress removed.[80]

Event after event, with words enflaming attitudes and deeds, the information competition between abolitionists and pro-slavers escalated from Congress down to the streets and back. The United States was rapidly growing westward, increasing its information ecosystem along with it. Territorial expansion led to a debate about the future of slavery, with critical events promoting antagonistic sectionalism or the prioritisation of one's part of the country over the whole.[81] For example, the *Wilmot Proviso* in 1846 aimed to restrict the expansion of slavery to newly acquired Texas.[82] Voting for the legislation fell along sectional lines as opposed to party lines, which had been the general practice.[83] The likes of Virginia slaver Edmund Ruffin began spreading fears that white people in the South were threatened with extinction because emancipation would surely mean their barbaric end.[84] Southern state conventions agitated for a swift response should something like the *Wilmot Proviso* ever be passed. Such fears led many in the South to believe they either had to entrench slavery within the Union or leave it."[85] While Southern fears and resentment were growing, anti-slavery efforts were gaining ground too. New publications supporting abolition popped up. The weekly *National Era* was launched in 1847 in Washington by the American and Foreign Antislavery Society.[86] The paper backed political parties like Liberty and, ultimately, the Republicans. Historian Eric Foner described the *National Era* as "the most consistently radical paper".[87]

In 1850 came the *Compromise*, which was a package of five bills passed by Congress with the hope of tempering sectional division. Far from dampening the flames, the 1850 *Compromise* poured gasoline on them. It included a ban on the slave trade in DC, a harsher *Fugitive Slave Act*, and left determination on the status of slavery on territory taken from Texas up to a new concept called "popular sovereignty".[88] Southern Nationalism after 1850 picked up a strain of manifest destiny (the idea that the United States was divinely preordained to spread capitalist democracy across the continent) to expand slavery, which some argued couldn't survive without expansion.[89] In the South, politicians saw each successive decision on slavery in newly acquired territories as some enduring means to relegate the South to a minority status in Congress, despite having enjoyed an inflated representation on the backs of the people they had enslaved.[90] Worked up in all this was the Southern concept of honour; taking away one's property, even enslaved people, was an attack on one's honour, particularly when Northerners helped those people escape.[91] In response to the 1850 *Compromise*, Russell Hunter Garnett Muscoe, a Virginian politician and lawyer, claimed that "The South has at stake, not merely the fourteen hundred millions of dollars, the value of her slave property, but all of honor and of happiness that civilization and society can give."[92] His tract entitled *Union Past and Future* was a litany of perceived injustices perpetrated on the South by the North, from its lack of representation federally to abolitionist plots and even disproportionate spending on lighthouses.[93]

Meanwhile, in the North, the 1850 *Compromise* was a propaganda gift for abolitionists. The implications of the *Fugitive Slave Act* specifically were a boon, as it compelled citizens in the Free States to help return people escaping slavery to those claiming ownership over them. It was no longer an issue that could simply be ignored, as the law was, in fact, forcing people to become involved in the institution, even in the Free States. Abolitionists focused their attention on the law, and according to historian David M. Potter, "from press, pulpit, and rostrum, a storm of denunciation burst forth."[94] Slavers and their supporters were tarred as sinners. Lithographs depicted brutal futures for African Americans, free and enslaved alike.[95] The *Act* inspired responses, including Harriet Beecher Stowe's hit novel *Uncle Tom's*

Cabin.⁹⁶ On its first day, the book sold 3,000 copies; the first run of 5,000 was sold within four days, and demand required presses to churn out copies around the clock.⁹⁷ Within its first year of being published as a book in 1852, it had sold 300,000 copies in the United States, and by the close of a decade, sales were up to 2 million, making the book one of the best sellers per population size of all time.⁹⁸ The novel depicted the flight of a woman from slavery and was based on the experiences of Josiah Henson, who published his autobiography in 1849 after making it to safety in Canada in 1830.⁹⁹ Reprints of Henson's account surged in sales following Beecher Stowe's work. The pro-slavery response to this informational flood was adding more information outputs into the information ecosystem. Southern authors responded, adding more than a dozen novels attempting to demonstrate that enslaved people lived better lives than Northern workers in the two years following *Uncle Tom's Cabin's* release.¹⁰⁰

While abolitionists were incensed, a growing body of Northern citizens were also agitated by the *Fugitive Slave Act*. The breaking point came with the *Act's* enforcement in 1854 by President Franklin Pierce when he turned the militia on Bostonians attempting to protect Anthony Burns, who had escaped slavery in Virginia. On 2 June 1854, Burns was convicted of being a fugitive. Buildings were adorned in black crepe, and tens of thousands watched from the streets as he was marched to a ship headed for Virginia.¹⁰¹ Burns' experience would become a topic for visual prints and abolitionist campaigning. The direct experience and high emotions galvanised by this episode pushed many towards the anti-slavery cause. In a letter to Giles Richards, the wealthy textile merchant Amos A. Lawrence recounted that "we went to bed one night old fashioned, conservative, *Compromise* Union Whigs & waked up stark mad Abolitionists." Lawrence then turned his fortunes to financing the next "battle" in Kansas.¹⁰²

At the time of the Burns case, in Congress, the *Kansas-Nebraska Act* was reopening the territorial dispute. The *Act* repealed an earlier *Compromise* in 1820, which limited slavery to the 36°30′ parallel when admitting Missouri and Maine into the Union.[103] The notion of popular sovereignty was again floated, which enabled people living in those territories, regardless of how recently they had migrated to them, to choose to ban or allow slavery, taking the decision away from Congress.[104] While the approach gained some traction for admitting the territories of Kansas and Nebraska, it was, perhaps ironically, unpopular with all sides, be they abolitionists and Republicans or southern newspaper editors and nationalists.[105] Sectional voting on *the Kansas–Nebraska Act* effectively split the Democratic party, which in general was Southern-leaning in their views and, by the 1850s, increasingly concerned with perceived Northern aggressions against the South.[106] They wanted to limit government and opposed federal policies that might restrict the individual liberties of white men.[107] Democrats drew their support from unskilled workers and farmers farther away from major urban centres, but also from Catholic immigrants, especially the Irish. The prospect of a sudden release of millions of enslaved people stoked fears of economic ruin for poorer people of European descent, such as Irish immigrants.[108]

In response to the *Kansas–Nebraska Act*, several politicians penned the 1854 *Appeal of the Independent Democrats*, published in the *Cincinnati Gazette* and reprinted elsewhere. The attack was, for Foner, "one of the most effective pieces of political propaganda in our history."[109] The *Appeal* was a manifesto signed by politicians Salmon Chase, J. Alexander De Witt, Joshua Giddings, Gerrit Smith, Charles Sumner, and Edward Wade. Reprinted in the Cincinnati Gazette, the *Appeal* positioned the Act:

As a gross violation of a sacred pledge; as a criminal betrayal of precious rights; as part and parcel of an atrocious plot to exclude from a vast unoccupied region, immigrants from the Old World and free laborers from our own States, and convert it into a dreary region of despotism, inhabited by masters and slaves.[110]

The passing of this act led to an open competition between North and South to populate Kansas with supporters to sway the vote in their favour, turning the territory into a hotly contested space in both the information and physical environments. In terms of information competition, the battle was between free labour and slavery, often resulting in physical violence.[111] Wealthy men like Amos A. Lawrence funded the migration of pro-abolitionists to the territory through the New England Emigrant Aid Company, and the brother of Beecher Stowe, Henry Ward Beecher, helped smuggle breech-loading Sharps rifles to the settlers in boxes marked "books and bibles", leading to the moniker "Beecher's Bibles".[112]

Before the vote, the situation grew increasingly unstable, leading to a period of violence that gained the name "Bleeding Kansas". Pro-slavers had not sat idly by while abolitionists moved in. They, too, migrated to the territory, often from just across the border in Missouri, and many pre-existing settlers were supportive of slavery. Ultimately, rival governments were put forward by both sides, murder followed, and armed clashes erupted.[113] A target for pro-slaver violence was the territory's centre for abolition, Lawrence, named after the textile magnate. Tensions escalated in 1856 when some 800 pro-slavers attacked the abolitionist newspapers there, the *Kansas Free State* and the *Herald of Freedom,* and fired a cannon on the Free State Hotel, setting it alight while pillaging the town.[114] The sacking of Lawrence provided abolitionists with more propaganda opportunities. Northern newspapers covered "Bleeding Kansas" heavily. Torchlit marches followed with chants of "'Free Soil, Free Speech, Free Men, Frémont!'"[115] Yet the more abolitionists pushed, the more pro-slavers did too, stoking fears over their eventual suppression within the Union and fanning hatred for Yankees.[116] The *Southern Literary Messenger* leaned into Southern nationalism and used Kansas as a warning to its readers. The *Southern Quarterly Review* endlessly covered slavery, issue after issue.[117] Ultimately, the proslavery camp won the 1857 vote in Kansas.[118]

The fight over slavery pulled on a host of disparate but oppositional threads. The North began to interpret Republicanism through the lens of free labour. In contrast, the South remained rooted in a concept of liberty, particularly around the freedom to own property, including enslaved people. The back-and-forth played out in the media, including in journals and periodicals.

In the North, the very practice of slavery was believed to corrupt labour, stifle economic development, and overall foster a backward, uneducated society dominated by an elite.[119] Given Northern dominance in printing and education, a superiority complex developed vis-à-vis the South, whereby the latter were perceived as uneducated.[120] In his 1857 influential work, Hinton Rowan Helper, a proud Southern and American diplomat, advocated for the abolition of slavery as a means of advancing the development in the South while retaining racial supremacy by stating, "Slavery is hostile to general education. Its strength, its very life, is in the ignorance and stolidity of the masses; it naturally and necessarily represses general literary culture."[121] Helper used statistics to argue that the South had fallen behind the North economically. While Helper was a Southerner, his book was used by politicians in the North to campaign against slavery.[122] This line of argument did not just diminish the institution of slavery and Southern society with it, but aggrandised the Northern capitalist approach.[123] It was expected that men would be responsible for improving their own conditions through hard work and that poverty would be alleviated by westward migration.[124] This perspective was reinforced by northern journalists filing reports from visits to the South.[125]

The South, on the other hand, took the view that labourers in the North were wage slaves, barely getting by and on the constant precipice of losing jobs and starving with no protection from uncaring masters, and attempted to juxtapose the position of those enslaved as somehow better.[126] In his work *Cannibals, All!*, the social theorist George Fitzhugh argued:

> You, with the command over labor which your capital gives you, are a slave owner—a master, without the obligations of a master. They who work for you, who create your income, are slaves, without the rights of slaves. Slaves without a master![127]

Pro-slavers developed and promoted a view of slavery as being a social good and morally just, championed by the likes of Southern Nationalists.[128] The Bible and science alike were trotted out to justify slavery in the 1851 *Diseases and Peculiarities of the Negro Race* by New Orleans doctor Samuel A. Cartwright.[129]

This tit-for-tat escalated the information competition between anti-slavery and slavery advocates. For example, when some states in the South criminalised the distribution of Helper's book, Republicans fundraised to run a new printing and distribute it *en masse*, attempting to flood the South with abolitionist messaging.[130] The onslaught helped foster a Southern media sphere. Both the number of newspapers and their circulation rates increased significantly in the 1850s.[131] By 1860, there were 700 political newspapers across the South.[132] In his analysis of Southern news media, historian Donald E. Reynolds found these publications were flanked on one extreme by Unionist newspapers arguing against secession and, on the other, secessionist outlets actively campaigning for the South to leave the Union in 1860. In the middle were the bulk of Southern rights papers, with some moderates less clear on secession before Lincoln's election and the larger group arguing secession should depend upon northern aggression, including the election of a Republican president.[133] But given a smaller market, the South had fewer newspaper subscribers than the North, which created cost considerations for editors, who were thus sensitive to their readers' desires. Reynolds pointed to an editorial in Raleigh's *La Grange* on 6 January 1860, in which the author lamented the lack of freedom in the press:

> The fact is, that no man has less freedom allowed him to express his opinions than an Editor. His patrons regard him as a penny trumpet through which not a note is to be sounded, unless it accords precisely with their own music.[134]

And so fears about the North's intention about slavery would be reflected to readers until the idea of secession was a self-fulfilling prophecy. Business models have long posed a problem for information ecosystems.

As arguments escalated, rhetoric became insulting. Abolitionists had long been painting slavers as immoral sinners, brutalising other humans, and Southern commentators depicted the North as lunatics.[135] In a letter to A. Hogeboom, Fitzhugh speculated that the free society was leading to crazy ideas, naming several radical movements that would tear itself apart:

> Why have you Bloomers and Women's Rights Men, and strong-minded women, and Mormons, and anti-renters, and 'vote myself a farm' men, Millerites, and Spiritual Rappers, and Shakers, and Widow Wakemanites, and Agrarians, and Grahamites, and a thousand other superstitious and infidel Isms at the North? Why is there faith in nothing, speculation

about everything? Why is this unsettled, half-demented, state of the human mind co-extensive in time and space, with free society? Why is Western Europe now starving? and why has it been fighting and starving for seventy years? Why all this, except that free society is a failure? Slave society needs no defense till some other permanently practicable form of society has been discovered. Nobody at the North who reads my book will attempt to reply to it; for all the learned abolitionists had unconsciously discovered and proclaimed the failure of free society long before I did.[136]

On and on the rebuttals went, touting racial superiority in books and journals, spilling over into math problems for students.[137] By the summer of 1860, the *Southern Literary Messenger* was digging into the Norman–Saxon myth discussed above about the different English roots between South and North to suggest that "Yankees *were* perhaps fit only to be slaves," pulling once again on that thread from the seventeenth-century English information ecosystem.[138]

As abolitionists agitated further and became more militant in their activities, many in the South feared uprisings supported by abolitionists, fuelling rumours in times of uncertainty.[139] Despite small numbers of people escaping slavery and rare occurrences of revolts, Southerners were preoccupied with the threat of both. Yet the measures southerners enacted to counter such eventualities, including censoring the press, further aggravated relations with the North in a manner reminiscent of Charles I.[140] The prospects of Republicans winning the 1860 election only fuelled these fears, which McPherson noted "brewed a volatile mixture of hysteria, despondency, and elation in the South." Southern newspapers reported on slave revolts "that followed the visits of mysterious Yankee strangers, reports of arson and rapes and poisonings by slaves crowded the southern press. Somehow, these horrors never seemed to happen in one's own neighbourhood."[141] Outsiders were not to be trusted. When a prolonged drought sparked a massive fire in Dallas in the summer of 1860, Southern newspapers were quick to blame it on abolitionists and slave revolts.[142] The story was quickly spread via the telegraph across the South.

Southern voices began decrying that a Republican rule would mean enslavement of the South to the North, preying on fear to raise emotions. The only answer was secession. Secessionist states sent commissioners to persuade other Southern states to join them in leaving the Union.[143] Indeed, by the presidential election, editors of Southern newspapers were claiming that a Republican presidential win would be tantamount to a declaration of war by the North on the South.[144]

For their part, the North wasn't quelling fears. Both sides believed they were in an all-or-nothing game. Lincoln stated that in his famous "House Divided" speech, as did William Seward in his speech "The Irrepressible Conflict", which was reprinted in the *New York Times*.[145] Communities in both the North and South had worked themselves up to a feverish pitch, and their worldviews were incompatible.

The decades leading up to Confederate shots which launched the Civil War on 12 April 1861 were full of change and activity, bringing about opportunities for some and uncertainties for others. The United States had become one of that age's most educated Western societies. Advances in printing increased the availability of various means of capturing and relaying information through lithographs, newspapers, journals, and books. Changes in transportation revolutionised the movement of information not just across the country but across the ocean. The introduction of the telegraph changed the lifespan of "news". These changes spurred the spread of new, radical ideas that challenged the *status quo* both in the North and in the South. As with all changes, people reacted to them differently in major part depending on their perceptions of possible losses or benefits. In the South, perhaps feeling itself more threatened by these changes, it appears that old ideas supported by new myths made even deeper roots. The increasing information flood presented the Northern abolitionists and Southern pro-slavers alike with sufficient content and justifications, with each community competing as if it were a niche species fighting for that ecosystem.

The more Southern interests attempted to control the information environment, the more distinct the two still interconnected ecosystems became. Controls over the spread of information in the South meant that most Southerners were not highly exposed to Northern publications, especially abolitionist literature, which was often censored. The most popular paper in the North, the *Tribune,* which espoused a free labour ideology, had a Northern circulation of 287,750 in early 1861 but only reached a few hundred in the South.[146] Attacking journalists, torching newspapers, censoring content, and controlling the mail only made it harder for Southerners to see different points of view, not that such exposure might have changed minds there. Meanwhile, leading Republicans subscribed to Southern publications to follow pro-slavery arguments and form rebuttals. The one place where political leaders from both sections infrequently met, the United States Congress, was, as Dickens had noted, paralysed. At a time when American society required sober decision-making in the public interest, the legitimacy of the very mechanism to conduct such assessments and deliberations was being questioned in favour of particular interests. As sectional divisions worsened, the ability of Congress to reach the necessary consensus to resolve disputes deteriorated. The two sides had lost touch to such a degree they were reacting, as Potter noted, to distorted perceptions of each other: "the North to an image of a southern world of lascivious and sadistic slavedrivers; the South to the image of a northern world of cunning Yankee traders and of rabid abolitionists plotting slave insurrections."[147] This was a tale of two countries.

Meanwhile, as events unfolded, information animals reacted. The Nullification crisis over an import tariff seeded Southern nationalism and origin myths. Southern attempts to control information flows in Congress with the Gag Rule gave abolitionists a platform. By the time of the *Wilmot Proviso* and *1850 Compromise,* both sides had their established playbooks that guided their responses. For every action, there was a reaction. Enforcing the *Fugitive Slave Act* increased support for abolition and the movement of people to Kansas in response to the *Kansas–Nebraska Act*, as did violently attempting to suppress those migrants. Just as the retributive killing of five pro-slavers by abolitionist John Brown and his failed attempt at an uprising helped feed Southern fears about revolts.[148] People were so conditioned to react by this point that even fantasy caused a response as with the Dallas fire. In the American information ecosystem, a flood of content about these events was often followed by a counter-flood with a different point of view.

As communities formed around both sides, various agents engaged, each with their own interest. Proselytisers emerged from religious and women's rights groups to spread abolitionism, drawing on the personal accounts and hardships of the people they aimed to help. Newspapers raised awareness but also pursued profits. Artists like Dickens and Longfellow weighed in, and others like Beecher Stowe used fiction to advance their cause. Politicians were courted, but activists took to politics as well, like Sumner. As support grew and events unfolded, wealthy benefactors like Lawrence joined in. It was a cross-section of European-descended Northern society, as Delany observed. Slavery's supporters also counted various actors, including fiction writers like Caroline Lee Hertz, journal editors like DeBow, and a host of politicians. Beyond slavers themselves, lawyers and other farmers rallied to their cause. But overall, the South's activities might be seen mainly as a reaction to an increasingly well-organised campaign from the North—with both supporting rather minority interests. The heat of these debates and their uncompromising nature left little room for either side to manoeuvre. The board was set.

Variances in factors and conditions across an information ecosystem can cause serious challenges, leading to different climates and outcomes. These differences can be so significant that an information ecosystem can effectively split into two or more smaller ones. Analysing changing conditions throughout an information ecosystem to understand regional differences is critical. To maintain a large information ecosystem, similar investments must be made across it into the people, the means for processing information, and available outputs to reduce imbalances and keep it connected.

7

ALPHABETS AND ALIENS

VIETNAMESE INDEPENDENCE

Having imposing neighbours is hard. If they feel powerful, they might come for what isn't theirs. Trưng Trắc knew this all too well. First, they took her land; then, they took her husband. What else could she do? Defiant, Trắc rallied her sister and then their compatriots, building an army of 80,000 led by thirty-six female generals to drive the invaders back.[1] These women were fierce. One even gave birth on the battlefield, strapped the newborn on her back, and continued to fight.[2] They succeeded—and for a time, Trưng Trắc became the first female ruler of Vietnam in the first century CE. As the poet Đặng Thanh Lê, wrote fourteen centuries later, "All the male heroes bowed their heads in submission. Only the two sisters proudly stood up to avenge the country."[3] The revolt happened nearly two millennia ago, but the heroism of the first major resistance against Chinese rule lives on in Vietnam. The sisters are depicted on statues riding elephants into battle. Temples commemorate their honour. Each year, festivals celebrate their victory. In part, the Trưng legend looms large thanks to their inspiration for more recent Vietnamese independence movements and how those activists used the sisters to garner support. Such are the long threads woven into some information ecosystems. The importance of these threads can be lost on outsiders, like French colonisers. Blinded not so much by the latest technology but by their sense of superiority and entitlement to an empire, these latecomers would miss how changing conditions within the Vietnamese information ecosystem, some of which they introduced, would only fuel ideas of independence. Growing literacy rates and an opening of the information ecosystem helped spark a nationalist movement supported by new technology in a simplified writing system and print, but also history.

Unfortunately for the Trưng sisters, Emperor Guangwu sent his best general with 20,000 troops to squash their rebellion, and both sisters died in 43 CE.[4] China would rule the country for a millennium, influencing education and spreading Confucianism, which the Vietnamese adapted to their needs.[5] For the most part, the Vietnamese threw off the Chinese yoke in the tenth century and, in turn, dominated some of their neighbours to the south, taking lands from several Cham peoples in the centuries that followed. This ultimately led to the creation of different regional Vietnamese identities. These differences persisted through stereotypes lingering for centuries, such as the view that the South was a frontier, more ethnically and culturally diverse, more individualistic and entrepreneurial than the North.[6] Throughout this period, the Vietnamese remained more or less independent for nearly another millennium, albeit with bouts of instability and a regular threat of Chinese intrusion, which helped further instil a strong sense of nationalism and hard-won independence. Then, European adventurers and missionaries began to arrive in the sixteenth century. In one moment of weakness, Emperor Gia Long asked the French to save him from unrest late in the eighteenth century, which had dire consequences for Vietnamese independence. By 1884, after decades of effort, Vietnam was forcibly subsumed under Indochina, the name the French gave the conquered region, which included Cambodia and Laos.[7] Despite changing names and external influences, a Vietnamese identity and drive for independence endured, which was central to the anti-colonial movements and struggle for freedom from alien domination that followed.

French rule was exploitative and sometimes brutal. After colonisation, many rural Vietnamese who owned land became increasingly dispossessed.[8] French policies were also racist and divisive, favouring white colonists and a minority of Vietnamese who adopted European practices, including converting to Catholicism.[9] The number of French who came to settle in Vietnam remained small compared to the overall population size, which left them dependent on this small French-trained elite they fostered, accounting for 5 per cent of the population, but who were increasingly out of touch with their compatriots.[10] This co-dependency cut off the colonisers and their supporters from the general population they ruled, a situation that leads to trouble, as we have seen in other information ecosystems. At their peak, the estimated size of these *colons* or *Français d'Indochine* ranged between 34,000 and 50,000.[11] The majority settled in Saigon, followed by Hanoi and Haiphong and were primarily men, as female *colons* only began to arrive after 1900.[12] The country overall, as a result, remained homogenous, with 85 per cent or more of the population being ethnic Kinh or lowland Vietnamese.[13]

To socialise and train a small number of emerging Vietnamese elite, the French introduced their education model and sent students to France. The process aimed to lead the Vietnamese away from Confucianism and, in so doing, introduced French philosophies and values like those inscribed in France's motto of "*liberté, égalité, fraternité*". This both opened the pre-existing Vietnamese information ecosystem to new influences and exposed those affected to the stark discrepancy between the colonisers' liberal values at home and oppressive actions in Vietnam.[14] The creation of a separate Vietnamese school teaching system in French in 1917 aimed to channel local students away from *colon* schools and thus limit their upward mobility vis-à-vis the colonists. The uptake among Vietnamese was low.[15] Nonetheless, the adoption of the Romanised script *quôc nhu* in education, replacing Chinese characters, meant that within the first few decades of the twentieth century, some 10 to 20 per cent of the population could read.[16] The new writing system was more accessible to a broader population, prompting growth in printed outputs in *quôc nhu*.[17] The script's simplicity and easy adoption made it an obvious tool for a growing movement of nationalists, influenced by the Western philosophies learned in the changed school system, to begin their fights against the country's occupation.[18]

With more people able to consume written outputs, the Vietnamese information ecosystem became increasingly connected to the outside world. The same changes in steam travel that connected America to England linked Vietnam to France. The opening of the Suez Canal sped that travel up, and an end to the French monopoly on shipping lines to Vietnam at the turn of the twentieth century helped increase Asia-bound traffic from Europe through these routes.[19] The number of travellers boomed. Some Vietnamese left the country of their own accord, albeit requiring permission from French authorities to do so, while others were forced to leave. Phan Bội Châu (1867–1940) and Phan Châu Trinh (1872–1926), two leading figures in the emerging independence movement, headed for Japan, where Vietnamese nationalists like the former created a "Go East" programme, which provided refuge and inspiration to Vietnamese émigré intellectuals.[20] Phan Bội Châu wrote his play about the Trưng sisters fighting invaders while in Thailand around 1911.[21] When the French authorities closed the "Go East" programme, Phan Bội Châu attracted the Vietnamese to Guangzhou in Southern China.[22] Others were exiled as political prisoners elsewhere in the French empire, exposing them to anti-colonialist sentiments developing, for example, in Northern Africa.[23] Some young men like Nguyễn Sinh Cung left the country to work on steamships, travelling to places like New York, London, and Paris, learning foreign languages, and returning home only decades later.[24] This broad exposure led this son of impoverished gentry to read not only classical Confucian texts but also the works of Phan Bội Châu and Châu Trinh, as well as Western philosophers.[25]

The increasing information flows facilitated by travel and education also swelled awareness of conditions in Vietnam and expectations for improving them. During the First World War, some 90,000 Vietnamese were mobilised and sent to fight in France, with many expecting to receive full citizenship or independence for Vietnam in return for their service, buoyed by the concept of self-determination the U.S. President Woodrow Wilson espoused after the war.[26] Among those on the sidelines of the 1919 Paris Peace Conference were Nguyễn Sinh Cung and Phan Châu Trinh, who drafted an appeal for independence, which they submitted to Wilson. The appeal was signed "For the Group of Vietnamese Patriots, Nguyễn Ái Quốc," or Nguyễn the Patriot, which became yet another moniker Nguyễn Sinh Cung adopted among many.[27] The high hopes for Vietnam at the Conference were squashed when the petition was ignored.

In this disappointment, and remaining in France, the now-named Nguyễn Ái Quốc found inspiration in writings like Vladimir Lenin's *Theses on the National and Colonial Questions*. The essay directed Communist parties to support the oppressed in overthrowing landlords and colonialists, including through entering "a temporary alliance with bourgeois democracy in the colonial and backward countries."[28] The Bolshevik leader proclaimed that the ultimate end of achieving a socialist revolution justified any means taken to achieve it. Building on these ideas and others, Nguyễn Ái Quốc, in turn, became a prolific writer advocating for greater national independence.[29] Meanwhile, at home in Vietnam, print continued to grow as a medium.

Vietnamese readers had growing access to various outputs, including pamphlets, books, and newspapers.[30] Some newspapers in urban centres enjoyed daily audience sizes in the thousands. The books published in the next couple of decades were a mixed bag covering religion, fiction, traditional literature, and theatre. Revolutionary materials propagating alternatives to the colonial *status quo* were becoming increasingly available. As historian Christopher Goscha noted:

> The French colonial police censored written material heavily and tightly controlled the licensing of papers and presses, but they could not stop the accelerating globalization of new ideas of which the French themselves were as much a part of as their colonies were.[31]

The two information ecosystems were part of an interconnected global information environment. Vietnam was becoming increasingly connected via wireless telegraphy to the outside world, including between Saigon and Paris, with two-way communication in 1924.[32] A brief relaxation of censorship in 1925 led to an indigenous publishing boom. In an outpouring flood of books, pamphlets, and periodicals, a new generation of reformers explored and re-examined how existing political philosophies applied to the realities of colonial Vietnam.[33]

Into this dangerous mix of heightened opportunities for some and broken expectations for others, widespread corruption permeated all ranks of the colonial elite, composed of French administrators and their co-opted Vietnamese client groups, adding more fuel to the fire.[34] While the French-trained elite was small, it doubled from 5,000 in 1925 to 10,000 in a decade, concentrating mainly in urban areas like Saigon but amassing rural property and extracting wealth from the people on it from a distance.[35] For historian Pierre Asselin, these Vietnamese were "complicit in the exploitation and dispossession of their own compatriots."[36] They had greater access to education and resources, while most Vietnamese were left out. It is little wonder that anti-colonial sentiments and demands for change, including increased schooling for Vietnamese students, grew.[37]

After the criminal sentencing of leading nationalist figure Phan Bội Châu in 1925 and the death of reformer Phan Châu Trinh in March 1926, there were mass protests and strikes.[38] French-educated Vietnamese channelled anti-colonialist sentiments into new associations such as Tân-Việt Kách-mệnh Đảng (New Vietnam Revolutionary Party) and the Việt Nam Quốc Dân Đản (the Vietnam Nationalist Party, or VNQDD) which staged events and produced pamphlets.[39] The long memory of Chinese domination centuries ago was used to push for independence and justify their means of pursuing it. Glorification of historical heroes played a central role in these calls to action, including the Trưng sisters.[40] Despite these anti-Chinese messages referencing past histories, the Vietnamese and Chinese information ecosystems continued to be interconnected due to shared interests at the time. This period shaped a new generation of nationalists demanding greater autonomy, including Vietnamese communist leaders, driven by anti-feudal and anti-colonial sentiments, something many Chinese could support as they also did not want foreign interference in the region.[41] The Vietnamese Communists used South China to recruit and learn, with many of their brightest studying at its Whampoa Military Academy.[42]

Starting with just nine members, the Communist Party of Vietnam was created in 1925.[43] Along with it, Nguyễn Ái Quốc launched the Vietnamese Revolutionary Youth Association (Thanh Niên), which trained young cadres on how to deliver speeches, write articles, and create cells to proselytise the Communist cause. Thanh Niên was among the first to focus on engaging the masses, including publishing articles in its papers targeting women.[44] The reach of Thanh Niên spanned across Vietnam and abroad to Thailand and Southern China.[45] Some of its best marketing was gifted by the French in their brutal treatment of the Vietnamese, pushing youths like Võ Nguyên Giáp, a future military commander, towards communism after his father and sister died in a French prison.[46] Through Thanh Niên, Giáp would read banned copies of Nguyễn Ái Quốc's journal *Le Paria* and his literary tract *French Colonialism on Trial*.[47] The creation of the "workers and peasants paradise" announced by the Soviet Union following the October 1917 revolution and Sun Yat-sen's blending of nationalism, socialism, and democracy all inspired Vietnamese intellectuals.[48] By 1930, Nguyễn Ái Quốc reconstituted the Communist Party of Vietnam into the Indochinese Communist Party.[49]

The 1930s were restive in Vietnam. The Great Depression drastically decreased prices for rice and rubber, leading to unemployment and social unrest. Nationalist cartoons were printed showing peasants attacking French colonial troops and yelling, "wipe out the gang of imperialists, mandarins, capitalists, and big landlords!"[50] The French met some of this dissent with violence, for example, in the brutal squashing of the peasant revolts in 1930–31 in Nghe Tinh. At the same time, Buddhism was experiencing a revival thanks to new communication and transportation methods.[51] Like the Communists, they tapped into modern communications and used print and the simplified script to proselytise.[52] Another censorship thaw in 1936 allowed the Communists to produce French and Vietnamese newspapers, which helped grow the Indochinese Communist Party.[53] And despite the risks of violence, workers continued to stage strikes, with more than forty occurring just in December 1936.[54]

Meanwhile, halfway across the world, France fell to Nazi Germany's invasion in just six weeks, ushering in the Vichy regime in 1940. A couple of months later, Japan occupied North Vietnam with France's approval. In response, the Indochinese Communist Party launched the Việt Minh, a unified anti-colonialist front fighting both France and Japanese occupation under the military leadership of Giáp. The Việt Minh's manifesto again drew on national heroes, like the Trưng sisters, Ngo Quyen, and Le Loi, who all fought Chinese occupation, but also others who had later resisted the French.[55] A long historical thread of independence was being rewoven into the fabric of the Vietnamese information ecosystem that, when plucked, would resonate with the people as part of a shared identity.

The Japanese occupation was a jumble for the Vietnamese. The French had not departed and were left to administer much of the South even after Japan's subsequent takeover there. Japan was still an occupying force, but its presence and easing of some restrictions over the information ecosystem opened a path to increased expression of desires for independence. Political freedom grew, with protests, political rallies, and public political discussions occurring on a nearly daily basis, which, according to historian Huỳnh Kim Khánh, "encouraged an unprecedented blossoming of political activity."[56] This coincided with concerted Japanese efforts to champion its ambitions to create a coalition of Asian states tied to Japan, for which calls to free Vietnam from French occupation might have seemed compatible. To their own ends, the Japanese supported youth groups and the religious sects, Cao Đài and the Hòa Hảo, protecting these groups and providing sanctuary for their leaders abroad when needed.⁵⁷ These Buddhist sects would go on to take military control over significant chunks of Vietnam after the war.⁵⁸ The Japanese funded movies and newspapers, too, in order to push a racialist agenda meant to pit Asians against European colonisers and instil awe and fear of Japanese might.⁵⁹ Naturally, the impact of these changes were mostly felt in urban centres like Hanoi, as the majority of the Vietnamese population still resided in the countryside. Life in rural Vietnam went on as before under French rule.⁶⁰

Perhaps in response to relative Japanese political easements, even the Vichy Governor, General Decoux, promoted a concept of quasi-independence for Vietnam under an Indochinese federation. Schools could now teach Vietnamese language and history, and enrolment increased by 56 per cent from 450,000 in 1939 to 700,000 in 1944.⁶¹ New organisations, like "Youth and Sports", were created to indoctrinate the young but also to encourage them to teach some 50,000 peasants how to read and write, which led to unintended consequences since many members adopted anti-colonial views.⁶² Even the heretofore prohibited name of Vietnam could be used. Despite this thaw, however, print publications were still censored, and more than a dozen newspapers were closed from 1940 to 1943.⁶³ These shifting levels of control over an information ecosystem are difficult to sustain. Ideas once free are difficult to eradicate.

By 1943, in the country's North, the Việt Minh had gained some measure of control over the information ecosystem there from French and Japanese occupiers, taking over the postal system and introducing means of communication and education. Along with these changes came yet another name for Nguyễn Ái Quốc, who was now called Hồ Chí Minh. Việt Minh leadership at this time displayed an uncanny understanding of the Vietnamese information ecosystem. Without official power, there was a recognition that the entire population must be engaged in independence efforts to succeed, a common tactic in guerilla warfare. Both Hồ and Giáp had a keen sense of how military activities and propaganda worked together, using them to promote further recruitment for the Viet Minh.[64] They published a newspaper and simple political pamphlets proselytising their version of self-governance in Vietnam. Public demonstrations were regularly staged, as Khánh explained: "Mobile teams brought propaganda materials to remote areas. In addition, the revolutionary regime established short-term, month-long courses in political and military tactics for its members."[65] In urban centres like Hanoi, "Viet Minh propaganda publications flooded the city. Selective terrorism also sowed fear, demonstrated Viet Minh power, and confirmed the rumors, deliberately exaggerated, about daring Viet Minh attacks on the Japanese."[66] In the meantime, various events affecting physical existence greatly impacted the information ecosystem.

A terrible famine brought on by wartime measures and a series of natural disasters lasted from late 1944 into the next year, killing somewhere between 500,000 and a million Vietnamese.[67] The Việt Minh called for the opening of granaries, breaking into rice stores to feed starving people.[68] French and Japanese action, as much as inaction, communicated to the Vietnamese how little their rulers cared about the ruled.[69] The devastation of the famine and the lack of response by the occupiers, deftly used by proselytising revolutionaries, pushed some Vietnamese towards the Communists. The interconnected nature of the physical and information environments was vividly demonstrated through those events. The vast majority (between 80 and 90 per cent) of Vietnamese lived in the countryside in 1945, widely ignored by anti-communist parties.[70] Crushed by taxation and debts, many rural dwellers struggled to survive.[71] Yet, the Vietnamese were traditionally tied to their village, believing this was where their ancestors' spirits resided and guided them.[72] Vietnamese communism appealed to the villagers because it framed their problems as unnecessarily caused by a foreign oppressor that could be overthrown by revolution, making the people the new master.[73] They didn't need to leave; they needed to rise up. Events like this offered the Việt Minh clear examples to demonstrate to Vietnamese audiences that France did not have their interests at heart. When a power vacuum opened after Japan's failed coup against the French colonial government, the Communists seized the opportunity with little resistance and declared Vietnam independent on 2 September 1945.

French authorities again attempted to reimpose control over the Vietnamese information ecosystem despite Hồ's declaration of independence. This included increasing censorship, as well as shutting down newspapers and harassing people openly engaging with Hồ. But the Việt Minh continued to campaign both in Vietnam and abroad, positioning their plight as an anti-colonial fight against France, often tapping into patriotic fervour to win support from the people. New history books drew upon the Vietnamese history of resisting foreign occupation, again hailing the Trưng sisters.[74] For Stanley Karnow, a historian and journalist who covered Vietnam, these accounts helped foster "the notion that every Vietnamese is potentially a soldier, the memory of these struggles has forged a fierce sense of national identity that pulsates through Vietnam theatre, literature and folk art."[75] School children were taught to recite these accounts by heart.[76]

This patriotic positioning, which asserted Vietnamese independence with the aim of connecting citizens under a sovereign state, also enabled the Communist Việt Minh to court unlikely allies periodically. Positioned around anti-colonialism, nationalism, and patriotism, Ho's cabinet at times included Catholics and Socialists, and in declaring independence, claimed that "the new government would include all "patriotic elements" in the society, not merely workers and peasants," going so far as to disband the Indochinese Communist Party in 1945 to downplay the role of Communism in the Democratic Republic of Vietnam.[77] Indeed, Hồ claimed that "patriotism, not yet communism, led me to have confidence in Lenin, in the Third International."[78] Here, the political science reader might cringe at the overlapping of the terms nationalism and patriotism, but that is a very narrow reading of the concepts from a Euro-centric vantage point. Directly applying the experiences from which those terms originate—in nineteenth-century nation-building in Europe—misses the nuances of this twentieth-century independence movement in Asia. In Vietnam and for Hồ, both concepts co-mingled. The Party exhorted one and all, including ethnic minorities whom the French regarded as savages, to commit fully to the anti-French struggle and to sacrifice everything for the common goal.[79] The majority ethnic Kinh and minority peoples were to be Vietnamese and build an independent nation-state together. This nationalistic version of communism spoke to the Vietnamese population and strengthened Hồ's image as independent of foreign interests. However, this often put him at odds with radicals and the Soviet Union, sometimes hindering his ability to win external support.[80] His talent for understanding the Vietnamese mindset helped Hồ craft a careful image of the desired leader as "Uncle Hồ", the nice man next door "who expresses in his life how the government and the society ought to behave."[81] This image of Hồ as the effortless and humble leader, dressed in his now-standard simple country garb, was reinforced by a cult of personality campaign.[82]

Understanding the physical realities on the ground and the pressing need to win the masses' attention, Hồ adopted new technologies for his cause. When announcing independence from Ba Đinh Square in Hanoi, Hồ broadcast his message with an improvised network of loudspeakers to reach tens of thousands.[83] Within a week, the *Voice of Vietnam* would begin broadcasting.

Hồ was an avid radio listener and understood its propaganda value, using it to agitate for independence. Commercial radio had been around for two decades, but its adoption was hindered in Vietnam. As with print, the French authorities attempted to control the rollout of radio. Access to radio licenses was restricted, and those wanting to broadcast had to commit to running colonial programming from *Radio Hanoi* and *Radio Saigon* and air only cultural content. The electric grid, particularly outside the major cities, was unreliable, stifling the ability to broadcast consistently. Nonetheless, the technology was gradually adopted. Upwards of a thousand new radio sets a year were installed in the late 1930s in southern Vietnam. Probably in a display of status and custom, Vietnamese families would display their radio in the window at home and play it loudly to share with others, which ensured important messages were amplified in a community.[84] The Việt Minh used radio domestically to push agendas but also as a means to influence external audiences, as Hồ attempted to persuade the West, in particular the United States, to support his cause of Vietnamese independence.[85] Again, there seemed to be a realisation that the Vietnamese information ecosystem was connected to others in a wider environment.

In what might now be considered a classic marketing technique, Hồ considered his audience when crafting messages. Despite Woodrow Wilson's earlier rebuff, Hồ remained hopeful that the Americans could be persuaded to favour the Việt Minh's cause. He capitalised on unfolding events as opportunities arose. When an American pilot was shot down by Japanese forces towards the end of the occupation, the Việt Minh rescued him to garner support from the United States. For domestic audiences, the incident was printed in simple pictorial propaganda to project the Việt Minh's benevolence.[86] Appealing to American patriotism and self-image as leader of the free world, Hồ drew heavily on the United States Declaration of Independence when making his own proclamation for Vietnam.[87] Hồ used every channel available to him to solicit American support. He sent several letters to President Truman seeking support via sympathetic contacts within the United States' intelligence agency, the Office of Strategic Services, then operating in Vietnam. However, these letters went unanswered.[88] Ho even created the Vietnam–U.S. Friendship Association in 1945, which promoted economic ties in a bid to encourage Washington to reconsider its relationship with the new country.[89] Alas, these overtures did little to gain American support.

For their part, the American leadership turned their attention to the Vietnamese public, rather than Hồ. In a bid to court Vietnamese popular opinion, the United States Information Service opened a library in Saigon in August 1946. The reading room promoted American values and accomplishments, airing films. The initiative caught the attention of the French, who were irritated. They saw this as an intrusion into their sphere of influence and did everything possible to delay its opening.[90]

Meanwhile, the French had begun paying lip service to the idea of independence. In 1946, the French colonial authorities created the Autonomous Republic of Cochochina, which was autonomous practically in name alone. The president, Dr. Nguyễn Văn Thinh, came from a Southern land-owning family, held French citizenship, and studied medicine in France. He also had nationalist *bona fides*. Two decades before, Dr. Thinh had sat on the organising committee for the independence leader Phan Châu Trinh's funeral—a high-profile event preceding mass protests. He was also a founder of the Indochinese Democratic Party. Months into this experiment with "autonomy", when Dr. Thinh realised it was a farce intent on thwarting Vietnamese nationalism, including his own, he undertook a form of public protest that would become symbolic in the country. Thinh hanged himself, leaving behind a letter calling on his compatriots to react, stating, "I die in order to show you the path of duty, liberty, and honor."[91] His ultimate act of sacrifice reached a wide audience, with the letter read on radio services and reprinted in newspapers.[92] This would not be France's last attempt at a puppet government. As if ignoring public sentiments, France installed the former emperor, Bảo Đại, a philandering wastrel who stood in stark contrast to Hồ's asceticism. Bảo Đại's appointment as little more than a figurehead was intended to appease nationalists and Catholics.[93] By the close of 1946, the French and Việt Minh were officially at war.

All three groups of agents were communicating to audiences that simply wouldn't hear them: the Việt Minh to the Americans, and the Americans and the French to the Vietnamese. Yet only one of these groups, the Việt Minh, seemed to understand the Vietnamese information ecosystem and what might appeal to audiences within it. Operating across information ecosystems can be a challenge, as the conditions in one might unhelpfully inform one's actions in another.

The Americans waded into the quagmire that was the Vietnam conflict initially in support of the French in 1950. They did so with very little apparent understanding of Vietnam, as few Americans had even been there.[94] By many accounts, it was the politically motivated fear of Communism stoked by Republican politicians in the American information ecosystem that pushed the Democratic president to take a tougher stance in the Cold War, particularly in Vietnam. Despite fewer than 1 per cent of Americans identifying as socialist, by 1949, 43 per cent of respondents to one poll believed socialism was active in the United States.[95] Many people believed socialism was a near and present danger, yet very few Americans were openly espousing it.

The Cold War featured in presidential campaigns, with candidates like Eisenhower committing to a tougher fight. With the Communist victory in China in 1949, figures like Senator

Joseph R. McCarthy relentlessly blamed the Democrats for the outcome of the Chinese civil war.[96] Further attacks accused Democrats of treason and even alleged that American accomplices helped the Soviets develop an atomic bomb.[97] Backers of the anti-Communist China Lobby financed conservative think tanks, such as American Business Consultants Inc., run by former Federal Bureau of Investigation agents, which in turn published reports including "Red Channels", claiming to expose more than 150 communist sympathisers in the American media sector.[98] This book caused disarray in newsrooms, who tried not to cover it, ultimately providing McCarthy with an opportunity to take his crusade of exposing closet communists to the small screen, where Congressional hearings were broadcast.[99] In a period of seven years, starting in 1945, there were 84 hearings to weed out so-called "un-American activities."[100] At the outset of these investigations, nearly half of those Americans familiar with the issue "thought it brought more good than harm."[101] The political witch hunt failed to produce evidence of treason, yet many reputations were ruined while information pollution created a climate of fear in the American information ecosystem that pushed policymakers to react to perceived Communist threats both at home and abroad.[102]

The French seized on the hysteria. Starting in late 1948, France reframed their efforts at retaining their Vietnamese colony as part of the Cold War against communism in Asia.[103] The French military commander in Vietnam, General de Tassigny, propagated a fear in American media that if the country toppled to communism, others would, too.[104] In fact, some American policymakers feared France itself might swing towards the Soviet Union.[105] France went so far as to blackmail the United States, who was building military programmes in Europe to counter communism, threatening to impede these efforts if they didn't get help in Vietnam.[106] American news media outlets, like *Time* and *Life* magazines, championed France's cause and increasingly called for support from the United States. Unfolding events, like a bombing in Saigon in 1949, which was attributed to Việt Minh despite dubious evidence, were well covered, further positioning the conflict in the context of the emerging Cold War. [107]

Fears were also heightened by ongoing geopolitical developments. On 15 January 1950, the Democratic Republic of Vietnam recognised the People's Republic of China, which reciprocated in kind four days later, followed by the Soviet Union on 30 January, along with Yugoslavia and several Warsaw Pact countries.[108] In response, a couple of weeks later, the United States officially recognised the Associated State of Vietnam, which the French had proclaimed as an independent country under Bảo Đại.[109] The invasion of South Korea by northern communist forces in June 1950 provided some validation of fears that countries would continue to fall to unchecked communism. This "Domino Theory" took hold among American policymakers, first outlined under Truman and furthered under Eisenhower.[110] True believers like McCarthy would help elevate the theory to a hysterical pitch. In the wake of the Korean War, Senate Republicans produced the report "Communism in Government", which purported to outline the Democratic government's "Red Record".[111] Across the American information ecosystem, this fear of communism was mixed with an older notion of America's manifest destiny, which was resurfacing through the repeated mantra of spreading democracy worldwide.[112]

During this period, the American information ecosystem was undergoing significant changes. On a societal level, the postwar United States was booming on most counts. The United States was in the midst of a baby boom, adding more and more information animals to the ecosystem.[113] The economy was also growing quickly, with American gross national product nearly doubling in the 1950s, helping spur developments in the information ecosystem.[114] Education rates across demographics had consistently been increasing over the preceding decades, with big jumps in college attendance.[115] At the same time, racist segregation policies were being openly challenged.[116]

The information ecosystem was becoming more complex. A new means of communication—the television—was being widely adopted, with household ownership jumping from just 9 per cent in 1950 to 85 per cent within a decade, while commercial TV stations grew four and a half times.[117] Daily newspapers declined slightly, however, from a peak of over 2,000 in 1925 to 1,760 in 1955.[118] Politicians were quick to make use of the new medium. The Republican and Democratic national conventions were the first televised in 1952, and the ensuing presidential campaign was covered with a mixture of print and electronic delivery.[119] News anchoring emerged as a new type of broadcasting that delivered news through engaging coverage in American homes daily. This increased the speed and reach at which news could travel. A limited number of national television stations mediated news coverage through a trusted and impartial news reader, a short-lived ideal that continues to live on as a nostalgic standard. Americans moved from listening about the remote events of the Second World War through radios and press reels to following the conflicts on television in their living rooms, effectively connecting the information ecosystem in the United States with that of Vietnam.[120]

Television was not the only means connecting the Vietnamese and American information ecosystems. Members of the French-trained Vietnamese elite had been actively making American friends to forge communities of interest. The Catholic politician from Central Vietnam, Ngô Đình Diệm, was on a charm offensive to court the Americans, much as General de Lattre had been. Through his brother Pierre Martin Ngô Đình Thục, a Vietnamese Bishop, Diệm used Catholic networks to lobby the United States for support against Hồ in the early 1950s.[121] Diệm spent two years in New York seminaries, pushing for Vietnamese independence from France and gaining the support of Democratic Senators Mike Mansfield and John F. Kennedy, who would found the American Friends of Vietnam, a lobby group connected indirectly to the Republican administration.[122] Like the French, Diệm drew on the raging fears of McCarthyism to court American support, although he blamed the colonisers for driving the Vietnamese into the hands of the Communists, for whom the war was turning in their favour.[123] These human-to-human links created personal connections that tugged American leadership further into the Vietnamese information ecosystem—and the quagmire of conflict.

By 1952, despite not officially entering the conflict until later, the United States was footing over a third of France's war costs in Vietnam.[124] With the French badly losing at Điện Biên Phủ in the spring of 1954, the Americans were feeling increased pressure to help their allies.[125] The United States Secretary of State led a public education campaign to inform the American public about the risks of losing Vietnam to Communism, giving public lectures to politicians and journalists.[126] But this didn't help the French. The defeat at Điện Biên Phủ led to the 1954 Geneva Accords and the division of Vietnam. When Diệm returned to Vietnam, first taking up the post of Prime Minister of the State of Vietnam under Bảo Đại's puppet government, Hồ viewed this as a precursor to American intervention.[127] Indeed, South Vietnam became entirely dependent on American funding, which created an illusion of prosperity but sent all the wrong messages about freeing the Vietnamese from foreign dominance.[128] The French defeat only raised the pressure from "hawks in Congress" to intervene.[129] Moreover, the idea emerged that the American status as leader of the so-called free world was being put to the test, and failure in Vietnam would result in a public loss of face among allies and the world.[130]

If the United States was upholding democracy in South Vietnam, Diệm continuously pushed the boundaries of what that meant. Far from understanding what was wanted, Diệm's actions appeared to convey less a path to independence and more a continuation of colonial repression with a Vietnamese face. The paymaster had changed, and the leadership was Vietnamese, but the corruption and brutal oppression remained the same. Diệm wasted no time in staging a thinly veiled coup to oust Bảo Đại in October 1955, claiming the fixed referendum ensured independence from France, only to keep the same flag, anthem, colonial leader's residence, and policy biases in favour of Catholics.[131] Indeed, he antagonised the Buddhist majority and, in the process, alienated potential allies against the Communists. With help from his American allies, he attacked the Cao Đài and the Hòa Hảo Buddhist sects, who were also anti-communist but were viewed as competition for having taken control of areas in the South.[132] Diệm seemed to be in a race to breach all the articles in the Constitution in his first years in power. Human rights abuses were rampant, including torture, forced labour, and concentration camps, targeting communists and non-communists alike.[133] Some of his measures bordered on the paranoid and absurd, such as banning gatherings of more than seven people.[134] Far from freedom, the Vietnamese people seemed to enjoy less and less independence. What autonomy village councils historically had enjoyed was destroyed, and the promised elections of the Geneva Accords were denied.[135] Adding insult to injury, Diệm closed the border with the North, effectively cutting some families in two. This was not an information ecosystem opening in freedom but closing in on itself through poor leadership decisions. In his bid to beat the Communists, Diệm mirrored their tactics, implementing rehabilitation programmes and public reckoning sessions whereby offenders prostrated themselves for forgiveness. As reforms were increasingly forgotten and repression grew, Diệm's efforts to crush the Communists drove ordinary people to join Hồ.[136] At the same time, Diệm offered no alternative ideology or vision; instead, he pushed a convoluted and inaccessible concept of "personalism".[137] Diệm was entirely out of touch with his environment; his only answer was to reach for more control.

Notwithstanding, the Americans supported Diệm. They trained and equipped his army and ran influence operations to help him as if a little bit of strategic communication would encourage the southern Vietnamese to hate the Communists more than their apparent oppressor.[138] In May 1957, Diệm was welcomed to the United States and publicly acclaimed by President Eisenhower as a freedom-loving hero despite his despotic tendencies.[139] This certainly sent mixed messages.

While Diệm opted for cruel repression, Hồ made mass education core to Việt Minh efforts. Literacy was necessary to foster societal mobilisation through political awareness, much like it had been for English Protestants to experience God. In 1952, Hồ claimed that the Democratic Republic of Vietnam had nearly doubled the number of schools and attendance rates over the year before and that "people's organisations opened 837 classes attended by 9,800 public employees."[140] In 1956, Ho congratulated "the mass education service on its achievements during the first six months of the year. Over the past six months, 2,100,000 persons attended classes."[141] In the same year, Hồ called on followers:

> To wipe out illiteracy among the great masses, where the overwhelming majority are peasants, the education movement should be a mass movement. We should stand close to the masses, discuss with them, apply forms and methods suitable to their life, and rely upon them to promote the movement.[142]

Communists set up reading libraries in the North to foster a revolutionary education, but it also brought material benefits by opening up economic opportunities.[143] By 1958, most adults in the North could read.[144] For Hồ, increasing Vietnamese capacity to engage meaningfully within the information ecosystem through greater literacy rates was critical to their success in winning popular support. An informed public could be mobilised and made more resilient to external pressures.

The emphasis on increasing literacy did not mean everything was perfect in North Vietnam's information ecosystem. Immediately following independence, the presence of Chinese troops in the north ensured a degree of political freedom for parties opposing the Communists that previously had not been seen in Vietnam.[145] In the 1950s, however, the Communists exerted significantly more control over the information ecosystem, at times brutally cracking down on dissenters with rehabilitation programmes.[146] Controls again loosened in 1956 after disastrous land reforms, allowing for a public venting of frustrations *within reason*. Hồ publicly apologised for the unpopular initiative, and leading figures associated with it were demoted. But by November, there was another harsh crackdown on public dissent.[147] The difference between Diệm and Hồ's approaches to controlling the information ecosystem under their authority was that the latter understood when to loosen control. The two leaders also differed considerably in understanding the relationship between actions and perceptions.

South of the border, Diệm continued to make poor choices. To secure and control the rural countryside, Diệm enacted two disastrous re-settlement plans. The first was his Agroville project in 1959, whereby the government forcibly moved peasants to fortified hamlets to cut them off from the Việt Minh, but also inadvertently from their ancestors.[148] Despite the lack of success with this initiative, Diệm followed this up a couple of years later with the Strategic Hamlets programme. In this new effort, villagers weren't forced to relocate but to construct a security perimeter around their village and train local forces to defend them.[149] Coupled with severe repression of anyone suspected of helping the Communists, this reform alienated villagers in the South even further. Landlords were fearful, and villages were left without local governance.[150] This disrupted a critical flow of information between the governed and their government (again reminiscent of Charles I), a void in which Communists could readily show that French and American-backed Vietnamese leadership in the South did not care for the people. This view was only reinforced repeatedly through Diệm's actions as propaganda of the deed, whereby his brutal physical repression spoke louder than words.

Acutely aware of the impact of tangible actions on perceptions and support, the Việt Minh introduced a code of behaviour. Historian Spencer C. Tucker noted that this included swearing "a ten-part oath containing a pledge to respect, help and protect the people."[151] For Fitzgerald, this approach also drew from the Confucian idea of "a social contract between the government and the governed."[152] The best behaviour approach would later help the National Liberation Front (NLF), set up by the Việt Minh at the end of 1960, to be perceived by villagers in South Vietnam as nice, polite, and friendly, unlike Diệm's officials.[153] A key difference between North and South operatives was that the former saw deeds and behaviour as communication. In contrast, the latter and its American backers later focused on the message alone. The difference in approaches would be manifested in recruitment numbers. Just a year after it was established, the NLF grew fourfold to 300,000 members.[154]

Concentrated in the South, the NLF set up cells in villages to organise all segments of society to campaign against Diệm.[155] These cells encouraged a handful of men to "fight, not for ideological abstractions, but to gain the respect of his comrades."[156] To that end, officers and operatives lived among and like the villagers, helping build a bottom-up support supply chain. Personal appeals were made, asking people: "How can you help your families, if the nation is in such trouble? The best thing you can do for your families is to fight for the Liberation."[157] Members fought once a month, spending the remaining time teaching and indoctrinating the masses. The villagers were co-opted rather than directed, entering a relationship with the NLF and becoming part of the organisation rather than being compelled from the top down. It was in stark contrast to the often-brutal approach taken by Diệm. The resulting network of intertwined organisations, from households to a bigger group of families in a village association, in turn connected across the country, created an information web binding the NLF and its members. Schooling was organised, and propaganda spread. Each village became capable of being an independent but interconnected node for producing and distributing information in support of the cause.[158]

Meanwhile, back in the United States, Kennedy narrowly beat Richard Nixon, who had played the "Red scare" card, for the Oval Office in 1960.[159] Vietnam wasn't Kennedy's only Communist concern. Early in his term, he was pressed into a disastrous outcome in the Bay of Pigs in Cuba, which was followed by the erection of the Berlin Wall. Coupled with his own expressed beliefs in the Domino Theory, referring to Vietnam as "the finger in the dike" at an American Friends of Vietnam meeting, Kennedy was in a position where he had no choice but to continue fighting Communism, regardless of Diệm's authoritarianism or potential for success.[160] As the Kennedy administration's rhetoric hardened its stance on being tough against Communism, its ability to disengage support for Diệm declined.[161]

At the close of 1961, while American commitments quietly grew, the public remained largely uninformed about America's involvement in Vietnam. But in early 1962, news outlets began covering it.[162] Prior to this, the flow of information about Vietnam was filtered from the Diệm regime through the United States government into domestic media, creating biases in interpreting what was happening on the ground.[163] The Kennedy administration attempted to stage-manage how the conflict was covered in the United States, with the president denying in a press conference that American troops were fighting.[164] As American news media grasped the truth, tensions between it and the government grew. Instead of censorship, American officials pressed the media to focus on the positive, and Kennedy unsuccessfully attempted to have problematic journalists bent on exposing the truth transferred by newspaper owners.[165] Attempts to control the American information ecosystem, far from being a successful measure to dissuade criticism, led to animosity between journalists who toed the official line and those who did not, while decreasing trust in official narratives about the United States' involvement in what would become a prolonged conflict.[166] With the two information ecosystems connected, the floodgates were now opened.

As the war progressed, the media was increasingly used by the American-backed South as well as the Communist North to champion their causes, playing the conflict out globally via television and other media. Other agents, like the Buddhist groups persecuted by the Diệm government, used the media to convey grisly messages. American journalists were invited to the scene of the monk Thích Quảng Đức's self-immolation in 1963. The monks would afterwards show his heart encased in glass and ensure journalists would cover another half dozen self-immolations on television.[167] Suicides were used as a public form of protest. Such acts conveyed a gruesome dissatisfaction with the existing order and, despite their hopelessness, signalled to others that faith in the South's government was misplaced.

In many ways, television turned war into a form of gruesome entertainment. Even the fall of Diệm's influential brother and sister-in-law was drama for television viewers.[168] Yet what American leaders failed to see in all this was that with increased technology, the information ecosystem of the United States had become inextricably linked to the that of the Vietnamese. The main difference was that with increased connectivity came an information flood about the distant conflict, which was causing ever more losses on both sides and ultimately worked in the favour of the Communist Vietnamese. Americans did not yet see the information environment of which they were a part.

Nor did the French seem to understand the information environment. At best, it was a space to be controlled, as demonstrated in their attempts to regulate the Vietnamese information ecosystem. Much like Charles I, the colonial government was misguided in believing that regulating the means of communication would somehow control the ultimate flow of information. They were too focused on specific technology, like the printing press and radio. They missed how other less novel innovations like a simplified script could lead to fundamental shifts in capacity among a wider population beyond the small elite they enriched and controlled at the same time. In trying to erase ideas about independence, colonialist authorities banned those people in which the desire was sparked. Removing them from Vietnam, however, had much the same outcome as it has had on digital platforms—people holding such views were banished to other corners of the empire, where they met like-minded anti-colonialists. Moreover, the movement of people, as much as technology, enabled the flow of information. It is definitively not strategic to not anticipate that sending tens of thousands of men to fight on France's behalf might create certain expectations and expose those soldiers to the same ideals of self-determination wrapped up in that conflict. As happened with so many colonisers, the underestimation of those colonised was gross. Not only did the French miss the forest (information ecosystem) for the trees (specific technology), but their sense of superiority and detachment from the people they governed deluded them into more poor decision-making. Despite glorifying their own revolution, the French forgot the importance of heeding the needs of society from the bottom up. Not only were puppet governments far from able to satisfy decades-long calls for independence, but in the brutal form of Diệm, it produced the opposite effect that the people desired. The French seemed not to realise that they, as aliens, entered and imposed upon an information ecosystem that, while different from their own, was nonetheless vibrant and comprised of many threads, like that of a nation's fierce independence, which was so interwoven into the local tapestry that no amount of deliberate cutting could remove it.

Conversely, it was as though agents like Hồ and Giáp intuitively sensed the information environment around them and its interconnected nature. Hồ certainly grasped that means of communication like radio and, later, television enabled direct links not just to American decision-makers but also to the wider public, who also held influence in their own right. As if learning from the English and American information ecosystems of previous chapters, the Communists saw literacy and education as a condition to plant new ideas. In trying to foster the right conditions, their efforts effectively constructed the analogue equivalent of a social network that strengthened the ties of people within it to the NLF and the Communist North. While serving indoctrination purposes, increased education also supported economic development, helping to meet the practical needs of the people involved. The Communists also recognised that behaviour was a form of communication. This fact seemed lost on the French and Diệm, who sought to win the information competition and subsequent conflict through repressive measures propped up by the Americans. Not only did this reliance on the United States convey the opposite of independence, but the violent repression also did little to win hearts and minds. It's little wonder why one side had more success in rallying the Trưng sisters' legend to their cause. An expensive statue of the Trưngs erected by Diệm's sister-in-law in Saigon in 1962, using her own face as inspiration, was destroyed after South Vietnam fell.[169] The Diệm family's deeds didn't live up to the reality of patriotism and independence the Trưng sisters embodied. Diệm's heavy handed response to dissenters including Buddhists, the main religion in Vietnam, alienated him and his family from the people. One side in this conflict was still a part of the information ecosystem from whence they came, whereas the other one had become more alien.

8

THE UKRAINIAN CURSE OF NONEXISTENCE

It's tiring constantly having to assert one's right to existence. You'd think it might get easier when millions of others share the same belief that together, you exist as a people. But there is the perpetual questioning of where your homeland is, or worse, the denial of your country's existence by neighbouring chauvinists that must be faced. It's a theme a generation of post-colonial writers, like Yuri Andrukhovych and Oksana Zabuzhko, tackled in the early decades of Ukrainian independence. It's a persistent challenge, not just at home, where your own information ecosystem is a hotly contested space, but also abroad, where so much about your newly independent country has been framed by the very centre of power from which you recently broke free. If geopolitics were a human relationship, Ukraine was the berated ex-wife struggling to escape a domineering husband in Russia, always telling her she's worthless. Yet, as Zabuzhko wrote in her influential novel, "We can break out, tear ourselves away from the beaten track—from that eternal Ukrainian curse of nonexistence"[1] The threads woven into the Ukrainian tapestry that is their information ecosystem are long and proving more resilient with each attack, regardless of how much Russian leaders try to cut them. Those threads were already woven in during the first decades as a new state at the turn of the twenty-first century. This was an information ecosystem undergoing rapid changes, such as a massive opening up to a wider information environment with the collapse of the Soviet Union, but also deteriorating economic conditions under the watch of a corrupt elite, some of which had strong ties to a neighbouring ecosystem in Russia, and whose focus on language use and media control rendered them unable to hear the people.

Ukraine and Russia share a long and storied history. Their languages, along with Belorussian, emerged from Old East Slavic. Both claim that their birthplace is Kyivan Rus', a state founded by a Viking in the ninth century, and the two might have been even more similar today had it not been for the Mongol invasion in the thirteenth century.[2] After Rus' was overrun, the northern part (modern Russia) remained under the Mongol yoke for over two centuries, whereas the south (modern Ukraine) fell under the Kingdom of Lithuania after only a hundred years of Mongol rule.[3] For the next five centuries, parts of the land on which modern Ukraine is situated would move back and forth under various rulers, creating the modern cultural differences between it and neighbouring Belarus and Russia.[4] This has led to different interpretations of claims on the myths and histories that tied people in these lands together. The Russians view ancient Rus' as their history, of which Ukraine is a part. Conversely, Ukrainians see Kyivan Rus' as their direct origin, with some in the west of the country referring to themselves as Rusyn or Ruthenians into the nineteenth century, a fact Russians have tried to use to deny Ukrainian existence.[5] Kyiv is the contested first capital of both peoples.

Much of Ukraine's existential angst comes from its location at a crossroads, her very name meaning "borderland".[6] Situated

THE UKRAINIAN CURSE OF NONEXISTENCE

in the middle of Eastern Europe, Ukraine shares borders with seven countries and, for centuries, housed a melange of languages, alphabets, ethnicities, and religions. Pinning down a single identity at this intersection of trade routes, cultures, and warring neighbours with contradicting, multi-layered narratives may seem like a fool's errand. This is why highly interconnected information ecosystems like Ukraine's must be studied as part of a wider environment. They do not exist in isolation, but as we've already seen in other chapters, few information ecosystems do.

The region has faced hundreds of invasions and conflicts, leading the political geographer Gerard Toal to quip that "Ukraine might not be interested in geopolitics, but geopolitics… is interested in Ukraine."[7] As invaders came and went, shifting their borders over Ukraine, regional identities were left behind. The Poles and Austro-Hungarians ruled the western region of Galicia. Some, like the Poles, pushed for assimilation, which influences the dialect of the Ukrainian language there to this day.[8] Architecturally, the city of Lviv is far more reminiscent of Kraków than Moscow. Thus, the Poles negated Ukraine, calling Galicia "Little Poland" or "Malopolska".[9] Whereas, nearby Transcarpathia fell under Hungarian rule for many centuries and was Magyarised.[10] There, an identity of Rusyn emerged from blending those of Ruthenian and Slovakian that local activists claimed is more Western, distinct from Ukrainian, and went so far as to foster a separatist movement after the country's independence supported by Slovak and Hungarian politicians.[11] Bukovina has been claimed by Romania, who has in the past treated Ukrainians as though they were amnesiac Romanians.[12] And then there was Russia.

For a nation claiming ownership of Kyiv, it took Moscow a while to return. In the middle of the 1600s, Cossacks revolted against their Polish overlords to establish the Hetmanate in central Ukraine, only to become a vassal of the Russian Tsar, which persistently eroded any hard-won autonomy gained and ultimately enserfed swaths of Ukrainians.[13] While Russian chauvinism has tended to negate Ukrainian's existence as a separate language, the negotiations between the Cossack leader Bohdan Khmelnytsky and Tsar Alexis I in 1648 had to be translated between the two, suggesting that the languages have been diverging for considerable time.[14] The partitions of Poland beginning in 1772 brought more of Ukraine up to the Dnieper, Drut, and Dvina rivers in the west, with its ethnic mix of Jews, Poles, and Ukrainians, under what by then had become the Russian empire. Not long after, Jews were restricted to living within the Pale of Settlement, encompassing most of modern Ukraine.[15] They would continue to be targets for Russian Imperial authorities to deflect discontent, with increasing limits on their freedoms.[16] In 1783, the Russians took Crimea from the Ottomans, with its Ukrainian population in the north and Tatars to the south, followed by encroachment into the lands around the Donets region of the now Donetsk and Luhansk oblasts.[17] Much has been made of this region as a melting pot of ethnicities, which, given its rich coal basin, gained the name Donbas and experienced an influx of migrants thanks to industrialisation, significantly increasing Russian representation.[18] Here, Russians and Ukrainians inter-married at high rates.[19] And like the Poles in Galicia, Russians took to calling this area "Novorossiia" or "New Russia" and the people within it "Malorossy" or "little Russians".[20]

Be it the Poles, Romanians, or Russians, many have had a hand in denying or questioning Ukrainian existence. It's little wonder that Ukrainians might have identity issues. As the Ukrainian diplomat Olexander Scherba explained: "We feel like a part of Europe, but may look like a part of Russia. With our thoughts, we are in the West. With our sins, we are in the East."[21] Identity is constructed in the mind, woven together with many different threads, but its acceptance outside of where it develops depends on others reflecting the same reality in return. Self-interest can lead others, like Poles and Russians, to focus on similarities over differences to weave their own mental tapestries about another people, thus negating their independence. As one side asserts its identity, and the other imposes its view, the process becomes dynamic and repeated. It is not isolated to the competing parties but often projected for a wider audience that both sides hope will reflect their version of reality in turn. In the example of Ukraine, the imposition of blending one's identity into something else often came with political pressure to suppress their sense of nation, making it harder to assert, let alone strengthen. Yet, the more the Poles and Russians tried to form the people of Ukraine in their own image, the more some resisted. A separate Ukrainian literary language can be traced from the eighteenth century.[22] The first publication to use vernacular Ukrainian, *Eneïda,* was printed in 1798.[23] The first Ukrainian patriotic poem was published by Russian journals in 1807 during the Napoleonic War.[24] The first Ukrainian grammar book was published in 1818, a short dictionary in 1823, and finally, a vernacular Bible in 1903.[25] In the geographically remote Galicia, farther from Russian imperial reach but scarred from Polish imposition, a nationalism emerged, drawing on Ukrainian Cossack experiences from the east to foster an identity.[26] By the turn of the twentieth century, Galicia developed its own sense of manifest destiny in its aspirations to lead Ukrainian unity while also acting as what historian Andrew Wilson described as "the keeper of the true faith on behalf of the rest of Ukraine."[27] At the same time, some 170,000 Ukrainians would move from Galicia and Bukovina to Canada, where their culture thrived and their political influence grew, in turn reflecting yet another construction of what Ukrainians are.[28]

At home, an attempt at independence was made during the turmoil of the Bolshevik revolution and civil war as the Russian empire disintegrated after October 1917. It was short-lived and followed by chaos in 1919, with six armed factions fighting in the country, during which Kyiv was conquered five times in less than a year.[29] Ukraine became a part of the Soviet Union, and the next couple of decades were tragic, to say the least. First came famine caused by the forced collectivisation of farms that killed millions of Ukrainians in a tragedy known as *Holodomor*, then the Stalinist purges of the 1930s, which tended to target Jews.[30] And yet worse followed.

During the Second World War Ukraine suffered terribly, losing millions of people. This figure ranges among historians from 5.3 million up to 8 million.[31] Of all Ukrainian casualties, between 1 and 2.25 million were Jews, and the country lost nearly two-thirds of the total Jewish population and more than 90 per cent in Galicia.[32] Of all Jews murdered in the Holocaust, one in six was from Ukraine.[33] Ethnic groups were purged *en masse*, and upwards of 1.25 million people were deported to the far reaches of the Soviet Union between 1939 and 1941, including some 180,000 Crimean Tatars.[34] While Ukrainians fought on both sides of the war, most people were caught between warring sides, with four-fifths of deaths being non-combatants.[35] Most Ukrainian combatants, between 2.5 and 7 million, fought in the Soviet army.[36] Another 2 million were forcibly sent to Germany as *Ostarbeitern*, little more than slave labourers.[37] Between 40,000 and 200,000 joined the Ukrainian Insurgent Army, created by the Organisation of Ukrainian Nationalists, who committed atrocities against the Poles and other minorities and collaborated for a time with the Nazis.[38] Additionally, upwards of 250,000 Ukrainians became Nazi auxiliaries as *Hilfswillige* (willing helpers).[39] This included Ukrainians who assisted in arresting, deporting, and killing Jews.[40] Between 13,000 and 20,000 Ukrainians were recruited in the SS Galicia Division, which was destroyed in its first battle.[41] On the other hand, over 3,500 Ukrainians were recognised as "Righteous Among the Nations" by Yad Vashem, the World Holocaust Remembrance Center, for protecting Jews in the Holocaust. Behind each of these dry statistics weaves an individual thread of mostly tragic human experience shaped by the complex and historically interconnected fabric of Ukrainian identities. For the Ukrainian population, the result of the Second World War was catastrophic. If the population was less than 30 million in the mid-1920s, according to historian Serhii Plokhy's count, and we take the lower end of estimates for both the famine and the war, Ukraine still lost at least a third of its population in two decades.[42]

Between the loss of people and the forced movement of survivors, the ethnic makeup of Ukraine was significantly changed. After the war, the Soviets forcibly moved entire populations of Ukrainians and Poles between the two states, reducing heterogeneity in both.[43] At the same time, the proportion of ethnic Russians was increasing, particularly in the country's east.[44] More were added when the Secretary General of the Soviet Union, Nikita Khrushchev—himself a Russian migrant to Donbas—added the Russified Crimean Autonomous Republic to the Ukrainian Socialist Soviet Republic in 1954, for reasons still unknown.[45] Ideas of ethnicity followed a gradient across the country, with greater Russian influence in the east and south and more people in the west identifying as Ukrainian.[46] Genocide, fratricide, deportations, and migration had left their mark, including on the languages and dialects spoken in Ukraine. These threads are still woven into Ukrainian worldviews, plucked by politicians using them for their own gain, often in ways that backfire. Such is the challenge for diverse information ecosystems surrounded by so many others.

Languages, much like the people speaking them, are living. They don't always follow political borders. In a country the size of Ukraine, which is more than four and half times the size of

England (with all its dialects), and with many bordering countries, variations on Ukrainian are only natural. For example, towards Belarus, the two languages form a transitional dialect, blending the former with Ukrainian.[47] Various forms of a pidgin tongue called *Surzhyk* have developed, mixing Ukrainian and Russian.[48] As with ethnicity, language-speaking patterns followed a gradient across the country. Ukrainian was more commonly spoken in the west of the country, like Galicia, while in the central regions, there were higher rates of bilingualism with Russian. Even further to the east and south, Russian was the predominant language, particularly in larger cities.[49] This linguistic diversity has often been used by self-interested neighbours to negate Ukrainian existence.

Keeping the Ukrainian language alive hasn't always been easy. At various times, Ukrainian has been disincentivised and discouraged. Under rule by others, whether Poles, Hungarians, Russians or Soviets, learning the language of the ruler presented opportunities for upward mobility.[50] This, at times, as in the post-Second World War period, led to decreased enrolment in Ukrainian-language schools.[51] Dissenters of Russification were targeted by the authorities in the 1960s and 1970s.[52] Speaking Ukrainian in many parts of the Union of Soviet Socialist Republics was considered bourgeois nationalism, and Russian was required to succeed in many professions.[53] Up to the 1980s, Ukrainians, regardless of what language they spoke, were still treated with suspicion regarding allegiances during the Second World War, and would have to answer additional questions on official forms about relatives who lived under German occupation or abroad, beyond the usual ones about criminal records.[54] This sort of continuous pressure was facilitated through the Communist Party's control over the Soviet Union's sprawling information ecosystem, where, despite comprising the second-largest ethnic group, Ukrainians were offered just two television channels and three radio stations in their language.[55] Russian language and content dominated.[56] However, with Mikhail Gorbachev in the 1980s came a thaw. The Soviet leader's policies *glasnost* and *perestroika* relaxed controls over the Soviet, and thus Ukrainian, information ecosystem, increasing civic activism, which helped lead to a resurgence of Ukrainian, once derided as a peasant tongue.[57]

At the same time, Ukraine was playing a pivotal role in the collapse of the Soviet Union. The inept handling of the 1986 Chornobyl Nuclear disaster, which occurred 152 kilometres from Kyiv and was hidden from the population for several weeks, gave rise to wild rumours and fuelled anti-communist sentiments.[58] When protests erupted across Eastern Europe in the summer of 1989, they easily spread into Lviv and from there to central Ukraine; the information ecosystem was fertile for discontent.[59] Miner strikes in Donbas in 1991 broadcasted over television news further undermined the Communist Party's authority by exposing weaknesses in the central planning system, adding to the Union's demise.[60] On 1 December 1991, with a turnout of 84 per cent, over 90 per cent of voters across Ukraine opted for independence, reaching 99 per cent in Ternopil in Galicia, 85 per cent in Odesa (another Russian-language stronghold), and 83 per cent in Donetsk, but just 54 per cent in Crimea, a pattern of voting variance that would persist in the decades after.[61] And with that, the three founding members of the Soviet Union still in existence—Belarus, Ukraine, and Russia—dissolved it.

The opening up of the Ukrainian information ecosystem increased immediately after independence, leading to a reckoning with long-suppressed regional history, as well as thinkers and writers whose works were republished.[62] The new declaration of independence spoke of a millennium of Ukrainian state building, harking back to Kyivan Rus'.[63] Ukrainian politicians inflamed the topic of language for their own gain, but in the early days after independence, much of it was empty rhetoric. Despite some major universities introducing Ukrainian literacy for entry exams, for example, most of the curriculum was still in Russian.[64] Attempts to reform Ukraine as a nation-state were controversial given the country's diversity, with some Russian speakers feeling alienated.[65] Films tugged on a Cossack past with its freedom and independence narratives, such as "Forward, to the Hetman's Treasures!" (1994) and "The Black Council" (1999). Soviet periodicals were privatised and unrestricted, leading to a growth in new publications and television stations alike. State-owned TV focused on promoting Ukrainian and aired poorly-funded folk concerts and educational programming that performed badly against higher-quality Russian productions.[66]

Given the historical legacy, in the early days of independence many Ukrainians could speak Russian, which left the information ecosystem susceptible to external Russian influence. With its larger market, the quantity and quality of content produced in Russia at the time dominated the former Soviet information space, including the Ukrainian information ecosystem. Ukrainian content had to compete with Russian material in television, film, and music until language laws came into force in 2016.[67] Perhaps unsurprisingly, bilingualism in Ukraine was one-sided as a result. Many first-language Ukrainian speakers learnt Russian in school, but this was far less the case in reverse.[68] Despite the widespread knowledge of Russian, first-language speakers were in the minority among Ukrainians in 2001, with just under a third of the population speaking Russian as their first language, compared to two-thirds who spoke Ukrainian.[69] After the Soviet Union collapsed, the number of schools teaching Ukrainian increased across the country except in Donbas and Crimea, where Russian remained dominant. Meanwhile, the exiled Tatars who returned to the peninsula accounted for just 13 per cent of the population there.[70] The attempt to increase Ukrainian as a dominant language and the reactive entrenchment of Russian in some places became a loose thread between regions within the information ecosystem that, when pulled by politicians, threatened to unravel the entire tapestry. Yet this risk was only made possible by the presence of certain conditions, like economic insecurity, regionalism, and corruption—all three a by-product of bad leadership. Coupled with attempts to manipulate and control the Ukrainian information ecosystem, this resulted in a heavily polluted space wherein public discontent festered.

The 1990s were particularly difficult in Ukraine with mass inflation and growing economic problems, which the elites proved themselves ineffective (at best) or unwilling to resolve through reforms. Crony capitalism and corruption were rife.[71] Oligarchs concentrated economic power and resources in their ownership during the transition from Communism, and in turn, political leaders leaned on oligarchs to win and maintain power. As the once mighty Donbas went into economic decline, its centrally planned economic networks helped foster a mistrust of authorities in Kyiv.[72] The area became dominated by local clans rather than central law, which relied on the rise of homegrown oligarchs, many of whom made their money from the Russian gas trade.[73] Here, the voter base remained more Soviet in outlook. At the same time, its population and industry enabled Donbas to hold sway over the country, providing some 13 per cent of all Ukrainian members of parliament, among them oligarchs, which predictably and consistently opposed any moves in Kyiv to break with Russia.[74]

Regionalism was a continuing concern. Fears of it were aggravated by Kyiv's lack of hegemony in Ukraine. The situation was grave enough that in 1996 regional parties were forced to become national to participate in elections.[75] Still, there was the spectre of separatism in a variety of regions. The fear was used by politicians from various sides of the political spectrum, with accusations thrown at Donetsk, Transcarpathia, and Bukovina. Crimea was a constant friction point with Russia, centring on the Black Sea Fleet and who should control it. Successionist rumblings in Crimea began as early as 1990 when the Communist Party called for the peninsula to rejoin Russia. In 1994, the Sevastopol city council voted to put itself under Russian jurisdiction, a precursor of what was to follow two decades later. Russia only recognised Ukraine's borders in 1997 with the "Friendship Treaty", which also extended its lease on the Sevastopol naval base.[76]

Unsurprisingly, given the history and outstanding issues with Russia, on the other side of the political spectrum in independent Ukraine was a loose group of politicians, mainly from the West of the country, who thought their neighbour threatened the future of the country. Their political opponents, mainly from the East, accused them of being right-wing nationalists, but, in reality, the very few that were extreme won only around 3 per cent of the vote in early elections, whereas the wider block accounted for 20 to 25 per cent. Nonetheless, movements like the Donbas *Interrukh* and the Communist party proclaimed themselves as the upholders of a Soviet Ukrainian legacy and defenders against Galician manifest destiny in its aim to spread its sense of shared sense of Ukrainian culture across the country.[77]

Meanwhile, as the media in Ukraine struggled, oligarchs began to buy and use outlets for their own agendas. The most popular media in the decades after independence was television, with nearly all Ukrainians accessing news weekly through it.[78] Many top television and news channels were established in the mid-1990s, including *1+1*, *Inter*, *Channel 5*, *ICTV*, and *STB*.[79] Determining who owned media outlets after independence in Ukraine was challenging as possession was often hidden behind complex vehicles of offshore ownership.[80] Simply tracking the total number of media outlets in the country was an issue.[81] The communications scholar Alla Nedashkivska estimated that upwards of 80 per cent of all Ukrainian television outlets by the mid-2000s were "owned either by Russians or by pro-Russian citizens of Ukraine."[82] Regardless, a handful of corporations controlled the majority of media outlets in Ukraine.[83] A similar concentration occurred with radio as well, which roughly a third of Ukrainians accessed every week, mainly middle-aged male car owners who tuned in while driving.[84] Within a decade, radio would be in the hands of four major owners with a combined audience share of 75 per cent.[85] These groups belonged to the wealthiest oligarchs: Rinat Akhmetov, Dmytro Firtash, Viktor Pinchuk, and Ihor Kolomoisky.[86] Other oligarchs owned media outlets, such as Petro Poroshenko who owned *Channel 5*.[87] Newspapers also remained a source of information for Ukrainians and were similarly captured by oligarchs, with the most influential belonging to Serhiy Kurchenko and Rinat Akhmetov.[88]

In the early days of independence media, by and large, remained free from government control, except for the unpopular state-owned outlets, although this situation would not last. With American financial backing, *ICTV* began buying Western programming and dubbing over foreign languages with Ukrainian. *ICTV*'s hit show *Terytoriya A* was, according to sociologist Tetyana Nikitina, "a tool for the soft Ukrainization of the youth as most songs in its hit parade were in Ukrainian."[89] The Russian *Channel One*'s broadcast was stopped by the government in 1996, as it had been critical of the Ukrainian government, which in turn boosted the popularity of *1+1* and *Inter*. The latter station was partly owned by the Russian *Channel One* and continued to broadcast Russian programming, including content strongly associated with a nostalgia for Soviet times and traditions. This trend continued well into the 2010s.

Using their captured media, the oligarchs continued to exert political influence over the country. They poured enormous amounts of money into influencing politics. As Andrew Wilson noted in the 1999 election, "the shadowy 'Social Protection Fund', controlled by Oleksandr Volkov, may have had over $1.5 billion to spend. Russian mogul Boris Berezovskii reportedly pledged $150 million at Volkov's birthday party to protect his investments in Ukraine."[90] What's more, intrinsic to Ukraine's economic woes were mounting energy debts to Russia soaring into the billions and threatening to default the country.[91]

The situation was not good. Journalists like Georgiy Gongadze began asking questions. Kuchma, in turn, clamped down on the media and went further, ordering Gongadze's murder, a directive which was caught on tape and leaked in late 2000.[92] The country's relationship with Western countries suffered. This, in turn, isolated Kyiv, pushing Kuchma back towards Russia.[93] Within a couple of years, the very close relationship between Kuchma and Putin, who would meet eighteen times, would result in back-to-back celebratory years marking the friendship between their respective countries.[94] In response, a series of street protests called for "Ukraine without Kuchma", led by left-leaning political actors.[95] The protests rallied tens of thousands in Kyiv but waned after sabotage efforts provided authorities with an excuse to violently crackdown, a common tactic to subvert rallies in Ukraine. All types of media, both oligarch-owned and independent, were squeezed.[96] During this period, Russian-language content continued to dominate the Ukrainian information ecosystem in particular, given co-production efforts with better-funded Russian outlets, which Nikitina noted "dictated not only the language but also the ideology that would be acceptable for the Russian audience and government," not to mention access to a much more lucrative post-Soviet market.[97] Language laws dictating percentages of Ukrainian in broadcasting, which had mostly been ignored, were now used by politicians to crack down on the media.[98] Kuchma touted the importance of the Ukrainian language and promoted it in schools, yet did little to support publishing or the media to adopt it.⁹⁹ At the same time, defamation was decriminalised.¹⁰⁰ As the Ukrainian non-profit Institute of Mass Information noted, oligarch-owned media turned "to gutter journalism, tabloidization. They did not need an audience that can think, an audience that can analyse different options."¹⁰¹

Increasing government control over the media led to a distortion of reality, with news coverage of carefully picked incomplete information about the president, a twisting of international relations, and the opposition attacked or left out entirely.¹⁰² Opposition media did the same in return but were also targeted by the authorities.¹⁰³ The situation was a farce, and each side mocked the other. There was little to stop information pollution, as what rules that did apply to the media were mostly self-governed, few were implemented in practice. A form of contamination entered the Ukrainian market, colloquially called *jeansa*, which was paid-for advertising dressed up like news media.¹⁰⁴ Like many influence activities, *jeansa* wasn't entirely new in Ukraine. For journalist Ivan Verstyuk, it was "a natural extension of Soviet media practices that included direct government interference in the editorial policy of broadcasters and publishers, all of which were state-owned."¹⁰⁵ Eventually, journalists pushed back, staging hunger strikes and covering the election interference in November 2004, ultimately leading to the Orange Revolution.¹⁰⁶ This was no small feat, as civil society barely existed in Ukraine at that stage.

The 2004 election was a filled with drama. The incumbent Prime Minister Viktor Yanukovych and opposition leader Viktor Yushchenko were the two primary candidates. From rough Donbas origins, Yanukovych had been jailed twice for violent crimes in the 1980s.¹⁰⁷ An ethnic mix of Belarusian, Polish, and Russian, Yanukovych spoke Ukrainian with an accent, played on fears over Ukrainianisation, and campaigned to make Russian an equal state language.¹⁰⁸ He drew support from hometown oligarchs like Akhmetov as well as former president Kuchma. Russia has long interfered with Ukrainian elections, making their desired outcome known, and in this instance, Yanukovych was unmistakably Russia's preferred candidate and received the open support of the Moscow Patriarchate.¹⁰⁹ Putin sent "political technologists" or what Wilson described as "ultra-cynical political manipulators", including Marat Gel'man, to help Yanukovych in 2004 with an estimated US$300 million for the campaign.¹¹⁰ In turn, Yanukovych attempted to build backing among Crimean Tatars, creating groups like the Kazan Party and the Crimean Tatar Popular Front, among others.¹¹¹

The other Victor was ethnically Ukrainian and married to an American Ukrainian who had worked in the State Department of the United States.¹¹² Yushchenko was a staid central banker who, while in office, dealt successfully with inflation and was, for a short while, Prime Minister for Kuchma.¹¹³ In his oligarchic corner stood Poroshenko. In retrospect, it was apparent how this contest would be framed with a corrupt Russian-speaking politician on one hand and a Ukrainian reformer on the other. Yanukovych painted Yushchenko as a Western plant and, with the support of state media, linking his name with the then United States President George W. Bush—rendering "Bushchenko" an American stooge.¹¹⁴ Whereas Russian press portrayed him as a fascist, Yanukovych supporters tried to make that a reality, faking far-right rallies in Yushchenko's name.¹¹⁵ In a similar vein, the Yanukovych camp whipped up regionalist fears, creating maps purportedly coming from the Yushchenko campaign that carved Ukraine up into three classes, with the west and centre at the top and the east at the bottom.¹¹⁶ But the real drama was in the accompanying violence. Someone tried to run Yuschenko's campaign car off the road. A deadly bombing in Kyiv was blamed on his extremist supporters.¹¹⁷ Then, in September, Yuschenko was poisoned with a chemical found in Agent Orange (dioxin), which also happened to be the colour of his campaign.[118] Despite facial disfigurement and severe illness, he stayed in the campaign, only to be beaten by Yanukovych in the second round of voting, which many believed to be rigged, thus sparking the Orange Revolution.

The Orange Revolution was like a bushfire, fast and ferocious in the pent-up power it suddenly released. Following the Rose Revolution in Georgia the year before, it too was a rejection of Russian influence in the country, based on the population's frustration with corruption, economic stagnation, and social inequalities.[119] Many Ukrainians took their outrage to the streets of Kyiv, with estimates ranging from 200,000 to 500,000 participating.[120] This was a well-organised, elite-driven protest, complete with a main stage in central Independence or "Maidan" Square, coordinated intake of protestors on busses, hundreds of tents to provide shelter, and considerable media presence.[121] Poroshenko's *Channel 5* covered the protest favourably.[122] Protestors made up jokes about Yanukovych, calling those quips "Yanekdoty", a pun on his name, and these along with protest details were spread using cell phones.[123] Meanwhile, Yanukovych dug into his thuggish roots and bussed in Donbas coal miners to Kyiv, ready for a fight with the Orange protesters.[124] The political unrest lasted two months. The Supreme Court of Ukraine eventually invalidated the results of the election, and a new ballot was held, which Yushchenko won.

Examining this period in retrospect, it becomes clear that Ukraine was headed toward a heated information competition. Would the country remain in the Russian fold or lean toward the West? The European Union (EU) expanded significantly with ten new members in 2004, mainly from the former Warsaw Pact countries, a fact that irritated Russia and that Brussels seemed to ignore.[125] These countries would, in turn, actively champion

Ukraine's potential ascension.[126] An information competition played out between domestic politicians and was aggravated by interference by both Russia and Western countries. Essentially, the EU and Russia were forcing Ukraine to make a binary choice. This resulted in tit-for-tat statements about the 2004 election, whereby the EU condemned another round of voting, and the Russians argued for it.[127] Russia did not sit idle. After the Orange Revolution, pro-Russian NGOs began to appear in Crimea.[128]

Opponents of European integration attempted to tarnish proponents of it as fascists, a hangover notion from the Second World War fostered by the Soviets and subsequently by Russians and Ukrainian politicians to attack political opponents.[129] Meanwhile, what few Ukrainian films were being made helped fuel these attacks, revisiting the controversial Organization of Ukrainian Nationalists and its Ukrainian Insurgent Army in movies like "The Undefeated" (2000), "Iron Hundred" (2004), and "Far Shot "(2005), and documentaries like "Between Hitler and Stalin" (2004), "History of the First Ukrainian Division UNA 1943–1945" (2005), and "Stepan Bandera Museum" in London (2006). Other films, such as the documentary "NATO: Friend or Foe" (2007) touted the benefits of NATO. Meanwhile, politicians, mainly from eastern Ukraine, railed against language reforms and policies aimed at fostering a Ukrainian identity while blaming the lack of real reform in the country on Western meddling.[130] This camp included the likes of Yanukovych, whose party also ran a campaign stoking fears about NATO expansion in 2006.[131] Abroad, the Bush administration actively promoted Ukrainian membership in NATO, which did little to quell the growing paranoia among the Russian elite about Western intentions.[132] A litany of events starting with the 1999 NATO bombing of Serbia, followed by a series of revolutions unsettled Russia: Serbia in 2000; Georgia in 2003; Ukraine in 2004; Lebanon and Kyrgyzstan in 2005. These events were all seen as clear indicators of Western encroachment and, with it, a loss of prestige and power (much like Sparta's reaction to Athenian defensive walls).[133] A persistent paranoia that the West was supporting such events with the aim of regime change and that it would try to do the same in Russia was expressed through political announcements and state-owned media coverage. Western support for protests, exit polling, election monitoring, and the promotion of democracy were all taken as proof.[134] Activities on the ground and an escalating information competition settled into a pattern. While Western rhetoric fuelled Russian fears, Putin's speeches (and later actions) did as much to stoke concerns in return.[135]

With Yushchenko came a thaw for the media in general. However, he amended the law "On Television and Radio Broadcasting" to introduce a control around language use, forcing TV stations to run a minimum of three-quarters of Ukrainian content.[136] Little stopped oligarchs from controlling their media outlets, though, and this period saw an increase in *jeansa*. Most media depended on advertising (or oligarchic backers) to survive in Ukraine. Both political and commercial advertising increased more than five times from 2001 to 2006, with the market for television advertising growing by 1,000 per cent.[137] Of over 1,000 radio and television organisations in the country by 2006, half were in private hands, with some estimates attributing those owners to just thirty individuals.[138] New technologies were changing how people communicated, and the population was now the most university-educated Ukraine had ever been, reaching enrolment rates of over 82 per cent.[139] Mobile cellular subscriptions increased dramatically, jumping from 14 per 100 people in 2005 to 119 in 2007.[140] Yet the economic situation was deteriorating badly. In 2008 alone, the external debt more than tripled to $105.4 billion.[141]

Despite the high hopes the Orange Revolution instilled, little change followed it. The squabbles between Yushchenko and Yulia Tymoshenko, a key politician, and Tymoshenko and Poroshenko were legendary and, in part, prevented real reform.[142] Corruption remained common and was even alleged among Yushchenko's own family.[143] When Yushchenko's chief of staff, Oleksandr Zinchenko, stepped down, he claimed that corruption had increased, pointing specifically to Poroshenko.[144] At the end of 2009 and with an election looming, members of Yanukovych's Party of Regions started spreading a claim that Yushchenko had poisoned himself in the last campaign. The Ukrainian newspaper *Segodnya*, which reportedly published an article suggesting Yushchenko faked his poisoning, was cited in other outlets, including Russia state-backed RT and Ukrainian outlet *Korrespondent*.[145] *Segodnya* was owned by Akhmetov, and *Korrespondent*, by Kurchenko, both close contacts of Yanukovych.[146] Instead of meaningful and necessary economic reforms, Yushchenko focused on commemorating the *Holodomor* as a genocide. In January 2010, during the election, he made Stepan Bandera, the leader of the Organisation of Ukrainian Nationalists, a Hero of Ukraine.[147] Bandera's recognition alienated Ukrainians in the east and south who had grown up with Soviet war movies and gave Russia another opportunity to stoke fear amongst Ukrainians.[148]

At the same time, Russia was pushing hard for Ukraine to join its newly created Customs Union with Belarus and Kazakhstan. To that end, Putin supported Yanukovych's 2010 election campaign with its framing of a choice between Russia and the West.[149] Yanukovych staked his campaign on the belief that the last election was stolen from him, and he turned to the Russians for help.[150] Yuri Luzhkov, the mayor of Moscow and a regular meddler in Ukrainian affairs, attended his rally, branding Yushchenko's campaign a "sabbath of witches".[151] Sergei Glazyev, Putin's aide to the Customs Union, made thinly veiled public threats about Ukraine joining the European Union.[152]

Yanukovuch also hired the American consultant Paul Manafort and other lobbyists from Washington to remake the Party of Regions for the election.[153]

The election was a three-way contest, all backed by competing clans of oligarchs. In Yanukovych's corner were Akhmetov and Firtash. Kolomoiskyi and Pinchuk supported Yushchenko. And backing the so-called "gas princess", Tymoshenko, were Poroshenko and oligarchic newcomers, Vitaliy Haiduk, Serhiy Taruta and Kostyantyn Zhevaho.[154] It was clear with backers like these that they were not serious about reform, which was especially difficult after the highly elevated hopes of change raised by the Orange Revolution. And on that lacklustre note, Yanukovych was at last returned to office and, in turn, went after political opponents like Tymoshenko, who was sentenced to seven years in prison in October 2011.[155]

At home, Russia began facing discontent, with protests erupting at the end of 2011. Putin blamed the demonstrations on American machinations, a claim only helped by the activities of American officials. United States Senator John McCain taunted Putin on Twitter in 2011, posting: "Dear Vlad, the Arab Spring is coming to a neighborhood near you."[156] Ambassador Michael McFaul regularly met with protestors.[157] The talk of continued EU and NATO expansion was solidly a symbol of deliberate Western encroachment in the minds of the Russian leadership.[158]

With no institutional changes to protect the newfound media freedoms, government control soon returned. Outlets that criticised Yanukovych had their broadcasting rights threatened, as happened to *TVi* and *Channel 5*.[159] Russian-language media still dominated the Ukrainian information ecosystem. Two-thirds of the newspapers by 2011, and even more of the content on the top television stations, were in Russian.[160] Just one Ukrainian film was shown in theatres in Ukraine.[161] As ever, though, the situation was more complex. If anything, Ukrainian media promoted bilingualism. In a study of language used in television, film, and print media, Nedashkivska found repeated representations of characters and presenters carrying on conversations where one person spoke Russian and the other Ukrainian.[162] Sometimes, language use showed social divides, with protestors speaking Ukrainian in the movie "Orange Sky" and those in power using Russian.[163] Nonetheless, Ukrainian usage increased in urban centres, given its role in bureaucracy as the official language.[164] Yet, if Ukrainian nationalists were attempting to eradicate Russian from the country, there was little evidence of its success. This did not prevent politicians from using the idea to provoke linguistic grievances for their own gain.

Conforming to the patterns already established on all sides, the Ukrainian relationship with the West again soured. Many EU leaders became fixated on the imprisonment of Tymoshenko, with some member countries boycotting the European football championships co-hosted by Ukraine and Poland in 2012. Her release became an unspecified condition of the European Union Association Agreement with Ukraine.[165] To commit Yanukovych, in turn, demanded ever more money (upwards of US$165 billion) from the EU, who were offering significantly less than US$1 billion.[166] The more the EU pushed for Tymoshenko's release, the more Yanukovych dithered on the agreement. The EU was also prescriptive with prospective members, dictating their terms.[167] While several Ukrainian politicians, including Kuchma, promoted greater integration with Europe, they failed to make the necessary reforms membership required.[168]

With a lack of change came more discontent. Protests erupted in Ukraine over violence against women that authorities did little to stop. The first occurred in March 2012 after eighteen-year-old Oksana Makar was gang raped and burned to death in Mykolayiv, but as the alleged culprits were sons of local government officials, the police initially did nothing.[169] The people wanted leaders to tackle corruption, but Yanukovych and the Party of Regions would rather enflame ethnic divisions. He turned his eye to the Russian language problem again. In his 2012 law, Yanukovych enabled any municipal or regional authority with 10 per cent of Russian speakers to declare it an official language.[170] This, too, sparked protests, demonstrations, and hunger strikes in the Rada.[171] These tactics mobilised pro-Russian voters while readily inflaming Ukrainian nationalists.[172] Meanwhile, everyone else, especially women, received a clear message about how little politicians care about them.

Information pollution continued apace. Newer means of communication, like websites, facilitated the creation and distribution of more low-quality content. Political *jeansa* was particularly widespread online by 2012, spiking in advance of yet another election that year, which Yanukovych again won.[173] By September, across all press coverage, 11 per cent was *jeansa*, which primarily supported the authorities.[174] That year, in its election report, the Organization for Security and Co-operation in Europe warned that paid content disguised as news "leaves citizens unable to distinguish between editorial and paid-for coverage that is de facto (political) advertising. Poor professional standards and the current economic crisis leave journalists even more vulnerable to corruption."[175] The problem was not just confined to *jeansa* in newspapers and online outlets. Political advertising outstripped news coverage about the election fivefold on the major television stations.[176] Where there was news coverage, it was biased for one side. Nearly half of the election campaign coverage of the state-owned channel *First National* went to Yanukovych's Party of Regions, while just 13 per cent covered the opposition.[177] Such informational pressure was matched with physical attacks on political opponents.[178]

Russia continued its push for Ukraine to enter its Customs Union, with some Russian intellectuals foreshadowing darker threats. The concept of *Novorossiia* was revived, and influential members of a pressure group called the Izborsky Club, such as Glazyev and Alexander Prokhanov, advocated for it to be reincorporated into Russia.[179] By the summer of 2013, Russia deliberately slowed international trade with Ukraine and sanctioned Ukrainian products.[180] A leaked document purporting to outline Russian strategy on Ukraine claimed these moves were intended to influence Yanukovych and his cronies and make the country more dependent on Russia.[181] In turn, Yanukovych cracked down on civil society organisations while enabling Russian donors to lobby for the Customs Union.[182]

Yanukovych was not popular at home. The concentration of power and resources in the hands of his nearest cronies and relatives, known as "the family", led to a loss in support from other oligarchs.[183] It was also clear he cared little for the people who suffered under systemic corruption. In July 2013, in the village of Vradiyivka, the same region where Makar had been murdered the year before, a twenty-nine-year-old woman was sexually assaulted by three police officers. Their colleagues and superiors covered up the brutal crime.[184] Protests again erupted, demanding action. At this point, 58 per cent of Ukrainians thought the country was on the wrong course, up 5 per cent from 2012, and 43 per cent felt their lives were worse. They were unhappy with the economy (87 per cent) and the politics (79 per cent). Just under half (43 per cent) questioned the freedom of Ukrainian elections.[185] They pointed to corruption, oligarchic greed, and the complicit political elite as the cause for a lack of reforms.[186] Ukraine needed no foreign interference; it was a political powder keg waiting to self-ignite.

Instead of addressing the concerns of the people, Yanukovych and his cronies did what many poor leaders have done before them—they tried to control the information ecosystem. Ukraine was ranked 126 out of 180 countries by Reporters Without

Borders that year, just a few places up from Zimbabwe.[187] While Ukraine had laws to protect press freedom, they were not implemented.[188] Changes to the Criminal Code narrowing the definition of slander put further pressure on journalists, who, at the behest of the oligarch owners, were already pressured by middle management.[189] Yanukovych put media outlets into the hands of his supporters. Inter Media Group went to Firtash, another major conglomerate to Kurchenko.[190] Control over the information ecosystem was tightening while pollution within it was increasing.

Media remained dependent on advertising, which was a booming field. Digital content became more accessible with increasing internet usage. Fixed broadband subscriptions had grown nearly four times over five years, up to 41 per cent by 2013.[191] Internet users were more likely to be younger, better educated, and better off. They began consuming digital news over radio and print, making online news media the second most popular weekly news source.[192] The lower cost barrier to entry rendered online media more pluralistic in ownership than radio and television, which was in line with similar trends worldwide. That said, the most popular online news media were still owned by conglomerates and the politically minded as most traditional media quickly launched online versions, supported by oligarchs and advertising.[193] Driven by high-stakes political competition during elections, the Ukrainian advertising market hit a frenzied peak, pushing US$1.4 billion, bringing with it yet more *jeansa*.[194] In October, *jeansa* reflected the ongoing political debate, with Medvedchuk and Communist leader Petro Symonenko championing the Customs Union with Russia and Mykola Katerynchuk paying for content to promote the European Union.[195] Unsurprisingly, trust in media sat at around 30 per cent.[196]

Such were the conditions when Yanukovych abruptly pulled out of the Association Agreement with the European Union nine years to the day of the start of the Orange Revolution, which he followed with the announcement that the government would resume negotiations with Russia on entering the Customs Union.[197] For a people whose only recourse against corrupt and inept leaders was to protest, that's what followed with the Euromaidan movement. Starting on 21 November 2013 and lasting for three months, the "Revolution of Dignity", as it was called, was the outburst of many Ukrainians across different age groups and socioeconomic statuses expressing deep disappointments of unmet calls for change following the Orange Revolution.[198]

An initial lack of central organisation made Euromaidan different from the Orange Revolution.[199] Most people just came out of their own accord, including driving for hours to get there. Estimates of attendance at the protest were anywhere between 50,000 to 1 million.[200] As the scale of demonstrations increased, they became better organised, spawning sub-protests like Auto-Maidan, which helped move participants and introduced the use of cars as a form of protest.[201] A stage was erected where famous Ukrainian musicians performed.[202] Very small single-digit percentages were brought out by civil society organisations or political parties; individuals were merely frustrated by the *status quo*.[203] Most affiliated protests took place in western and central Ukraine, although some occurred in the south and east, where counter-protests also took place.[204]

Despite the scale of the protest, the overall population remained mixed about what they wanted for Ukraine. At the time of the demonstrations, roughly the same number of Ukrainians fell on either side of the EU versus Customs Union debate, at 38 per cent. These rates ranged across the country, with more leaning towards Europe in the west and central parts and those in the southeast towards Russia.[205] Perhaps unsurprisingly, younger Ukrainians favoured European Union integration, which was associated with greater opportunities and liberalisation.[206] Demographics of protestors changed over time to become more male and more rural.[207] According to one survey, nearly 70 per cent of participants were over thirty, and 24 per cent were over fifty-five.[208] Nearly two-thirds were employed, and 76 per cent had higher education.[209] More than 80 per cent said Ukrainian was their first language, whereas it was for just 56 per cent of the total population then.[210] For nearly 40 per cent, this was their first protest.[211] Entrepreneurs also turned out, drawing on the same network that led the Tax Maidan protests a few years prior.[212] Consecutive Ukrainian leaders had sold the public on EU integration as an answer to all of Ukraine's problems while making few reforms that would ensure that outcome.[213] Ukrainians were fed this myth so often that it could be argued the disappointment of Yanukovych's about-face provoked the protests.[214]

Social media was used to encourage people to protest, initially drawing a few thousand participants after journalist Mustafa Nayem posted on Facebook and emailed friends.[215] Another journalist, Yuri Andreev, then tweeted about the protests.[216] Nayem worked for the paper Gongadze founded, *Ukrainska Pravda*, and co-led the youth group *Pora!*[217] Traditional media played a key role too. When the violence of authorities was caught on camera and aired on the internet and television, even more protestors came out.[218] Indeed, 70 per cent of participants said their motivation for turning out was the repression.[219] This happened despite journalists being issued editorial instructions to "de-emphasize the protest actions".[220] Websites were created such as www.yanukovich.info, documenting "The Family's" wealth; www.personalaccountability.info which reported on corruption; and www.skoty.info tracked protest violence. Drones were used to expose the affluence of public officials.[221] According to a survey taken at the protests, just under half learned about the events from Facebook, 35 per cent from VKontakte, and 51 per cent from online news outlets.[222] While social media was novel and played a part, it was a role among many other means and outputs in an increasingly complex, if polluted, information ecosystem.

Rumours spread that Yanukovych had signed a secret deal in Sochi to join the Customs Union.[223] This rumour was furthered by a subsequent meeting and press conference between Yanukovych and Putin in Moscow on 17 December, where Russia announced a US$15 billion loan and a dramatic cut in gas rates.[224] Opposition media promoted the claim, with headlines like "The Rada Gave Ukraine Away," published by digital outlet *Ukrains'ka Pravda*.[225] Opposition politicians were quick to take up the narrative.[226] Emotions were provoked, and tensions rose.

More information pollution followed, with *jeansa* quickly deployed to discredit the protests.[227] This included articles published by *Obozrevatel* claiming protestors spread diseases, were hospitalised with mental disorders, and overall had no right to determine which direction Ukraine took.[228] For others, the idea of greater European integration was a perceived threat to traditional values. The Communist leader Symonenko called to replace so-called "gay ministers from Europe" who were currently sitting in the Ukrainian parliament.[229] Oligarch-backed media outlets pushed fears about degeneracy imported from Europe.[230] There were also reports that security services were encouraged to view the Euromaidan protestors "as paid sub-human representatives of gayropa ('Gay Europe')".[231] Fear and bigotry were commonly used to inflame the masses for political ends. For those who claimed to be on the side fighting fascists, the rhetoric denouncing the protests seemed oddly far right.

The presence of far-right politicians and nationalistically-minded activists at Euromaidan helped Russian officials brand

Euromaidan as a fascist coup.²³² Many of the extremists present were thought to be fakes brought in or collaborating with authorities.²³³ A march in Kyiv honouring Bandera helped bolster claims of a fascist presence.²³⁴ Protestors began using a slogan coined by the Organisation of Ukrainian Nationalists, "Glory to the Heroes!" [Heroyam Slava!]."²³⁵ One far-right group that garnered much attention was Pravy Sektor (Right Sector), which peaked in its all-time overall membership of several thousand.²³⁶ Oddly, the group's values echoed more of those denouncing the protest than those of the EU. In one post on 11 May 2014, below a photo of Eurovision song-winner, drag queen Conchita Wurst, they asked: "Ukrainians! Do we need such a 'Europe'? Could it be better to revive a real Europe at home and build a strong nation-state that would be free not only from the Moscow imperialists, but also from the Western Liberals?!"²³⁷ The post garnered under 1,000 likes, 463 comments, and 159 shares some ten years later, which is not overly remarkable for a page with a following of over 50,000. As others noted, even Pravy Sektor followers condemned the post.²³⁸ The group's use of violence as a tactic also helped give Yanukovych the excuse he sought to crack down on the protest.²³⁹ On 16 January 2014, Yanukovych signed a draconian bill to break up the protests, which only further inflamed the situation.²⁴⁰

Russian fears, which their pressure helped provoke, were coming true. This view was helped in part by Western support for the protests.²⁴¹ United States Secretary John Kerry publicly stated: "The United States stands with the people of Ukraine. They deserve better."²⁴² Visits to the protest were made by high-level United States officials and politicians, including Victoria Nuland and senators John McCain and Chris Murphy, as well as the European Commission's Catherine Ashton.²⁴³ Russia publicly censured these visits, condemning them as interference in Ukrainian domestic affairs, which was hypocritical given their meddling.²⁴⁴

A wiretapped call between American officials discussing the make-up of the new government heightened Russian fears about Western-backed regime change. In it, the officials discussed their interactions and advice to the opposition leaders.[245] Meanwhile, Ukrainian flags decorated Warsaw streets in neighbouring Poland, and its colours lit up official buildings.[246] Then, on 22 February 2014, Yanukovych left a power vacuum when he disappeared.[247] In that void, Russia seized Crimea under the pretext of countering a fascist coup to protect its naval interests.[248]

It's tempting to reduce the information competition occurring at that time to one between Yanukovych, backed by Russia, on one side, portraying Euromaidan as a fascist coup, and pro-Euromaidan politicians supported by the West, on the other, promoting freedom. Public comments clearly show that foreign actors had few qualms about wading into Ukrainian affairs, both in its information ecosystem and abroad. Indeed, that simplified information competition about Ukraine's future played out as much in other ecosystems, like that of the United States, as it did in the Ukrainian one. It was abroad in English-speaking information ecosystems beyond Ukraine where fake accounts were increasingly used to engage in that information competition on news sites there.[249] However, the situation was far more complex, with many information competitions occurring simultaneously, only adding further to the confusion. The Ukrainian information ecosystem was a crowded cacophony in the first decades after independence. A melange of politicians and oligarchs jostled for power within it, aligning with foreign interests as needs arose.

As we've seen in all the information ecosystems explored in this book, from Ancient Greece to modern Ukraine, each is connected to others around it, particularly to those in near physical proximity, but also increasingly to others farther flung. Very few information ecosystems are voids unto themselves; instead, they are part of a global information environment.

THE UKRAINIAN CURSE OF NONEXISTENCE

The ties binding Ukraine to other information ecosystems were significant and diverse, not just to Russia and other neighbours but farther afield to America and Canada. These connections are part of the tapestry, which is an information ecosystem, intertwining threads that are human relationships, mediated communications, and ideas. However, those connections do not always translate into a true understanding of the Ukrainian information ecosystem, leading to missteps by domestic leaders and neighbours alike.

The Ukrainian information ecosystem reflected its history as a crossroads between many cultures and peoples. This made the country less homogenous than other information ecosystems explored here, such as historic England, America, and Vietnam. The diversity in languages and identities across the many regions of this vast space, at least leading up to 2014, formed less of a tapestry and more of a patchwork whereby the various pieces were not always so tightly stitched together. All too often, the self-interest of Ukrainian leaders made this situation worse. Instead of finding ways to make a quilt out of the diverse communities, attempts to choose one identity from among many led those not reflected in that vision to fear a loss of status, which in turn was readily inflamed by politicians who gained in so doing. Similarly, Russian chauvinism blinded Moscow to the limits of using language and identity to galvanise mass support for their interests in Ukraine. While the annexation of Crimea went easily enough for Russia, subsequent invasions of Ukraine have not, suggesting merely speaking Russian does not make a Russian. In fact, continued Russian aggression has had the opposite effect, pushing Ukrainians farther from their neighbour. Coupled with years of domestic neglect, each Russian encroachment has strengthened Ukrainian civil society, too. Before Euromaidan, civil society was weak and even mistrusted in Ukraine.[250] The conflicts in 2014 sparked a resurgence, with regular Ukrainians stepping into the government's void to support the military, rendering it far more able to push back on Russian aggression.[251] The more the Russians disregard average Ukrainians, the stronger they become, as if determined to remove their curse of nonexistence.

The fact is that the Ukrainian information ecosystem had long been a hotly contested space, poorly managed by its successive leaders, who had grown so corrupt that they deluded themselves into believing that the mass discontent felt by people whose needs continued to be unmet would somehow be quelled through control of the information ecosystem. At the same time, the Ukrainian information ecosystem was growing increasingly complex with new means of communication, adding novel outputs that the power-hungry elite quickly co-opted to pollute the environment further for their own self-interest. The internet and web added more means of information production and exchange to an already turbulent ecosystem, enabling some plurality of voices in online sources, but as has been the case in many of the cases explored in this book, often of dubious quality. Like other information ecosystems studied here, new technologies like social media did not displace existing means of communication but became part of an increasingly complex system. Cell phones and social media helped people coordinate, but mainstream media and journalists, coupled with coverage of violence by authorities, brought people out on the streets. Despite all the manipulation and information pollution, a sizeable group of people were still able to communicate their dissatisfaction in the only way left to them: in protest.

This exploration of Ukraine highlights the interconnected nature of information ecosystems and the role of news media within them. News media does not exist in a void but is connected through relationships between outlets and their owners, advertisers, staff, and consumers. For the most part, news media is a business. So much ink has been spilt on the business model of social media companies, but the same can be said of news media. Ownership and revenue models matter just as much in newsrooms and can shape the quality of their outputs. Outside of political commercials, particularly during elections, advertising is often overlooked as an essential aspect of the modern information environment. However, in capitalist societies like Ukraine during the period explored, advertising revenues were an indicator of increased manipulation of the information ecosystems. Looked at in conjunction with the quality of outputs, ownership of outlets, and media regulation, rates of advertising revenue can provide insights into the state of an information ecosystem.

At the turn of the twenty-first century, the Ukrainian information ecosystem should stand as a cautionary tale for any policymaker who cares about democracy. Anecdotally, I've heard it often said in circles concerned with information integrity that Ukrainians are now very resilient to Russian disinformation. This is thought to have come about from over-exposure to Russian propaganda and, at the time of writing, its brutal and prolonged invasion of Ukraine—hardly the sort of conditions a sane leader should want to foster to increase societal resilience to disinformation. However, Ukrainians in the decades leading up to this conflict were also highly educated and extremely self-sufficient, given so many neglectful and dishonest governments. These factors and conditions could just as well explain Ukrainian resilience. But if policymakers hope to unlock those secrets, a shift to studying information ecosystems must occur, starting with the development of information ecology to facilitate systemic and comparative analysis.

9

ALL HAIL FINLAND?

It was the so-called year of elections. More than sixty countries were expected to count ballots, giving over 4 billion eligible voters an opportunity to express their choice for the future.[1] Along with the voting came a growing panic that 2024 would be the year that elections would be undermined by artificial intelligence. News coverage stoked fears about the potential impact of fake content. Many of the most feared threats, though, were not new, including hate speech, disinformation, harassment of election officials, and suppression of opposition; the worry was that they would now just be supercharged by generative artificial intelligence (AI) tools.[2] First in the cycle in January was Finland's presidential election, which, despite the AI hype, went smoothly. Maybe it was all of Finland's past efforts related to disinformation; maybe AI played no role.[3] It's hard to say, but the reported absence of significant attacks will likely continue to fuel a persistent belief in democratic policy circles that Finland is a shining example other countries should follow in the fight against disinformation. Putting measures Finland took to protect itself aside, how practical is the hope that Finland can be a beacon for other democracies? Ecologically speaking, not very.

All too often, issues related to information ecosystems are reduced to simple, singular topics. In Finland's case, its apparent success in addressing disinformation is thought to result from investments in media literacy programmes and education that fosters the ability to critically assess mass media.[4] Media literacy is an offshoot of traditional literacy, but instead of just reading comprehension, it also considers things like people's ability to critique the source and evaluate its quality. While media literacy might be the reason for Finnish success, without looking at the information ecosystem, the claim is little more than a hunch based on a correlation: the Finnish government raises awareness about disinformation, and the society isn't having problems like Canada or the United States, so the two must be connected. On traditional adult literacy rates, Finland ranks second overall, with Canada and the United States falling below the Organisation for Economic Development's (OECD) average.[5] Nearly half of adult Canadians struggled with literacy as of 2012.[6] Similarly, just over half of Americans aged sixteen to seventy-four lacked literacy proficiency in 2020.[7] There is one multi-country ranking on media literacy, which is less a test of Finnish ability as much as a compilation of other indices on press freedoms, literacy, interpersonal trust, and e-government participation.[8] Finland has consistently topped that list, but it still isn't a measure of media literacy. However, the index takes a more systemic approach in that it considers multiple factors. In so doing, it hints at the fact that it is more likely that a combination of various factors and conditions leads to greater resilience to threats rather than a single intervention, but finding that answer requires an ecological approach.

Taking an ecological approach to studying information ecosystems is challenging. It requires not just looking at one aspect of an information ecosystem, like news media, and hoping to make sense of everything. Instead, an ecological approach assesses a variety of factors, including about the people, tools, and outputs, as well as conditions in the wider environment that could impact them, like economics, education, politics, and pressing threats. Most research programmes are not geared this way. The system produces specialists, but at some point, to study the system, we'll need subject-matter generalists who can bring it all together. The focus on specialisation also means that much of the available data is piecemeal, like literacy and education rates, or is based on small sample sizes from surveys, such as what news people consume or the social media they use. A lot of other data that would be insightful is not currently collected or readily available, such as breakdowns about what various types of content information animals are foraging or how they go about finding it. Bringing what is available together to make sense of an information ecosystem, as the examples in this book demonstrate, is often sprawling and messy—and researchers aren't currently trained to do so. Yet it is a first step towards where research needs to head for an ecological approach to emerge to understand how information animals relate to the information environment around them. Moreover, given the international nature of that environment, data must also be generated in a way that lends itself to fair comparisons between information ecosystems. This last part is absolutely necessary if policymakers hope to learn lessons from one information ecosystem that can be applied to another.

Hoping to replicate Finland's success, many researchers have called on governments to invest in media literacy programmes. It's become the Holy Grail for curing all that ails polluted information ecosystems. As of 2024, media literacy was one of the most recommended interventions for countering disinformation. However, media literacy comes in various forms, and as my colleagues at the Carnegie Endowment for International Peace noted, "variation in pedagogical approaches means the effectiveness of one program does not necessarily imply the effectiveness of another."[9] (This is to say nothing of the challenges in scaling it to reach an entire society.) The few examples studied in this book demonstrate that information ecosystems are complex, and each has its own characteristics. Even if we concretely knew what did work in Finland, that approach might not work in Canada or the United States. Based on available data, what can be said about the factors and conditions surrounding the Finnish information ecosystem, vis-à-vis the Canadian and American ones? Well, at a quick glance, they are not much alike.

To begin with, Finland's information ecosystem is more insular than those of Canada or the United States, in part because of language but also because of cultural norms. While we might speak of a European information biome stitched together by shared governance, linguistically, Finland is a separate island within it. Finnish hails from an entirely different language family than most of those spoken in Europe and coupled with the fact that there are so few Finns, it is a lot less common as a second language, much less a mother tongue. Even within the Finno-Ugric language family, Finnish is only somewhat mutually intelligible with Estonian (another small population) and not at all so with Hungarian. This provides an advantage in any competition for Finnish hearts and minds. When fake Twitter accounts were created purporting to be Finnish candidates or experts during the 2023 parliamentary elections, they were mocked for their terrible language skills.[10] Compare this to, say, Canada or the United States, which are part of an English-speaking information biome that spans dozens of countries and results in considerable cross-border information sharing. Moreover, as an international *lingua franca*, the English language is taught almost everywhere, making the mostly free American and Canadian information ecosystem extremely porous. It certainly enables cross-border news consumption. Some Anglo-Canadians are tuning into British and American news media weekly, with CNN attracting 19 per cent of Canadians and both BBC and Fox News each garnering 13 per cent.[11] Similarly, 12 per cent of Americans are consuming BBC as well.[12] This foreign news consumption is slightly less prevalent in Finland, where just 9 per cent are watching foreign television and 6 per cent are reading foreign news online.[13]

The Finns aren't just challenging to reach in their own language; they are also tough nuts to crack socially. A well-known joke about them asks how can you spot the extroverted Finn? The answer is that they'll be the one staring at your feet instead of their own. Introversion, self-deprecation, and modesty are all promoted alongside their pristine forests and lakes on the Finnish government's tourism website, *Visit Finland*.[14] Breaking into Finnish culture can be such a challenge for foreigners, there are social media groups and services to help newcomers understand the quirks of Finland. Another defining characteristic of Finns is their self-reliance. Varpu Rusila, founder of *Her Finland* noted in an email that "Finnish society celebrates agency and independence."[15] People are taught to be self-reliant and think critically for themselves. Children take themselves to and from school by the first grade, and when they are provided with their meals at school, they "take their own food to their plates, and they are not served." This sense of agency and responsibility follows into work as well. A person is expected to execute projects with minimal direction. In many ways, the Finns have developed a worldview that is their own, partly based on a concept of inner strength or "sisu", which provides a grounding factor. As Rusila noted, "Many elements in the Finnish lifestyle and culture allow you to be connected with who you are. There's freedom and there's trust". It's quite possible that Finnish culture just lends itself to a more resilient information ecosystem, making its people well-grounded, independent critical thinkers.

Their information ecosystem might be insular, and the people introverted, but that doesn't make the Finns unworldly.[16] While 13 per cent of Finns haven't travelled abroad, 28 per cent do so a few times *a year*. Compare that to the United States, where nearly a quarter (23 per cent) of Americans haven't travelled abroad, and of the vast majority who have (50 per cent), it was to fewer than five other countries. Canadians are getting out a bit more than their neighbours, with 43 per cent having visited five or more countries, and just 9 per cent having never travelled abroad. Travelling more might be encouraging greater multilingualism, too. Most Finns (93 per cent) speak a foreign language.[17] It is almost the reverse in both the United States and Canada. Most Americans (78 per cent) only speak English.[18] In Canada, a country that is proud of its bilingualism, only 18 per cent of Canadians say they can have a conversation in both French and English, whereas half the total population speaks only English, and 10 per cent speak only French. Still, Canadians are more multilingual than Americans, with 21 per cent able to speak a non-official language beyond French or English.[19] This might account for the Canadian tendency to feel more connected to the world (51 per cent) than Americans do (35 per cent).[20] Unfortunately, the same survey didn't include Finns. Here is where the comparative statistics begin to fail us, for either being differently captured across countries or incomplete. Greater ability to engage with the world might be a key to resilience, particularly if the threat is foreign interference, but better measurements would need to be made for comparisons to work.

Population size and diversity might also be factors, with smaller, more homogenous information ecosystems having a leg up on resilience. Here, Finland is quite different from the United States and Canada. Finland is a small country. According to World

Bank data, in 2023 Finland had a little more than 5.5 million people.[21] The population of Finland is extremely homogenous, where 90.9 per cent "has a Finnish background", and two-thirds follow the same religion, the Evangelical Lutheran Church of Finland.[22] The country is considered so homogenous it is often a study for gene mapping.[23] As of 2019, just 7 per cent of Finland's population was foreign-born, compared to 13 per cent in the United States and 23 per cent in Canada.[24] While Finland has small populations of other ethnicities, including Swedes, Russians, Estonians, Romani, and Sami, the percentages are tiny. The Sami people are Europe's only recognised indigenous people, living across northern Finland, Sweden, Norway, and Russia. In Finland, Sami number some 10,000, which is less than 1 per cent of the overall total population.[25] Finland is also more homogenous in terms of income levels than either Canada or the United States, with comparatively stable and lower levels of income inequality.[26] Such homogeneity in demographic factors and economic conditions might leave fewer loose threads that could be pulled to divide the Finnish tapestry, which is its information ecosystem.

Compare that to the United States, with nearly 335 million people, following a kaleidoscope of Christian variants among other established religions and smaller cults, each with its own information bubble. From here, demographic comparisons can get a little tricky. Finland measures diversity differently from the United States, which takes a less ethnicity-focused approach and is more race-based, with lingering Civil War echoes. It's unsurprising that in the latest 2020 census, the United States Census Bureau did some mental gymnastics to adjust to a changing world. Using their terms, "The most prevalent racial or ethnic group for the United States was the White alone non-Hispanic population at 57.8 per cent. This decreased from 63.7 per cent in 2010." This was followed by 18.7 per cent of the total population who were "Hispanic or Latino" and 12.1 per cent who were "Black or African American alone not-Hispanic."[27] This suggests that two-fifths of Americans identify as something other than White and that the diversity rate continues to increase. Although these statistics must be taken with a grain of salt, as before an announcement in 2024, the United States Census had been counting Americans with Middle Eastern and North African heritage (still a very broad category) as White.[28] While the United States is more diverse than Finland, comparing different approaches to capturing ethnicity is challenging. In some countries, like France and Germany, collecting data on ethnicity is discouraged, if not prohibited, limiting what can be assessed about the diversity of people within those information ecosystems.[29] Historical events led to these restrictions, and such data can be abused, but ethnicity informs identity and experiences and thus plays a role in how realities are formed. Modern societies will need to find a way to study these aspects of people that discourages abuse but also still helps inform understanding of information ecosystems.

Canada's population is significantly smaller than that of the United States, but with more than 40 million people, it is seven times larger than Finland's.[30] Geographically, Canada is also huge as the second biggest country globally and nearly thirty times the size of Finland. Not only does this make infrastructure costly to maintain (and, as telecommunication service providers here in Canada try to argue, justifies the high costs for subscribers), but it also lends itself to regionalisms whereby each province and territory can feel aggrieved by confederation.[31] According to the Canadian census, the country is far more diverse than Finland. As of 2022, a quarter of Canadians were part of a racialised group, with Statistics Canada noting that "more than 450 ethnic and cultural origins, 200 places of birth, 100 religions and 450 languages have been included in this census."[32] This includes

6 per cent of the population who are Indigenous and 19 per cent of Canadians who speak French at home.[33] There are also 144,055 ethnic Finns in Canada, roughly the equivalent of 3 per cent of Finland's population.[34] Nearly a quarter of the Canadian population as of 2022 was foreign-born, the highest rate since the country was confederated in 1867 and topped the G7.[35] In fact, immigration has led to Canada having one of the fastest population growth rates in the world. More than 1.3 million people immigrated to Canada between 2016 and 2021, with 471,771 alone in 2023.[36] This movement of people, and with them information, connects Canada to ecosystems throughout the global information environment. In general, these factors related to the movement of people and information across borders, coupled with the connections those processes create and their impact on information ecosystems, are some of the most challenging aspects to study.

As information animals coalesce around identities and interests to form communities, likewise different communities can intersect and form networks, which, along with the means for processing and sharing information, form the basis of an interconnected system. As with most attempts to categorise the physical world, information ecosystems, communities, and ideas can often overlap and blend across borders. Communities intersect across borders and geographies in more diverse countries like the United States and Canada (or as we saw in Ukraine). With that movement of people can come new ties to the information ecosystems from whence they came. The United States and Canada share the longest undefended border in the world, which has led to a lot of cross-border traffic and intermarriages. As of 2020, some 353,495 Americans lived in Canada, whereas around 800,000 Canadians were living in the United States, with a further 126,340 moving there in 2022 alone.[37] With strong interpersonal relations, long-standing economic relations and cultural influences, the two information ecosystems are interconnected despite Canadian content laws restricting foreign programming in the country. Canada is connected to other information ecosystems as well. As mentioned in Chapter 8 on Ukraine, the population of the Ukrainian diaspora in Canada, accounting for just 3.5 per cent of Canadians, has enjoyed considerable national political influence. A Ukrainian church was prominently featured in the middle of the national Canadian Museum of History. Immigrants helped foster Ukrainian culture and maintained those links back home for a century.[38] Canada was the first Western country to recognise Ukrainian independence and was quick to come to Ukraine's aid in the face of Russian invasions.[39] This diversity, which is very much the basis of the modern Canadian information ecosystem, has been viewed as a potential point of vulnerability. Diaspora communities have been targeted in Canada as part of foreign interference in our elections.[40] Some prominent American news, business, and political figures have had few qualms about how their commentary about Canada might impact the information ecosystem here. Intended or otherwise, the actions of information animals elsewhere can make ripples (if not waves) in the Canadian information ecosystem.

Even the most homogenous information ecosystems can experience ripples caused by agents elsewhere. Invasions and changes to the flow of information have, to varying degrees, affected the information ecosystems explored in this book. Often, these reverberations result in enduring threads woven into that information ecosystem's tapestry. This means that history and geography are conditions that must also be considered alongside direct factors related to people, means, and outputs when assessing the state of an information ecosystem. For example, Finland might be more resilient to disinformation because of its proximity and history with Russia. The two countries have had a troubled past. Russia occupied Finland as part of its empire from

ALL HAIL FINLAND?

1809 to 1917, and the older architecture in Helsinki is identical to that across Russia, albeit in much better shape. Then, in the 1940s, Finland fought the Winter and Continuation Wars against the Soviet Union. The Finns have a threat to their independence on their doorstep, which might lead to a heightened awareness of informational threats. Indeed, Finland has alleged that Russia has used migrants to destabilise its neighbour, blaming these actions for their introduction of a new law contradicting its human rights commitments.[41] For Finland, Russia is a clearer and more present threat than, say, the United States is to Canada, despite American attempts to take Canada over in the other War of 1812 (remembered mostly by Canadians). Although this might change given comments by returning President Trump about Canada becoming the fifty-first state.[42] Finns might be more resilient to Russian disinformation because of language and cultural barriers. Yet, the proximity of a domineering adversary on one's border might also make the population's awareness of the threat more acute. Whereas Canadians and Americans are practically cousins, and our star entertainers seamlessly enter and lead in Hollywood, often without anyone but Canadians really noticing. Similarly, as allies, we Canadians might not even detect when disinformation seeps across our border and are unaware of what might be a friendly threat. Proximity to and awareness that there even is a threat might create resilience.

There are, however, some shared factors across these three information ecosystems. In the early decades of the twenty-first century, Finland, Canada, and the United States all experienced the introduction of new technological means that have changed how people process and share information. This also puts these three modern information ecosystems in a similar position to the historic ones explored in this book. The internet has widely been adopted across Finland, Canada, and the United States, albeit a little faster in Finland between 2004 and 2014, at times outstripping Americans by 20 per cent. However, across all three information ecosystems, more than 90 per cent of people were using the internet by 2021.[43] Social media has had a similar comparative uptake rate across the three information ecosystems, with just shy of two-thirds of people using Facebook and slightly less for YouTube. Half that many uses social media to access news, though, and just 15 per cent of Finns use YouTube for news, compared to 31 per cent of Americans and 29 per cent of Canadians.[44] At the same time, journalism across all three information ecosystems is experiencing the same crunch in declining revenues, often blamed on digital technologies. And here is where things begin to diverge again.

Overall, the structure of the news media market and people's relationships with it differ across the three information ecosystems. For example, in Finland, news content is less polarised than in the United States, where more than a third of Americans want journalists to share their political views.[45] Finland is also known for its strong public broadcaster (*Yle*) and regional press. Two-thirds of Finns tune into *Yle* weekly, which has an 85 per cent trust rating. Finns generally have much higher rates of trust in news than other countries, sitting at 69 per cent overall. [46] Finland also ranks consistently high in media freedom, sitting at five out of 180 countries in the Reporters Without Borders 2024 ranking, compared to Canada at fourteen and the U.S. at fifty-five.[47] Like Finland, the Canadian media market is small, and it's shrinking. It is also starkly cut in two between English and French. Canada still has a public broadcaster in the CBC, and 41 per cent of Anglo- and 24 per cent of French-Canadians tune into some form of its broadcast weekly. Moreover, 63 per cent of Anglo-Canadians trust the CBC, and 74 per cent of French speakers trust its radio coverage.[48] This is higher than the average trust in news overall in Canada which sat at just 39 per cent in 2024, down from 45 per cent in 2021.[49] Canadian media, however, is consolidated in the hands of five powerful companies that control telephone, mobile, internet, cable, and, in some cases, news outlets themselves, like Bell and Quebecor. Meanwhile, newspapers have been consolidated, with just three out of seventy-one dailies being independently owned in Canada as of 2022.[50]

By comparison, the American media market is massive compared to either Finland or Canada, and it is almost entirely corporate. To call NPR and PBS a public broadcaster in the same vein as *Yle* and CBC is a bit of a stretch, as it is mainly supported directly by viewers. As of 2023, just 8 per cent of Americans were tuning into either PBS or NPR, which takes less than 1 per cent of its $300 million annual budget from the federal government.[51] However, 47 per cent of Americans trusted NPR, compared to just 32 per cent trusting news overall.[52] And while trust in news media is declining across the political spectrum in the United States, far fewer Republicans (11 per cent) than Democrats (58 per cent) trust mass media to be accurate and fair, with Independents falling in the middle (29 per cent).[53] All these numbers demonstrate not only the disparities in ownership, variety of media, or trust in it but, more importantly, the differences in how people relate to news media within the information ecosystems of Finland, Canada, and the United States. In other words, it might not be that Finns are better trained to critically analyse news media, but that the quality of their news is also better, leading to a healthier relationship with it.

Then again, it might be that the overall conditions that impact the Finnish information ecosystem are better than those of Canada or the United States. In index after index, Finland fares well. Indeed, Finns are regularly ranked the happiest in the world.[54] According to the OECD, Finland outstrips both Canada and the United States on issues such as community, education, environment, life satisfaction, safety, and work-life balance.[55]

Whereas in the United States, a quarter of teachers reported working at a school experiencing a gun-related lockdown in the year before the survey.[56] On Transparency International's *Corruption Perceptions Index*, Finland is nearly at the top of the world for having the least perceived corruption, ranked second out of 180 countries, with Canada at twelve and the United States at twenty-four.[57] Maybe the reason why more Finns trust their government is because it's working for them. Nearly half of Finns (47 per cent) said they had high or moderately high levels of trust in their national government in 2023, and 82.7 per cent were satisfied with administrative services. The Canadians fared a bit better, with 48.5 trusting the government but just 68.8 per cent satisfied with services.[58] In the same period, just 22 per cent of Americans said they had trust in their government.[59] In poll after poll by Pew Research Center, the picture is bleak in the United States, with 80 per cent of Americans believing their politicians don't care what the people think, 72 per cent thinking their democracy is no longer a good example, and two-thirds feeling exhausted at the mere thought of politics they frequently describe as divisive.[60]

In Finland, children walk themselves to school safely; in the United States, children are at a real risk of being shot in schools. One might think a country worried about its population's susceptibility to disinformation might consider simply trying to do better for its people. That's certainly a message some leaders covered in this book could have heeded. An information ecosystem reflects physical realities as much as it shapes them. That's what makes the information environment a complex and dynamic system. The Finnish information ecosystem might simply be more resistant to disinformation because the society there is better equipped to meet more of its citizens' needs than Canada or the United States. We won't know conclusively, however, until the field of information ecology develops to the point where enough knowledge is systematised about information ecosystems that proper comparisons can be made to find that answer.

Should democracies all hail Finland? It's worth investigating, but so far the evidence is inconclusive. Without an ecological understanding of information ecosystems, it's imprudent to jump to conclusions and foolhardy to apply those leaps to other countries. Any number of things might make Finland special, from the factors related to the people, tools, and outputs within the Finnish information ecosystem to the conditions affecting them, such as history, geography, and social stability. Any number of combinations of factors and conditions might lead to greater resilience. Even with a cursory glance through an ecological lens, it's clear that the Finnish, American, and Canadian information ecosystems are quite different. For example, the highly homogenous yet multilingual and literate Finns enjoy excellent conditions supporting a good quality of life and trust in government, along with a strong public broadcaster and less polarisation in news coverage. A policy measure that might work for Finland, such as increased funding for the public broadcaster, might have the opposite effect elsewhere. In the United States, with people's love of freedom and low levels of trust in government, increasing funding for public broadcasting might lead people to question if this would co-opt the independence of PBS or, worse, simply be viewed as a liberal conspiracy aimed at brainwashing the population, a claim that has been made by some American lawmakers and covered on Fox News.[61]

While what little research that exists on polarisation in Canada suggests the country isn't as divided as our southern neighbours, but there is a growing sense that we are becoming more so.[62] Despite a concern over news media consolidation, most Canadians (59 per cent) do not think the government should intervene to support private newsrooms, rising to 83 per cent of respondents who support the Conservative party versus

48 per cent who support the Liberals. However, less than half (47 per cent) overall also do not agree with entirely defunding the CBC.[63] For all our smugness towards the Americans, we Canadians are but a few steps away from fostering a mimicry of their information ecosystem—at least, that's far more likely than it ever becoming more like Finland's. But that's the point: without information ecology, humans won't have a great grasp on the information environment or what they are already doing to information ecosystems, much less what they should be doing to foster healthier ones.

10

THE FUTURE OF THE INFORMATION ANIMAL

Brain implants could destroy democracy, warns a government-commissioned report

A new report commissioned by the Department of Homeland Security raises the alarm over the rapid spread of human-brain interfaces (HBI), warning that they pose "cataclysmic" risks to national security and that the federal government must act now or face imminent disaster. The report, released last week by Palmerston HBI, was based on several roundtables involving more than 100 top tech executives, national security officials inside government, and researchers.

The report warns that "the potential for cognitive manipulation and mental exploitation poses serious risks to freedom and democracy".

Stressing that the report does not represent the views of the U.S. government, an official confirmed that the department commissioned the report as part of its ongoing assessment of how the latest technologies are aligned with protecting American interests.

The report is a reminder that with all the potential benefits of HBI come tangible risks, too.

"Human-brain interfaces, which enable direct communication between the brain and external devices, offer remarkable possibilities", explains Mary Judge, the Executive Director of Palmerston HBI. "They can restore lost functions for individuals with disabilities, offering hope for those with spinal cord injuries or neurodegenerative diseases, and help people instantly acquire new skills or languages, or researchers to share knowledge and insights directly through neural networks."

However, the head of Palmerston HBI, which aims to promote responsible development and use of the new technology, also warns:

"Malicious actors could exploit HBIs to alter thoughts, beliefs, or behaviours, raising concerns about autonomy and psychological safety. In the wrong hands, this technology could become a tool for coercion or control, creating a dystopian scenario where personal freedom is compromised and citizens are co-opted to revolt."

White House spokesperson Joe Bauers said that the Global Declaration on HBI, spearheaded by the United States, "establishes a set of high-level international commitments by participating States to seize the promise and manage the risks of HBI, and the President remains committed to its implementation."

Others aren't so sure. As these interfaces allow unprecedented access to individuals' thoughts and cognitive processes, the potential for misuse and unauthorised surveillance is alarming.

"We know very little about the impact of these technologies on society because few researchers have access to the data related to their use," explains Robert Cheavins, a researcher at Wellington University. "Most of the findings about HBI come from the companies selling the technology or what little trickles out from FDA oversight. The data and access needed for independent research is proprietary and not publicly available."

* * *

To quote the Four Tops, "It's the same old song." I admit, that was tongue-in-cheek. This fake news story hasn't happened yet. However, I expect that once brain implant technology rolls out, many news stories will be very similar to this one, based on others about existing tools.[1] It's a pattern I've noticed throughout my career. In fact, this type of story has been so common about social media and, more recently, artificial intelligence that my friends and I have quipped that a chatbot could write them. This hype-to-fear process drives the research-and-response cycle on the information environment outlined in the introduction to this book, ultimately encouraging a short-term and reactive focus on studying the latest technology. The cycle is kicked off by an innovation, like artificial intelligence. The innovators selling the new technology hype it for all it's worth in the media because they need investors and profits. At first, all the amazing benefits will be touted. If it might provide organisations with an advantage, businesses and governments will rush to figure out how they should adopt the new tool. Then come the concerns. Researchers might worry about privacy risks, increased disinformation, or other harms that arise with the use of the technology—the media hype moves from hope to fear. Calls grow for more funding for research on the innovation, which follows, creating a bubble on that topic as more people chase scarce resources and begin studying it too. In the mix might be a dissatisfied whistle blower or two from one of the tech companies who releases highly coveted internal data feeding fears. Advocates start demanding technology regulation; some will focus on data access. In a few years, the new rules might come into play to help researchers get access, but in the meantime, the innovation is pervasive, and the changes it was likely to make on the information ecosystem have occurred. And what's more, something new has already come along. Such is the pace of current innovations in the information ecosystem.

In many ways we are in a never-ending cycle of adding more technology that increases the speeds at which information can be processed and shared, which, in turn, demands more technology to cope with those changes. In so doing, we are also outsourcing fundamental aspects of the human experience that are the basis of the information environment, in so much as it exists because of us as information animals: that is to say, our abilities to process information and remember it. In essence, we are caught in a trap of acceleration based on a need to adapt, but dependent on technology to do so at the expense of our ability as information animals to naturally adapt. What might be the long-term consequences? Species need to adapt to survive. Technology can't save us from ourselves.

Meanwhile, because this research-and-response cycle follows innovation, no one is any farther ahead in understanding those changes because of a lack of baselines about the information ecosystem into which the technology was added. It's like investing the bulk of research funding into studying DDT without making longer-term investments into understanding ecosystems—but worse because the current approach on the information environment jumps from topic to topic following media coverage. Research on both the new technologies and information ecosystems is required to understand the impact of one on the other. Unless a different approach to studying the information environment is taken, the same pattern will be repeated regarding any new technology introduced into the ecosystem. Research will be piecemeal and reactive, as will the response. Granted, there are some key differences between the physical and information environments. For example, there is unlikely to be a pristine information ecosystem like ecologists had in northern Ontario to assess the effects of pollution and interventions to it. However, the good thing about baselines is they just have to be started. The earth scientists started tracking acid rain after it became a problem, too—they just persisted in their measurements for a very long time. Nothing but a lack of

THE FUTURE OF THE INFORMATION ANIMAL

will and resources precludes us from starting measurements today to create baselines against which tomorrow's comparisons can be made. What's needed is an approach that endures no matter what innovation comes along in the future.

While it is in very early stages, taking an ecological approach already tells us that the hype-to-fear process isn't the only pattern that emerges vis-à-vis new technology and information ecosystems. If humans continue the current trajectory of innovation, any new technology added to ecosystems will likely speed up how information is produced and shared between people. Given what was found by exploring historical information ecosystems in this book, innovation is more likely to be developed with profit in mind than not. Once on the market, various agents will undoubtedly use the new tools to make money or persuade people of something. The information ecosystem where this occurs will become more complex as more means of communication and content are added. New ideas could emerge, challenging existing beliefs, and both will find receptive audiences as information animals touting these ideas compete for hearts and minds. This pattern has happened throughout two millennia of human history; it will likely play out again regardless of the innovation. Beyond hinting at what information ecology might be able to tell us if further developed, identifying this pattern opens opportunities to prepare.

A pattern offers anticipated points of intervention before something happens. That doesn't mean necessarily that we should intervene or that doing so will have positive results, but that the option becomes possible. For humans to know whether an intervention is a good idea, we will still require information ecology to find the answers. However, long before intervening, democratic societies must also have some open and frank conversations on topics that are likely to be difficult, given how they are wrapped up in the sacred, if ethereal, concept of freedom. This is a thread that comes in many varieties and is woven into the information ecosystems of most democracies. Its manifestation and the tapestries it creates differ between ecosystems and countries.

Freedom is an exceptionally tricky thread in the context of information ecosystems, given how it is knotted into the very legitimacy of democracies, which is dependent on citizens making free and informed decisions. What if ensuring that freedom comes at the cost of freedom elsewhere? For example, as per the pattern above, one point of intervention is to control the introduction of innovations into information ecosystems, much like many societies do for pharmaceuticals until their impact can be ascertained (which still requires baselines). Free market capitalists will be screaming at me, but should market freedoms trump the freedom needed for the legitimacy of democracy? A common argument hindering independent research on existing technologies, like artificial intelligence, has been the risk to companies of losing a competitive market advantage. Is the freedom of companies to make money more important than the ability of citizens to make free and informed decisions, especially when the profit is made from tools and outputs that might be undermining this freedom of choice? When freedoms conflict, where does one end and the other begin? It blurs quickly when it comes to the information environment because the very innovations that worry us can potentially both inform and disinform people depending on how they are built and used. This is why it is paramount to understand information ecosystems to guide governance decisions over them with science about the system rather than mere value judgments.

Technology companies aren't the only ones with incentives whose freedoms clash with those needed for democracy's legitimacy. The problem with business models extends as much to most news media and politicians as it does to technology companies. A free press is generally accepted as a requirement for democracy, but if the business model demands competition for audiences, leading to sensationalism and partisanship, where does informing end and manipulation begin? Answering that question requires understanding the news media's role, in all its forms, in the information ecosystem. Similarly, the politician's business model is to raise the funds to enable efforts to persuade voters to support them. This means first convincing donors and then the electorate. As citizens, politicians have freedom of speech the same as everyone else, which they exercise in courting popular support. In so doing, they use all the means available to them, such as those worrying technologies and the media, to convey their message. In a complex and crowded information ecosystem, many politicians are leaning into populist tactics, disinformation, and entertainment to win votes. Does a politician's freedom to say whatever they like to win office impinge on citizens' freedom to be informed? Does such behaviour provide advantages in media coverage? What's the relationship between this sort of behaviour and the use of technology? What's the tipping point between voters having agency and not? Fundamentally, these are all questions that can only be answered through information ecology because they require more than one type of research or study to do so.

I'm picking on these agents—technology companies, media, and politicians—because they often play an outsized role in any information ecosystem. In that role, they also have greater responsibility. It stands to reason that those who build and use the means within an information ecosystem to profit and persuade, at least in a democracy where its legitimacy is at stake, should have to open their activities to independent researchers to inform rulemaking around such pursuits. And if the only fear in doing so is loss of competitive advantage, there may be bigger questions around the incentives democracies are fostering in relation to how their information ecosystems are developing. Again, it's this complexity that demands an interdisciplinary field to address.

We live in an Age of Complexity. The fact that the world is complex isn't itself new, but humans are newcomers to that awareness in many ways. We now know how complex and fragile the physical environment is. But we have also built increasingly complex systems in the global economy, governance models, and the information environment. All three of these complex systems are intertwined with each other, but all of them are absolutely dependent on the physical environment, which is under threat of collapse. At the same time, all decision-making takes place in the information environment, or rather, many information ecosystems are more complex than ever, noisier and more chaotic, making it harder to win support for difficult long-term decisions that might address climate catastrophes. Similarly, the more problems experienced in the physical environment, particularly those impacting the economy or governance, the worse things become in those information ecosystems affected. It's the hallmark of a polycrisis, whereby interconnections between systems lead to a situation where a crisis occurring in one triggers significant strain and a crisis in another.[2] A warming planet is expected to push people from warmer regions, and migration is already a contentious issue. As people move, the societies where they arrive will inevitably become more diverse. Even the most homogenous countries, like Finland, will be faced with these challenges, leading to uncomfortable situations where fear and hate will make people susceptible to provocation. This raises questions about how to foster diverse information ecosystems capable of making long-term decisions in the public interest—which will probably include new people. It is unreasonable to expect that everyone there will always share the same opinions. Any society hoping to weather the coming storm should invest in determining what factors and conditions in an information ecosystem enable constructive disagreement.

All of this isn't to suggest that problems in the physical world can somehow be managed in the information environment. If this book has found anything, it is that social problems are seldom just a matter of information. Ideas take root in the information ecosystems where the factors and conditions allow it. Controlling the information ecosystem will not address underlying issues of economic inequality. Events like repeated "once-in-a-lifetime" storms and fires, more than strategic communication, will change people's minds. However, how those problems play out in the information ecosystem can worsen the situation. Again, this is why information ecology is needed. It's not enough to study the information animals or their tools and outputs, but how they relate to those factors and surrounding conditions, like the economy and climate. That is the key that will ensure not just the survival of democracy but also humanity.

The information environment is an unexplored terrain, at least systematically so. At present, different types of researchers are wandering into various information ecosystems and exploring the bits that are relevant to them: a spot of news media here, some social media posts over there, elsewhere someone is assessing education and literacy levels, or maybe infrastructure developments. If we're really lucky, some of those stats might be repeated over time, but more often than not, when looking across the global information environment, these are one-time studies. Even the information ecosystems explored here are limited, looking specifically at conflicts and after a new technology was introduced. Information ecosystems where conflict did not happen or before a new technology was added also need to be studied. So much research must be built up. Without an umbrella field to connect disparate research, humans will never see the forest for the trees—and if we do not understand the information ecosystems and their role in society, we will never understand how our interventions within it impact societies. Other complex systems have been understood through the development of umbrella fields, and those fields provide a path that democracies should follow to get ahead of future challenges. That path is information ecology. Without a systematised long-term approach to studying the information environment, humans are doomed to repeat the same mistakes within ecosystems over and over again. We'll never fully understand what it means to be an information animal.

GLOSSARY OF TERMS

Information	Anything that is processed to provide meaning.
Information animal	A living being who has and acts on their agency to process information to understand the world.
Information competition	A state where two communities of information animals compete for supremacy of their idea in the information environment
Information disruption	Disruption to the flow of information between types or groups of information animals within an information ecosystem, commonly between those holding power within an information ecosystem and the public.
Information ecology	The study of the information environment, including the entities within it and their relation to each other and the wider system.

GLOSSARY OF TERMS

Information ecosystem	Information animals interacting with each other, tools, outputs, and the information environment as part of an interconnected system.
Information environment	The space where information exists, comprising all its myriad forms as well as the surrounding conditions affecting it.
Information flood	A disturbance in the information environment consisting of a marked increase in an output type and/or specific narrative such that it dominates the information ecosystem in which this occurs, drowning out other types of information.
Information pollution	The presence of low-quality information that degrades the overall information ecosystem.
Means	The tools information animals use to produce and share information, such as language, signs, digital tickers, printing presses, and mobile applications.
Outputs	Content produced by information animals that can be shared with others like chatter, directions, timetables, characters, and weather forecasts.
Political animals	Information animals that use means and outputs with the aim of seeking power over public decision-making processes.

GLOSSARY OF TERMS

Profiteers	Information animals who control and use means to process, produce, and distribute outputs for financial gain.
Proselytisers	Information animals who use means and outputs with the aim of encouraging others to adopt their beliefs.

NOTES

INTRODUCTION

1. Jonah Berger, *Contagious: Why Things Catch On* (Simon & Schuster, 2016).
2. Behrouz Ehsani-Moghaddam, Ken Martin, and John A Queenan, "Data Quality in Healthcare: A Report of Practical Experience with the Canadian Primary Care Sentinel Surveillance Network Data," *Health Information Management* 50, no. 1/2 (2021): 88–92, https://doi.org/10.1177/1833358319887743.
3. See: Robert Burton, *The Anatomy of Melancholy* (The Gutenberg Project, 1621), https://www.gutenberg.org/ebooks/10800.
4. Paul Dover, *The Information Revolution in Early Modern Europe*, vol. 62 (Cambridge University Press, 2021).
5. William F Channing, "Lecture III: The American Fire-Alarm Telegraph," in *Annual Report of the Board of Regents by the Smithsonian Institution* (A. O. P. Nicholson, 1855), 148; "Latest By Telegraph: Our Washington Correspondence. The Ocean Telegraph—Relative Benefits and Evils—The President and His Companion—Bigler and Stanton, Etc.," *The New York Times*, 19 August 1858, https://timesmachine.nytimes.com/timesmachine/1858/08/19/78859815.html?pageNumber=4.

1. WHAT CAN ECOLOGY TEACH US ABOUT THE INFORMATION EVIRONMENT?

1. Antony J. Blinken, "Building a More Resilient Information Environment—United States Department of State" (Summit for Democracy, Shilla Hotel, Seoul, Republic of Korea, 18 March 2024), https://www.state.gov/building-a-more-resilient-information-environment/.

2. Jaboury Ghazoul, *Ecology: A Very Short Introduction* (Oxford University Press, 2020), 4.
3. Elton, *Animal Ecology*, 565.
4. Whittaker, *Communities and Ecosystems*, 76.
5. Manuel C. Molles Jr. and Anna A. Sher, *Ecology: Concepts & Applications*, 8th ed. (McGraw-Hill Education, 2019), 17.
6. Sybryn L. Maes et al., "Environmental Drivers of Increased Ecosystem Respiration in a Warming Tundra," *Nature*, 17 April 2024, https://doi.org/10.1038/s41586-024-07274-7.
7. Gene E. Likens et al., "Acid Rain," *Scientific American* 241, no. 4 (1979): 43–51.
8. Alina Bradford and Ben Biggs, "Acid Rain: Causes, Effects and Solutions," livescience.com, 16 March 2022, https://www.livescience.com/63065-acid-rain.html.
9. Lesley Evans Ogden, "The Bittersweet Story of How We Stopped Acid Rain," *BBC*, 7 August 2019, https://www.bbc.com/future/article/20190823-can-lessons-from-acid-rain-help-stop-climate-change.
10. Peringe Grennfelt et al., "Acid Rain and Air Pollution: 50 Years of Progress in Environmental Science and Policy," *Ambio* 49, no. 4 (1 April 2020): 849–64, https://doi.org/10.1007/s13280-019-01244-4.
11. For the expansive view see: Gordon Pask and Susan Curran, *Micro Man: Computers and the Evolution of Consciousness* (Macmillan, 1982). For the others: Werner Kunz and Horst W. J. Rittel, "Information Science: On the Structure of Its Problems," *Information Storage and Retrieval* 8, no. 2 (1 April 1972): 95–98, https://doi.org/10.1016/0020-0271(72)90011-3; Richard T. Barth and Ilan Vertinsky, "The Effect of Goal Orientation and Information Environment on Research Performance: A Field Study," *Organizational Behavior and Human Performance* 13, no. 1 (1 February 1975): 110–32, https://doi.org/10.1016/0030-5073(75)90008-2; Philip Bromiley and John P. Crecine, "Budget Development in OMB: Aggregate Influences of the Problem and Information Environment," *The Journal of Politics* 42, no. 4 (1980): 1031–64, https://doi.org/10.2307/2130735.
12. John Arquilla and David Ronfeldt, "The Emergence of Noopolitik: Toward An American Information Strategy" (RAND Corporation, 1 January 1999), https://www.rand.org/pubs/monograph_reports/MR1033.html; "Joint Publication 3–13: Information Operations" (U.S. Joint Chiefs of Staff, 27 November 2012), https://irp.fas.org/doddir/dod/jp3_13.pdf; "Analysis and Assessment of the Information Environment" (Zentrum Operative Kommunikation der Bundeswehr: Multinational Information Operations Experiment Applied Concept, 30 April 2014); David Ronfeldt and John Arquilla, "Whose Story Wins: Rise of the Noosphere, Noopolitik, and Information-Age Statecraft" (RAND

Corporation, 27 July 2020), https://www.rand.org/pubs/perspectives/PEA237-1.html.

13. Lawrence M. Hanser and Paul M. Muchinsky, "Work as an Information Environment," *Rganizational Behavior and Human Performance* 21, no. 1 (1978): 47–60; Maureen McNichols and James G. Manegold, "The Effect of the Information Environment on the Relationship between Financial Disclosure and Security Price Variability," *Journal of Accounting and Economics* 5 (1983): 49–74; Frank Heflin, K. R. Subramanyam, and Yuan Zhang, "Regulation FD and the Financial Information Environment: Early Evidence," *The Accounting Review* 78, no. 1 (2003): 1–37; Santanu Mitra and William M. Cready, "Institutional Stock Ownership, Accrual Management, and Information Environment," *Journal of Accounting, Auditing & Finance* 20, no. 3 (2005): 257–86; Kee-Hong Bae, Warren Bailey, and Connie X. Mao, "Stock Market Liberalization and the Information Environment," *Journal of International Money and Finance* 25, no. 3 (2006): 404–28; Nuno and Ferreira, "Does International Cross-Listing Improve the Information Environment"; Piotroski and Wong, "Institutions and Information Environment of Chinese Listed Firms."; Carlos-Alberto Dorantes et al., "The Effect of Enterprise Systems Implementation on the Firm Information Environment," *Contemporary Accounting Research* 30, no. 4 (2013): 1427–61; Horton, Serafeim, and Serafeim, "Does Mandatory IFRS Adoption Improve the Information Environment?"; Nemit Shroff, Rodrigo S. Verdi, and Gwen Yu, "Information Environment and the Investment Decisions of Multinational Corporations," *The Accounting Review* 89, no. 2 (2014): 759–90; John Gallemore and Eva Labro, "The Importance of the Internal Information Environment for Tax Avoidance," *Journal of Accounting and Economics* 60, no. 1 (2015): 149–67; Nemit Shroff, Rodrigo S. Verdi, and Benjamin P. Yost, "When Does the Peer Information Environment Matter?," *Journal of Accounting and Economics* 64, no. 2–3 (2017): 183–214; Xu Li, Chen Lin, and Xintong Zhan, "Does Change in the Information Environment Affect Financing Choices?," *Management Science* 65, no. 12 (2019): 5676–96.

14. Kim M. Nazi, "The Personal Health Record Paradox: Health Care Professionals' Perspectives and the Information Ecology of Personal Health Record Systems in Organizational and Clinical Settings," *Journal of Medical Internet Research* 15, no. 4 (2013): e70.

15. Natalia V. Morze, Olena Kuzminska, and Galyna Protsenko, "Public Information Environment of a Modern University," in *ICTERI*, 2013, 264–72; Bok Baik et al., "Managerial Ability and the Quality of Firms' Information Environment," *Journal of Accounting, Auditing & Finance* 33, no. 4 (2018): 506–27.

16. Nicole Yankelovich et al., "Intermedia: The Concept and the Construction of a Seamless Information Environment," *Computer* 21, no. 1 (1988): 81–96; Hugh Davis et al., "Towards an Integrated Information Environment with Open Hypermedia Systems," in *The ACM Conference on Hypertext*, 1993, 181–90; Michael X. Delli Carpini, "Gen.Com: Youth, Civic Engagement, and the New Information Environment," *Political Communication* 17, no. 4 (2000): 341–9; Ronald J. Faber, Mira Lee, and Xiaoli Nan, "Advertising and the Consumer Information Environment Online," *American Behavioral Scientist* 48, no. 4 (2004): 447–66; Jorge Arango, "What Is an Information Environment?," *Medium*, 20 March 2018, https://jarango.medium.com/what-is-an-information-environment-b4709521c4d6#.
17. Jennifer Jerit, Jason Barabas, and Toby Bolsen, "Citizens, Knowledge, and the Information Environment," *American Journal of Political Science* 50, no. 2 (2006): 266–82; Bruce A. Williams and Michael X. Delli Carpini, *After Broadcast News: Media Regimes, Democracy, and the New Information Environment* (Cambridge University Press, 2011); Jennifer Jerit and Jason Barabas, "Partisan Perceptual Bias and the Information Environment," *The Journal of Politics* 70, no. 3 (2012): 672–84; Frank Esser et al., "Political Information Opportunities in Europe: A Longitudinal and Comparative Study of Thirteen Television Systems," *The International Journal of Press/Politics* 17, no. 3 (2012): 247–74; David J. Betz, *Carnage & Connectivity: Landmarks in the Decline of Conventional Military Power* (Oxford University Press, 2015); Peter Van Aelst et al., "Political Communication in a High-Choice Media Environment: A Challenge for Democracy?," *Annals of the International Communication Association* 41, no. 1 (2017): 3–27; Erik Peterson, "The Role of the Information Environment in Partisan Voting," *The Journal of Politics* 79, no. 4 (2017): 1191–1204; Anna Brosius, Erika J. Van Elsas, and Claes H. de Vreese, "Trust in the European Union: Effects of the Information Environment," *European Journal of Communication* 34, no. 1 (2019): 57–73.
18. Jennifer Allen et al., "Evaluating the Fake News Problem at the Scale of the Information Ecosystem," *Science Advances* 6, no. 14 (2020); Galen Stocking et al., "The Role of Alternative Social Media in the News and Information Environment" (Pew Research Center, 2022).
19. For example: Fernandes Nuno and Miguel A. Ferreira, "Does International Cross-Listing Improve the Information Environment," *Journal of Financial Economics* 88, no. 2 (2008): 216–44.; Joseph D. Piotroski and T. J. Wong, "Institutions and Information Environment of Chinese Listed Firms.," in *Capitalizing China 2*, ed. Joseph P. H. Fan and Randall Morck (Chicago, IL: University of Chicago Press, 2012), 201–42; Joanne Horton, George Serafeim, and Joanna Serafeim, "Does

Mandatory IFRS Adoption Improve the Information Environment?," *Contemporary Accounting Research* 30, no. 1 (2013): 388–423; Nazi, "The Personal Health Record Paradox: Health Care Professionals' Perspectives and the Information Ecology of Personal Health Record Systems in Organizational and Clinical Settings."

20. John McHale, *The Changing Information Environment* (Elek Books, 1976), 107.
21. Luciano Floridi, *The Fourth Revolution: How the Infosphere Is Reshaping Human Reality*, Kindle (Oxford University Press, 2014), 829, 831.
22. Paul Röttger and Balazs Vedres, "The Information Environment and Its Effects on Individuals and Groups" (The Royal Society, 30 April 2020), https://royalsociety.org/-/media/policy/projects/online-information-environment/oie-the-information-environment.PDF.
23. Edward Osborne Wilson, *Consilience: The Unity of Knowledge* (Vintage Books, 1999), 56.
24. Ronald E. Doel, "The Earth Sciences and Geophysics," in *Science in the Twentieth Century*, ed. John Krige and Dominique Pestre (Routledge, 2013), 391, 392.
25. Doel, "The Earth Sciences and Geophysics," 414.
26. Andrea Wulf, *The Invention of Nature: Alexander von Humboldt's New World* (Vintage Books, 2015).
27. Robert P. McIntosh, *The Background of Ecology: Concept and Theory* (Cambridge University Press, 1985), 22.
28. Donald Worster, *Nature's Economy: A History of Ecological Ideas*, Second Edition (Cambridge University Press, 1977); McIntosh, *The Background of Ecology: Concept and Theory*, 30.
29. Ghazoul, *Ecology: A Very Short Introduction*, 21.
30. McIntosh, *The Background of Ecology: Concept and Theory*, 1.
31. McIntosh, *The Background of Ecology: Concept and Theory*.; Edward J. Kormondy, "A Brief Introduction to the History of Ecology," *The American Biology Teacher* 74, no. 7 (2012): 441–3.
32. Kormondy, "A Brief Introduction to the History of Ecology," 442.
33. Matthew Wills, "The Case of the Thinning Eggshells," *JSTOR Daily* (blog), 24 October 2019, https://daily.jstor.org/the-case-of-the-thinning-eggshells/.
34. Donald H. White et al., "Elevated DDE and Toxaphene Residues in Fishes and Birds Reflect Local Contamination in the Lower Rio Grande Valley, Texas," *The Southwestern Naturalist* 28, no. 3 (1983): 325–33, https://doi.org/10.2307/3670793; Ozden Bastürk et al., "DDT, DDE, and PCB Residues in Fish, Crustaceans and Sediments from the Eastern Mediterranean Coast of Turkey," *Marine Pollution Bulletin* 11, no. 7 (1 July 1980): 191–5, https://doi.org/10.1016/0025-326X(80)90491-9.

35. Richard F. Bernard, "DDT Residues in Avian Tissues," *Journal of Applied Ecology* 3 (2 June 1996): 193–98, https://doi.org/10.2307/2401459; Robert Kesic et al., "Continuing Persistence and Biomagnification of DDT and Metabolites in Northern Temperate Fruit Orchard Avian Food Chains," *Environmental Toxicology and Chemistry* 40, no. 12 (December 2021): 3379–91, https://doi.org/10.1002/etc.5220.
36. David B. Peakall, "DDE: Its Presence in Peregrine Eggs in 1948," *Science* 183, no. 4125 (15 February 1974): 673–4, https://doi.org/10.1126/science.183.4125.673; David B. Peakall et al., "DDE-Induced Egg-Shell Thinning: Structural and Physiological Effects in Three Species," *Comparative and General Pharmacology* 4, no. 15 (1 September 1973): 305–13, https://doi.org/10.1016/0010-4035(73)90013-X; David B. Peakall, David S. Miller, and William B. Kinter, "Blood Calcium Levels and the Mechanism of DDE-Induced Eggshell Thinning," *Environmental Pollution* 9, no. 4 (1 December 1975): 289–94, https://doi.org/10.1016/0013-9327(75)90061-0.
37. Xiwei Wang et al., "Information Ecology Research: Past, Present, and Future," *Information Technology and Management* 18 (2017): 27–39.
38. Mark Guzdial, "Information Ecology of Collaborations in Educational Settings: Influence of Tool," in Proceedings of the 2nd International Conference on Computer Support for Collaborative Learning, International Society of the Learning Sciences, 1997, 86–94; Bonnie A. Nardi and Vicki O'Day, Information Ecologies: Using Technology with Heart (MIT Press, 1999); Brian Detlor, "The Influence of Information Ecology on E-commerce Initiatives," Internet Research 11, no. 4 (2001): 286–95; Bernardo A. Huberman, *The Laws of the Web: Patterns in the Ecology of Information* (MIT Press, 2001); Robert Hassan, "Time and Knowledge in the Information Ecology," Southern Review: Communication, *Politics & Culture* 35, no. 2 (2002): 37–54; Victor Bekkers and Vincent Homburg, *Information Ecology Of E-Government: E-Government As Institutional And Technological Innovation in Public Administration* (Informatization Developments and the Public Sector) (IOS Press, 2005); Seonyoung Shim and Byungtae Lee, "Evolution of Portals and Stability of Information Ecology on the Web," in The 8th International Conference on Electronic Commerce: The New e-Commerce: Innovations for Conquering Current Barriers, Obstacles and Limitations to Conducting Successful Business on the Internet, 2006, 584–88; Tim Finin et al., "The Information Ecology of Social Media and Online Communities," *AI Magazine* 29, no. 3 (2008): 77–92; Brian J. McNely, "Exploring a Sustainable and Public Information Ecology," 2010, 103–8; Ling Zhu and Sherry Thatcher, "National Information Ecology: A New Institutional Economics Perspective on

Global e-Commerce Adoption," *Journal of Electronic Commerce Research* 11, no. 1 (2010); Michal Lorenz, "Information Ecology of a University Department" (International Conference organised on the occasion of the 90th anniversary of the establishment of the Faculty of Philosophy at Comenius University in Bratislava, Information Ecology and Libraries, 2011), 53–65; Barbara B. Moran, "Adaptation, Evolution, or Extinction: Libraries and the New Information Ecosystem" (International Conference organised on the occasion of the 90th anniversary of the establishment of the Faculty of Philosophy at Comenius University in Bratislava, Information Ecology and Libraries, 2011), 15–26; Nazi, "The Personal Health Record Paradox: Health Care Professionals' Perspectives and the Information Ecology of Personal Health Record Systems in Organizational and Clinical Settings"; Aditya Johri et al., "Millennial Engineers: Digital Media and Information Ecology of Engineering Students," *Computers in Human Behavior* 33 (2014): 286–301; Christina Vasiliou, Andri Ioannou, and Panayiotis Zaphiris, "Understanding Collaborative Learning Activities in an Information Ecology: A Distributed Cognition Account," *Computers in Human Behavior* 41 (2014): 544–53; Anne M. Perrault, "The School as an Information Ecology: A Framework for Studying Changes in Information Use," in *Librarians and Educators Collaborating for Success: The International Perspective*, ed. Marcia A. Mardis (International Association of School Librarians, 2017), 161–73; Catherine Gomes and Shanton Chang, "The Digital Information Ecology of International Students: Understanding the Complexity of Communication," in *Digital Experiences of International Students*, ed. Shanton Chang and Catherine Gomes, vol. 1 (Routledge, 2021), 1–24; Annett Heft et al., "Toward a Transnational Information Ecology on the Right? Hyperlink Networking among Right-Wing Digital News Sites in Europe and the United States," *The International Journal of Press/Politics* 26, no. 2 (2021): 484–504.

39. Thomas H. Davenport, *Information Ecology: Mastering the Information and Knowledge Environment* (Oxford University Press, 1997); Tadashi Takenouchi, "Information Ethics as Information Ecology: Connecting Frankl's Thought and Fundamental Informatics," *Ethics and Information Technology* 8 (2006): 187–93; Karen S. Baker and Geoffrey C. Bowker, "Information Ecology: Open System Environment for Data, Memories, and Knowing," *Journal of Intelligent Information Systems* 29, no. 1 (1 August 2007): 127–44, https://doi.org/10.1007/s10844-006-0035-7; Brian G. Eddy et al., "An Information Ecology Approach to Science–Policy Integration in Adaptive Management of Social-Ecological Systems," *Ecology and Society* 19, no. 3 (2014); Mark Burgin and Yixin Zhong, "Information Ecology in the Context of General Ecology,"

Information 9, no. 3 (2018); Christian Unkelbach, Alex Koch, and Hans Alves, "The Evaluative Information Ecology: On the Frequency and Diversity of 'Good' and 'Bad,'" *European Review of Social Psychology* 30, no. 1 (2019): 216–70; Y. X. Zhong, "Information Ecology: The Methodology for Information Studies," in *Philosophy and Methodology of Information: The Study of Information in the Transdisciplinary Perspective*, ed. Gordana Dodig Crnkovic (Singapore: World Scientific, 2018), 525–51; Peter L. Pulsifer et al., "Information Ecology to Map the Arctic Information Ecosystem," in *Governing Arctic Seas: Regional Lessons from the Bering Strait and Barents Sea:*, ed. Oran R. Young, Paul Arthur Berkman, and Alexander N. Vylegzhanin, vol. 1 (Springer Cha, 2020), 269–91; Ping Wang, "Connecting the Parts with the Whole: Toward an Information Ecology Theory of Digital Innovation Ecosystems," *Mis Quarterly* 45, no. 1 (2021): 397–492.

40. Jela Steinerova, "Information Ecology as a Framework for Reconsidering Information Usage," *Mousaion* 30 (2012): 87–102; Eleonora Barkova, Marina Ivleva, and Elena Agibalova, "Information Ecology in Structuring Sociocultural Space of Modern Society," in *2nd International Conference on Contemporary Education, Social Sciences and Humanities* (Atlantis Press, 2017), 1146–50.
41. Timothy B. Norris and Todd Suomela, "Information in the Ecosystem: Against the 'information Ecosystem,'" *First Monday*, 2017, https://firstmonday.org/ojs/index.php/fm/article/view/6847/6530.
42. John R. Stepp, "Prospectus for Information Ecology," *Journal of Ecological Anthropology* 3, no. 1 (1999): 39–73.
43. Kenneth A. Schmidt, Sasha R. X. Dall, and Jan A. Van Gils, "The Ecology of Information: An Overview on the Ecological Significance of Making Informed Decisions," *Oikos* 119, no. 2 (2010): 304–16, https://doi.org/10.1111/j.1600-0706.2009.17573.x.
44. Thore J. Bergman and Jacinta C. Beehner, "Information Ecology: An Integrative Framework for Studying Animal Behavior," *Trends in Ecology & Evolution*, 2023, 1041–50.
45. Alicia Wanless, "The More Things Change: Understanding Conflict in the Information Environment Through Information Ecology" (Ph.D. Dissertation, London, UK, King's College London, 2023); Alexei L. Eryomin, "Information ecology—a viewpoint," *International Journal of Environmental Studies*, 54, no. 3–4 (1998): 251.
46. Laura Courchesne, Julia Ilhardt, and Jacob N. Shapiro, "Review of Social Science Research on the Impact of Countermeasures against Influence Operations," *Harvard Kennedy School Misinformation Review*, 13 September 2021, https://doi.org/10.37016/mr-2020-79.

47. Kubin and Sikorski, "The role of (social) media"; Arora, Singh, Chakraborty, and Maity, "Polarization and social media"; Tucker, Guess, Barberá et al., "Social media, political polarization, and political disinformation."
48. Sigal Samuel, "Lots of Bad Science Still Gets Published. Here's How We Can Change That," *Vox*, 6 December 2022, https://www.vox.com/future-perfect/23489211/replication-crisis-project-meta-science-psychology; Monya Baker, "Over Half of Psychology Studies Fail Reproducibility Test," *Nature*, 27 August 2015, https://doi.org/10.1038/nature.2015.18248; Youyou Wu, Yang Yang, and Brian Uzzi, "A Discipline-Wide Investigation of the Replicability of Psychology Papers over the Past Two Decades," *Proceedings of the National Academy of Sciences* 120, no. 6 (30 January 2023): e2208863120, https://doi.org/10.1073/pnas.2208863120.
49. Colin F. Camerer et al., "Evaluating the Replicability of Social Science Experiments in Nature and Science between 2010 and 2015," *Nature Human Behaviour* 2, no. 9 (September 2018): 637–44, https://doi.org/10.1038/s41562-018-0399-z.
50. Johannes Breuer and Mario Haim, eds., *Reproducibility and Replicability in Communication Research*, vol. 12, Media and Communication (Cogitatio, 2024), https://doi.org/10.17645/mac.i429.
51. Tom E. Hardwicke et al., "An Empirical Assessment of Transparency and Reproducibility-Related Research Practices in the Social Sciences (2014–2017)," *Royal Society Open Science* 7, no. 2 (19 February 2020): 190806, https://doi.org/10.1098/rsos.190806.
52. Will Douglas Heaven, "AI Is Wrestling with a Replication Crisis," *MIT Technology Review*, 12 November 2020, https://www.technologyreview.com/2020/11/12/1011944/artificial-intelligence-replication-crisis-science-big-tech-google-deepmind-facebook-openai/.
53. Naomi Orestes and Erik M. Conway, *Merchants of Doubt* (Bloomsbury Press, 2010).
54. Robert Zubrin, "The Truth About DDT and Silent Spring," *The New Atlantis* (blog), 27 September 2012, https://www.thenewatlantis.com/publications/the-truth-about-ddt-and-silent-spring; Deepak Lai, "Bring Back DDT," *CATO Institute* (blog), 26 April 2016, https://www.cato.org/commentary/bring-back-ddt.
55. Kamya Yadav et al., "What Makes an Influence Operation Malign?" (Carnegie Endowment for International Peace, 2023), https://carnegieendowment.org/research/2023/08/what-makes-an-influence-operation-malign?lang=en.
56. Oliver Milman, "Climate Scientists Face Harassment, Threats and Fears of 'McCarthyist Attacks,'" *The Guardian*, 22 February 2017, https://www.

theguardian.com/environment/2017/feb/22/climate-change-science-attacks-threats-trump; Evan Bush, "Almost 2 in 5 Covid-19 Researchers Have Faced Harassment, Survey Finds," *NBC News*, 24 March 2022, https://www.nbcnews.com/science/science-news/almost-2-5-covid-19-researchers-faced-harassment-rcna21060; Nick Robins-Early, "'A Deranged Ploy': How Republicans Are Fueling the Disinformation Wars," *The Guardian*, 10 July 2023, https://www.theguardian.com/world/2023/jul/10/republicans-fuel-the-disinformation-wars.
57. "About Causal Assessment," United States Environmental Protection Agency, https://www.epa.gov/caddis/about-causal-assessment.

2. FOR YOUR INFORMATION

1. Fred I. Dretske, *Knowledge and the Flow of Information* (The MIT Press, 1983), Kindle, Loc. 42.
2. Dirk Bouwmeester and Anton Zeilinger, "The Physics of Quantum Information: Basic Concepts," in *The Physics of Quantum Information* (Springer, 2000), 1–14, https://doi.org/10.1007/978-3-662-04209-0_1; Jan Van Leeuwen, *Handbook of Theoretical Computer Science*, vol. 1 (Elsevier, 1990), https://mitpress.mit.edu/9780262720144/handbook-of-theoretical-computer-science/; Yehoshua Bar-Hillel and Rudolf Carnap, "Semantic Information," *The British Journal for the Philosophy of Science* 4, no. 14 (1953): 147–57; Anthony G. Oettinger, "Information Resources: Knowledge and Power in the 21st Century," *Science* 209, no. 4452 (4 July 1980): 193, https://doi.org/10.1126/science.7280661.
3. Timothy Hutchin and Gino Cortopassi, "A Mitochondrial DNA Clone Is Associated with Increased Risk for Alzheimer Disease," *Proceedings of the National Academy of Sciences of the United States of America* 92, no. 15 (18 July 1995): 6892–95; Martin Frické, "Information Using Likeness Measures," *Journal of the American Society for Information Science* 48, no. 10 (1997): 882, https://doi.org/10.1002/(SICI)1097-4571(199710)48:10<882::AID-ASI4>3.0.CO;2-Y; James Gleick, *The Information: A History, A Theory, A Flood*, Kindle (Random House, 2012), 147.
4. Benjamin Schumacher, *The Science of Information*, Lecture 1, Audible (The Great Courses, 2018), https://www.audible.ca/pd/The-Science-of-Information-From-Language-to-Black-Holes-Audiobook/B07K8XTV5K.
5. Walter Bryce Gallie, "Essentially Contested Concepts," *Proceedings of the Aristotelian Society* 56 (1955): 167–98.
6. Andrea Scarantino and Gualtiero Piccinini, "Information without Truth," *Metaphilosophy* 41 (April 1, 2010): 314, https://doi.org/10.1111/j.1467-9973.2010.01632.x; Michael Buckland, *Information and Society*, Kindle

(The MIT Press, 2017), 51; Luciano Floridi, "Philosophical Conceptions of Information," in *Formal Theories of Information: From Shannon to Semantic Information Theory and General Concepts of Information*, ed. Giovanni Sommaruga, Kindle (Springer, 2009), 15, https://doi.org/10.1007/978-3-642-00659-31.
7. Davenport, *Information Ecology: Mastering the Information and Knowledge Environment*, 8–9.
8. Alex Wright, *Glut: Mastering Information Through the Ages* (Cornell University Press, 2007), 10.
9. Matthew Cobb, *The Idea of the Brain: The Past and Future of Neuroscience* (Basic Books, 2020).
10. Wright, *Glut: Mastering Information Through the Ages*, 30.
11. John Maynard Smith, "The Concept of Information in Biology," *Philosophy of Science* 67, no. 2 (2000): 177.
12. Dretske, *Knowledge and the Flow of Information*; H. Paul Grice, *Studies in the Ways of Words* (Harvard University Press, 1989); Floridi, "Philosophical Conceptions of Information"; Frické, "Information Using Likeness Measures."
13. Don Fallis, "Floridi on Disinformation," *Etica an d Politica / Ethics and Politics* XIII, no. 2 (2011): 201–14; James H. Fetzer, "Information: Does It Have To Be True?," *Minds and Machines* 14, no. 2 (1 May 2004): 223–9, https://doi.org/10.1023/B:MIND.0000021682.61365.56; Christopher John Fox, *Information and Misinformation: An Investigation of the Notions of Information, Misinformation, Informing, and Misinforming* (Greenwood Publishing Group, 1983); Scarantino and Piccinini, "Information without Truth."
14. Friedrich Nietzsche, *The Philosophy of Nietzsche*, ed. Geoffrey Clive, trans. Oscar Levy (Mentor Books, 1965), 508.
15. Marlene Habib, "Sam Panopoulos, Canadian Inventor of Hawaiian Pizza, Dies at 82," *CBC News*, 10 June 2017, https://www.cbc.ca/news/hawaiian-pizza-sam-panopoulos-1.4155044.
16. Jürgen Habermas, *Philosophical Introductions*, Kindle (Polity, 2018), 96, 102.
17. Jesse Bering, *The Belief Instinct* (W.W. Norton & Company, 2012), 11.
18. Elizabeth L. Eisenstein, *The Printing Revolution in Early Modern Europe* (Cambridge University Press, 2005), 22.
19. Richard Dawkins, *The Selfish Gene* (Granada Publishing, 1979), 3.
20. Buckland, *Information and Society*, 79.
21. Cailin O'Connor and James Owen, *The Misinformation Age: How False Beliefs Spread* (Yale University Press, 2019), Kindle, Loc. 148.
22. Buckland, *Information and Society*, 12.
23. Walter Lippman, *Public Opinion* (Simon & Schuster, 1997), 9.

24. Philip M. Taylor, *Munitions of the Mind* (Manchester University Press, 1990), 6–7; Kevin Moloney, *Rethinking Public Relations: PR Propaganda and Democracy* (Routledge, 2006); W.C. Garrison, *Information Operations and Counter-Propaganda: Making a Weapon of Public Affairs* (Army War College Carlisle Barracks, 1999); Anna Elżbieta Fotyga, "Report on EU Strategic Communication to Counter Propaganda against It by Third Parties" (Brussels: European Parliament Committee on Foreign Affairs, 2016), https://www.europarl.europa.eu/doceo/document/A-8-2016-0290_EN.html.
25. Daniel Funke and Daniela Flamini, "A Guide to Anti-Misinformation Actions around the World," *Poynter* (blog), https://www.poynter.org/ifcn/anti-misinformation-actions/.
26. Plato, "Phaedrus," in *The Dialogues of Plato Vol. 1*, trans. Benjamin Jowett (MIT Classics, 1892), http://classics.mit.edu/Plato/phaedrus.html, 453.
27. Floyd J. Brock and Gurpreet S. Dhillon, "Managerial Information, the Basics," *Journal of International Information Management* 10, no. 2 (2001): 46, https://scholarworks.lib.csusb.edu/cgi/viewcontent.cgi?article=1237&context=jiim.
28. Nichola Carr, *The Shallows: How the Internet Is Changing the Way We Think, Read and Remember* (W.W. Norton, 2010), 209.
29. Claude Shannon, "The Lattice Theory of Information," *Transactions of the IRE Professional Group on Information Theory* 1, no. 1 (1953): 105–7.
30. Andrei Nikolaevich Kolmogorov, *Theory of Information Transfer* (Publishing House of the USSR Academy of Sciences, 1956).
31. Smith, "The Concept of Information in Biology," 179.
32. Schumacher, *The Science of Information*, Lecture 1.
33. Oettinger, "Information Resources," 194.
34. Brooke Gladstone, *The Influencing Machine* (Norton, 2011), 116.
35. Andy Wood, *Riot, Rebellion and Popular Politics in Early Modern England* (Palgrave, 2022).
36. Ali Swenson and Kelvin Chan, "Election disinformation takes a big leap with AI being used to deceive worldwide," *AP News*, 14 March 2024, https://apnews.com/article/artificial-intelligence-elections-disinformation-chatgpt-bc283e7426402f0b4baa7df280a4c3fd.
37. Eric Berlow, "Simplifying Complexity," TED Global 2010, video, 1:21, https://www.ted.com/talks/eric_berlow_simplifying_complexity.

3. THE INFORMATION ENVIRONMENT

1. Miguel Civil, "Sumerian Riddles: A Corpus," *Aula Orientalis: Revista de Estudios Del Próximo Oriente Antiguo* 5, no. 1 (1987): 17.

2. David M. Buss, *Evolutionary Psychology: The New Science of the Mind* (Routledge, 2019).
3. Vivek V. Venkataraman, "The Origins of Human Society Are More Complex than We Thought," *The Conversation*, 2 November 2022, http://theconversation.com/the-origins-of-human-society-are-more-complex-than-we-thought-179137.
4. "Rock Art of the Mediterranean Basin on the Iberian Peninsula," UNESCO World Heritage Centre, 2 December 1998, https://whc.unesco.org/en/list/874/.
5. Jo Marchant, "A Journey to the Oldest Cave Paintings in the World," *Smithsonian Magazine*, January 2016, https://www.smithsonianmag.com/history/journey-oldest-cave-paintings-world-180957685/.
6. Michael Tomasello, *Origins of Human Communication*, Kindle (The MIT Press, 2008), Kindle, Loc. 153.
7. Alexander Stille, "The World's Oldest Papyrus and What It Can Tell Us About the Great Pyramids," *Smithsonian Magazine*, October 2015, https://www.smithsonianmag.com/history/ancient-egypt-shipping-mining-farming-economy-pyramids-180956619/.
8. Thucydides, *The History of the Peloponnesian War*, trans. Richard Crawley (Amazon, 2012), 3; Paul Roche, "Introduction," in *Euripides: Ten Plays*, trans. Paul Roche (First Signet Classics, 1998), ix–xii, ix; Lisa Kallet, "The Athenian Economy," in *The Cambridge Companion to the Age of Pericles*, ed. Loren J. Samons II (Cambridge University Press, 2007), 96; Loren J. Samons II, "Introduction: Athenian History and Society in the Age of Pericles," in *The Cambridge Companion to the Age of Pericles*, ed. Loren J. Samons II, Cambridge Companions to the Ancient World (Cambridge University Press, 2007), 2, https://doi.org/10.1017/CCOL9780521807937.001; Deborah Boedeker, "Athenian Religion in The Age of Pericles," in *The Cambridge Companion to the Age of Pericles*, ed. Loren J. Samons II (Cambridge University Press, 2007), 53; Geoffrey E.M. de Ste. Croix, *The Origins of the Peloponnesian War* (Cornell University Press, 1972), 74.
9. Edward Hyde, Earl of Clarendon, *The History of the Rebellion: A New Selection*, ed. Paul Seaward, Oxford World Classics (Oxford University Press, 2009).
10. Alicia Wanless and Michael Berk, "The Audience Is the Amplifier: Participatory Propaganda," in *The SAGE Handbook of Propaganda*, ed. Paul Baines, Nicholas O'Shaughnessy, and Nancy Snow (SAGE, 2019), 85–104; Alicia Wanless and Michael Berk, "Participatory Propaganda: The Engagement of Audiences in the Spread of Persuasive Communications," in *Social Media and Social Order*, ed. David Herbert

and Stefan Fisher-Høyrem (De Gruyter Open Poland, 2022), 111–37, https://doi.org/10.2478/9788366675612-009.
11. "10 Facts about Cane Toads," World Wildlife Foundation, 22 September 2019, https://wwf.org.au/blogs/10-facts-about-cane-toads/.
12. "Introduction of Cane Toads," National Museum of Australia, https://www.nma.gov.au/defining-moments/resources/introduction-of-cane-toads.
13. "Children Should Hunt and Kill Cane Toads: Bob Katter," *Sky News*, 11 January 2019, https://www.skynews.com.au/australia-news/politics/bob-katter-encourages-children-to-kill-cane-toads-with-40c-bounty/video/1ac37965cc3714a76944d769f3797041.
14. "The Online Information Environment: Understanding How the Internet Shapes People's Engagement with Scientific Information" (The Royal Society, January 2022), https://royalsociety.org/-/media/policy/projects/online-information-environment/the-online-information-environment.pdf?la=en-GB&hash=691F34A269075C0001A0E647C503DB8F.
15. Jonah Berger, *Contagious: Why Things Catch On* (Simon & Schuster, 2016).
16. McLuhan and Lapham, *Understanding Media: The Extensions of Man*; Ong, *Orality and Literacy: The Technologizing of the World*; Robert K. Logan, *The Sixth Language: Learning a Living in the Internet Age* (Stoddart, 2000); Asa Briggs and Peter Burke, *A Social History of the Media: From Gutenberg to the Internet*, Kindle (Polity, 2010).
17. *Ancient Writing and the History of the Alphabet*, Audible, The Great Courses (06:18:00, 2023), https://www.audible.ca/pd/Ancient-Writing-and-the-History-of-the-Alphabet-Audiobook/B0C4ZN9QNV.
18. David Hockney and Martin Gayford, *A History of Pictures: From the Cave to the Computer Screen* (Abrams, 2020), 11.
19. Dover, *The Information Revolution in Early Modern Europe*, 2.
20. Gleick, *The Information: A History, A Theory, A Flood*.
21. McLuhan and Lapham, *Understanding Media: The Extensions of Man*, 24, 64.
22. Simon Hornblower, *The Greek World 479-323 BC*, Fourth Edition (Routledge, 2011), 141.
23. David Hochfelder, "The Communications Revolution and Popular Culture," in *A Companion to 19th Century America*, ed. William L. Barney (Blackwell Publishers, 2001), 306.
24. Victor Davis Hanson, *A War Like No Other* (Random House Trade Paperbacks, 2005); Hornblower, *The Greek World 479–323 BC*, 132.
25. Mark Atwood Lawrence, *The Vietnam War: A Concise International History* (Oxford University Press, 2008); Christopher Goscha, *The Penguin History of Modern Vietnam* (Penguin Books, 2017), 222.

26. Manuel C. Molles Jr. and Anna A. Sher, *Ecology: Concepts & Applications*, 8th ed. (McGraw-Hill Education, 2019).
27. Charles Darwin, *The Five Essential Works* (Titan Read, 2015), 1149.
28. Rafe Sagarin, *Learning from the Octopus: How Secrets from Nature Can Help Us Fight Terrorist Attacks, Natural Disasters, and Disease* (Basic Books, 2012), xxiii, 33.
29. Lawrence B. Slobodkin, "The Strategy of Evolution," *American Scientist* 52, no. 3 (September 1964): 349–50.
30. Sagarin, *Learning from the Octopus*, 120–3.
31. Peter Paret, "The Genesis of On War," in *On War*, ed. Michael Howard and Peter Paret (Princeton University Press, 1976), 9.
32. Charles S. Elton, *Animal Ecology*, Kindle (Macmillan, 1927), 325.
33. Robert H. Whittaker, *Communities and Ecosystems* (The Macmillan Company, 1970), 16–17.

4. PULLING THREADS TOGETHER: ANCIENT GREECE

1. Harl, *The Peloponnesian War*.
2. Hermann Hesse, *Demian: The Story of Emil Sinclair's Youth*, 1919.
3. William George Grieve Forrest, *A History of Sparta, 950–192 B.C.* (W.W. Norton & Company, 1968).
4. Antony Andrewes, "The Government of Classical Sparta," in *Sparta*, ed. Michael Whitby (Edinburgh University Press, 2002), 50.
5. Michael Whitby, "Introduction," ed. Michael Whitby (Edinburgh, UK: Edinburgh University Press, 2002), 1–20; Paul Cartledge, "The Origins and Organisation of the Peloponnesian League," in *Sparta*, ed. Michael Whitby (Edinburgh University Press, 2002), 224.
6. Thucydides, *The History of the Peloponnesian War*, 5.
7. Hanson, *A War Like No Other*, 6; Harl, *The Peloponnesian War*, 23.
8. Stephen Hodkinson, "Social Order and the Conflict of Values in Classical Sparta," in *Sparta*, ed. Michael Whitby (Edinburgh University Press, 2002), 105; Powell, "Dining Groups, Marriage, Homosexuality," 10; Donald Kagan, *The Peloponnesian War* (Harper Perennial, 2003), 4.
9. J. E. Lendon, "Athens and Sparta and the Coming of the Peloponnesian War," in *The Cambridge Companion to the Age of Pericles*, ed. Loren J. Samons II, Cambridge Companions to the Ancient World (Cambridge University Press, 2007), 258, https://doi.org/10.1017/CCOL9780521807937.012; Harl, *The Peloponnesian War*, 17.
10. Aristophanes, "Lysistrata," in *Aristophanes: The Complete Plays*, trans. Paul Roche, Kindle (New American Library, 2005), 423.
11. Paul Cartledge, "Spartan Wives: Liberation or License?," in *Sparta*, ed.

12. Michael Whitby (Edinburgh University Press, 2002), 141, 143; John Lewis Gaddis, *On Grand Strategy* (Penguin Books, 2019), 31.
12. Thucydides, *The History of the Peloponnesian War*, 3.
13. Kagan, *The Peloponnesian War*, 3; Hornblower, *The Greek World 479–323 BC*, 121.
14. Hornblower, *The Greek World 479–323 BC*, 121.
15. Cartledge, "The Origins and Organisation of the Peloponnesian League," 224; de Ste. Croix, *The Origins of the Peloponnesian War*, 108.
16. Geoffrey E. M. de Ste. Croix, "Sparta's 'Foreign Policy,'" in *Sparta*, ed. Michael Whitby (Edinburgh University Press, 2002), 218.
17. Kagan, *The Peloponnesian War*, 4.
18. Robert Parker, "Religion in Public Life," in *Sparta*, ed. Michael Whitby (Edinburgh University Press, 2002), 170.
19. Harl, *The Peloponnesian War*.
20. Rein Taagepera, "Size and Duration of Empires: Growth-Decline Curves, 600 B.C. to 600 A.D.," *Social Science History* 3, no. 3/4 (1979): 115–38, https://doi.org/10.2307/1170959.
21. Tom Holland, *Persian Fire: The First World Empire and the Battle for the West* (Anchor Books, 2005).
22. Thucydides, *The History of the Peloponnesian War*, 24.
23. Simon Hornblower, *Thucydidean Themes* (Oxford University Press, 2011).
24. Hornblower, *The Greek World 479–323 BC*, 163; Kagan, *The Peloponnesian War*, 8; Boedeker, "Athenian Religion in The Age of Pericles," 47.
25. Chris Carey, "In Search of Drakon," *The Cambridge Classical Journal* 59 (2013): 29–51.
26. Vincent J. Rosivach, "The Tyrant in Athenian Democracy," *Quaderni Urbinati Di Cultura Classica* 30, no. 3 (1988): 43–57, https://doi.org/10.2307/20546964.
27. Samons II, "Introduction," 14.
28. Kagan, *The Peloponnesian War*, 8; Samons II, "Introduction," 15.
29. Kallet, "The Athenian Economy," 79.
30. Jeremy McInerney, *The Age of Pericles: Course Guidebook* (The Great Courses, 2004), 34; Hornblower, *The Greek World 479–323 BC*, 132.
31. Aristophanes, *Aristophanes: The Complete Plays*, trans. Paul Roche (New American Library, 2005), 33.
32. Paul Roche, "Introductory Note to Knights," in *Aristophanes: The Complete Plays*, trans. Paul Roche, Kindle (New American Library, 2005), 64.
33. Hanson, *A War Like No Other*, 6; Hornblower, *The Greek World 479–323 BC*, 132.

34. de Ste. Croix, *The Origins of the Peloponnesian War*, 176; Gaddis, *On Grand Strategy*, 36.
35. Kurt A. Raaflaub, "Warfare in Athenian Society," in *The Cambridge Companion to the Age of Pericles*, ed. Loren J. Samons II, Cambridge Companions to the Ancient World (Cambridge University Press, 2007), 111, https://doi.org/10.1017/CCOL9780521807937.005.
36. Samons II, "Introduction," 15; Kallet, "The Athenian Economy," 129.
37. Thucydides, *The History of the Peloponnesian War*, 3; Roche, "Introduction," ix–xii, ix; Kallet, "The Athenian Economy," 96; Samons II, "Introduction," 2; Boedeker, "Athenian Religion in The Age of Pericles," 53; de Ste. Croix, *The Origins of the Peloponnesian War*, 74.
38. Hanson, *A War Like No Other*, 13.
39. de Ste. Croix, "Sparta's 'Foreign Policy'", 221.
40. Dabney Park Jr., "History's Catch-22: The Peloponnesian War," *The History Teacher* 5, no. 4 (May 1972): 25, https://doi.org/10.2307/491318.
41. Lendon, "Athens and Sparta and the Coming of the Peloponnesian War," 261.
42. Kagan, *The Peloponnesian War*, 57.
43. Thucydides, *The History of the Peloponnesian War*, 18.
44. Thucydides, *The History of the Peloponnesian War*, 19; de Ste. Croix, *The Origins of the Peloponnesian War, 179–80*; Kagan, *The Peloponnesian War*, 14.
45. Park Jr., "History's Catch-22," 25; Thucydides, *The History of the Peloponnesian War*, 17; de Ste. Croix, *The Origins of the Peloponnesian War*, 203; Kagan, *The Peloponnesian War*, 28–9.
46. de Ste. Croix, *The Origins of the Peloponnesian War*, 111.
47. Cartledge, "The Origins and Organisation of the Peloponnesian League," 224.
48. de Ste. Croix, "Sparta's 'Foreign Policy,'" 220.
49. Kagan, *The Peloponnesian War*, 46.
50. *Thucydides, The History of the Peloponnesian War*, 16.
51. *Thucydides, The History of the Peloponnesian War*, 17.
52. *Thucydides, The History of the Peloponnesian War*, 16–17.
53. *Thucydides, The History of the Peloponnesian War*, 16–17.
54. *Thucydides, The History of the Peloponnesian War*, 48.
55. Aristophanes, "Archarnians," in *Aristophanes: The Complete Plays*, trans. Paul Roche (New American Library, 2005), 29.
56. Hanson, *A War Like No Other*, 19.
57. Plato, "Phaedrus."
58. Charles Mathewes, *Why Evil Exists, Lecture 4: Greek Philosophy—Human Evil and Malice*, Audible (The Great Courses, 2013), https://www.audible.ca/pd/Why-Evil-Exists-Audiobook/B0711PKTTP.

5. TYRANNICAL TIES: CHARLES VERSUS THE GODLY

1. Neil Johnston, "The Trial of Charles I," text, *The National Archives Blog* (blog) (The National Archives, 30 January 2019), https://blog.nationalarchives.gov.uk/trial-charles-i/.
2. "Settlers: Genetics, Geography and the Peopling of Britain," Oxford University Museum of Natural History and University of Oxford, https://oumnh.ox.ac.uk/settlers.
3. Hugh M. Thomas, *The English and the Normans* (Oxford University Press, 2003).
4. John H. Fisher, "Chancery and the Emergence of Standard Written English in the Fifteenth Century," *Speculum* 52, no. 4 (October 1977): 870–99, https://doi.org/10.2307/2855378.
5. Stephen Broadberry et al., *British Economic Growth, 1270–1870* (Cambridge University Press, 2015), http://www.cambridge.org/gb/academic/subjects/history/economic-history/british-economic-growth-12701870?format=PB.
6. Eleanor Russell and Martin Parker, "How the Black Death Made the Rich Richer," *BBC*, 1 July 2020, https://www.bbc.com/worklife/article/20200701-how-the-black-death-make-the-rich-richer; Adrian R. Bell, Andrew Prescott, and Helen Lacey, "What Can the Black Death Tell Us about the Global Economic Consequences of a Pandemic?," The Conversation, 3 March 2020, http://theconversation.com/what-can-the-black-death-tell-us-about-the-global-economic-consequences-of-a-pandemic-132793.
7. Simon Horobin and Jeremy Smith, *An Introduction to Middle English* (Edinburgh University Press, 2002).
8. William Caxton, *Caxton's Eneydos*, ed. M.T. Culley and F. J. Furnivall (Kegan Paul, Trench, Trübner & Co., 1890).
9. Laura Wright, "About the Evolution of Standard English," in *Studies of English Language*, ed. M. J. Toswell and E. M. Tyler (Routledge, 1996), 99–115.
10. Briggs and Burke, *A Social History of the Media: From Gutenberg to the Internet*, 13.
11. Jared Diamond, *Guns, Germs, and Steel: The Fate of Human Societies* (Norton, 1999); Briggs and Burke, *A Social History of the Media: From Gutenberg to the Internet*, 14.
12. "First Printed Book in English Sold for over £1m," *BBC News*, 17 July 2014, https://www.bbc.com/news/entertainment-arts-28344300.
13. Diamond, *Guns, Germs, and Steel: The Fate of Human Societies*; Briggs and Burke, *A Social History of the Media: From Gutenberg to the Internet*, 14.

14. Joseph Needham and Tsien Tsuen-Hsuin, *Science and Civilisation in China* (Cambridge University Press, 1985).
15. Dover, *The Information Revolution in Early Modern Europe*, 20.
16. Diarmaid MacCulloch, *Reformation: Europe's House Divided, 1490–1700* (Penguin, 2004), Kindle, Loc. 2388.
17. Dover, *The Information Revolution in Early Modern Europe*, 141.
18. MacCulloch, *Reformation*, Loc. 2388.
19. Raymond, P*amphlets and Pamphleteering in Early Modern Britain*, 124.
20. Dover, *The Information Revolution in Early Modern Europe*, 167–8.
21. Raymond, *Pamphlets and Pamphleteering in Early Modern Britain*, 72.
22. Richard Leslie Hills, *Papermaking in Britain 1488–1988: A Short History* (Bloomsbury, 2015), 5.
23. Raymond, *Pamphlets and Pamphleteering in Early Modern Britai*n, 55–6.
24. "The Age of Early Printing: 1450–1550," *Encyclopedia Britannica*, https://www.britannica.com/topic/publishing/The-age-of-early-printing-1450-1550.
25. MacCulloch, *Reformation*, Loc. 5689.
26. Raymond, *Pamphlets and Pamphleteering in Early Modern Britain*, 68.
27. Raymond, *Pamphlets and Pamphleteering in Early Modern Britain*, 80.
28. MacCulloch, *Reformation*, Loc. 1101.
29. MacCulloch, *Reformation*, Loc. 5490.
30. MacCulloch, *Reformation*, Loc. 614, 624.
31. Martin Brecht, *Martin Luther: His Road to Reformation 1483–1521, Volume 1*, trans. James L. Schaaf (Fortress Press, 1981), 201–5.
32. MacCulloch, *Reformation*, Loc. 349, 3903.
33. Christopher Haigh, *English Reformations: Religion, Politics, and Society Under the Tudors* (Clarendon Press, 1993).
34. Haigh, *English Reformations: Religion, Politics, and Society Under the Tudors*, 58.
35. Elizabeth Vandiver, Ralph Keen, and Thomas D. Frazel, "Introduction," in *Luther's Lives: Two Contemporary Accounts of Martin Luther* (Manchester University Press, 2003), 2.
36. David Daniell, *William Tyndale: A Biography*, New edition (Yale University Press, 2001).
37. MacCulloch, *Reformation*, Loc. 4555; Broadberry et al., *British Economic Growth, 1270–1870*.
38. MacCulloch, *Reformation*, Loc. 4567.
39. MacCulloch, *Reformation*, Loc. 4475, 6261.
40. Diane Purkiss, *The English Civil War: A People's History* (HarperPress, 2012), Kindle, Loc. 1737.

41. John Morrill, "The English Revolution as a Civil War," *Historical Research* 90, no. 250 (November 2017): 729, https://doi.org/10.1111/1468-2281.12200.
42. MacCulloch, *Reformation*, Loc. 6462.
43. "Witchcraft and Demonology In: Scotland," University of Glasgow Archives & Special Collections, https://www.gla.ac.uk/myglasgow/archivespecialcollections/digitisedcollections/damnedart/scotland/; King of England James I, *Daemonologie in Forme of a Dialogue, Diuided into Three Bookes*, 1597, https://name.umdl.umich.edu/A04243.0001.001.
44. Caroline M. Hibbard, *Charles I and the Popish Plot*, Kindle (University of North Carolina Press, 1983), 665.
45. Christopher Hill, *Puritanism and Revolution* (Vintage Books, 2011), 499.
46. Raymond, *Pamphlets and Pamphleteering in Early Modern Britain*, 218–20.
47. Katherine Schaap Williams, "Form, Deformity, and Frankenstein's Predecessors," Electra Street, November 2014, https://electrastreet.net/2014/11/form-deformity-and-frankensteins-predecessors/.
48. Ethan Howard Shagan, "Constructing Discord: Ideology, Propaganda, and English Responses to the Irish Rebellion of 1641," *Journal of British Studies* 36, no. 1 (1997): 8–9.
49. Raymond, *Pamphlets and Pamphleteering in Early Modern Britain*, 214.
50. Morrill, "The English Revolution as a Civil War," 726.
51. Leonard Hochberg, "The English Civil War in Geographical Perspective," *The Journal of Interdisciplinary History* 14, no. 4 (1984): 739–40, https://doi.org/10.2307/203463.
52. Adam Fox, "Rumours, News and Popular Political Opinion in Elizabethan and Early Stewart England," *The Historical Journal* 40, no. 3 (September 1997): 603, https://doi.org/10.1017/S0018246X97007346.
53. Raymond, *Pamphlets and Pamphleteering in Early Modern Britain*, 163.
54. William Craig, "Hampton Court Again: The Millenary Petition and the Calling of the Conference," *Anglican and Episcopal History* 77, no. 1 (2008): 46–70.
55. Naomi Tadmor, *The Social Universe of the English Bible: Scripture, Society, and Culture in Early Modern England* (Cambridge University Press, 2010); Jon Nielson and Royal Skousen, "How Much of the King James Bible Is William Tyndale's?: An Estimation Based on Sampling," *Reformation* 3, no. 1 (1 January 1998): 49–74, https://doi.org/10.1179/ref_1998_3_1_004.
56. Lawrence Stone, "The Educational Revolution in England, 1560–1640," *Past & Present* 28, no. 1 (1 July 1964): 43, https://doi.org/10.1093/past/28.1.41.
57. Stone, "The Educational Revolution in England, 1560–1640," 42.

58. Blair Worden, *The English Civil Wars: 1640–1660* (Orion, 2009); Purkiss, *The English Civil War*, 2354; Raymond, *Pamphlets and Pamphleteering in Early Modern Britain*, 58, 91.
59. Stone, "The Educational Revolution in England, 1560–1640," 43.
60. Stone, "The Educational Revolution in England, 1560–1640".
61. Stone, "The Educational Revolution in England, 1560–1640," 78–9.
62. Stone, "The Educational Revolution in England, 1560–1640," 79.
63. Hibbard, *Charles I and the Popish Plot*, 665, 679.
64. Hochberg, "The English Civil War in Geographical Perspective," 748; Hill, *Puritanism and Revolution*, 3323.
65. Hill, *Puritanism & Revolution*, 4653.
66. Hill, *Puritanism & Revolution*, 4735.
67. William W. MacDonald, "John Pym: Parliamentarian," *Historical Magazine of the Protestant Episcopal Church* 38, no. 1 (March 1969): 44; Hibbard, *Charles I and the Popish Plot*, 665; Henning Hillmann, "Mediation in Multiple Networks: Elite Mobilization before the English Civil War," *American Sociological Review* 73, no. 3 (June 2008): 437; Oliver Thomson, *Zealots: How a Group of Scottish Conspirators Unleashed Half a Century of War in Britain* (Amberley Publishing, 2018), 98.
68. Purkiss, *The English Civil War*, 255, 259, 343; Peter Gaunt, *The English Civil War: A Military History*, Kindle (Osprey Publishing, 2014), 228.
69. Thomas Cogswell, "The Politics of Propaganda: Charles I and the People in the 1620s," *Journal of British Studies* 29, no. 3 (1990): 194.
70. Purkiss, *The English Civil War*, 412.
71. Kevin Sharpe, "Crown, Parliament and Locality: Government and Communication in Early Stuart England," *The English Historical Review* 101, no. 399 (April 1986): 324.
72. Sharpe, "Crown, Parliament and Locality: Government and Communication in Early Stuart England," 326.
73. Sharpe, "Crown, Parliament and Locality: Government and Communication in Early Stuart England," 337.
74. Sharpe, "Crown, Parliament and Locality: Government and Communication in Early Stuart England," 330–1.
75. Purkiss, *The English Civil War*, 2193; Sharpe, "Crown, Parliament and Locality: Government and Communication in Early Stuart England," 336.
76. Sharpe, "Crown, Parliament and Locality: Government and Communication in Early Stuart England," 341.
77. Purkiss, *The English Civil War*, 2086.
78. Hyde, *The History of the Rebellion: A New Selection*, 7.
79. Hyde, *The History of the Rebellion: A New Selection*, 9.

80. Michael Lynn, "Scarcity Effects on Value: A Quantitative Review of the Commodity Theory Literature," *Psychology & Marketing* 8, no. 1 (1991): 43–57, https://doi.org/10.1002/mar.4220080105.
81. Purkiss, *The English Civil War*, 2354
82. Purkiss, *The English Civil War*, 534; Charles W. A. Prior, "Religion, Political Thought and the English Civil War," *History Compass* 11, no. 1 (2013): 25–6, https://doi.org/10.1111/hic3.12025.
83. MacCulloch, *Reformation*, Loc. 10836.
84. Hyde, *The History of the Rebellion: A New Selection*, 20.
85. Raymond, *Pamphlets and Pamphleteering in Early Modern Britain*, 151.
86. Hyde, *The History of the Rebellion: A New Selection*, 3; Hibbard, *Charles I and the Popish Plot*.
87. Raymond, *Pamphlets and Pamphleteering in Early Modern Britain*, 67.
88. Morrill, "The English Revolution as a Civil War," 729.
89. Hibbard, *Charles I and the Popish Plot*, 63.
90. Cogswell, "The Politics of Propaganda," 195, 197–9.
91. Purkiss, *The English Civil War*, 428; Hyde, *The History of the Rebellion: A New Selection*, 6, 10.
92. Hibbard, *Charles I and the Popish Plot*, 404, 516.
93. Wood, Riot, *Rebellion and Popular Politics in Early Modern England*, 47.
94. Fox, "Rumours, News and Popular Political Opinion in Elizabethan and Early Stewart England"; Hibbard, *Charles I and the Popish Plot*, 492.
95. Raymond, *Pamphlets and Pamphleteering in Early Modern Britain*, 149.
96. Raymond, *Pamphlets and Pamphleteering in Early Modern Britain*, 168.
97. D. Alan Orr, "Sovereignty, Supremacy and the Origins of the English Civil War," *History* 87, no. 288 (October 2002): 490; Hill, *Puritanism and Revolution*, 776.
98. Prior, "Religion, Political Thought and the English Civil War," 25.
99. Hibbard, *Charles I and the Popish Plot*, 63, 4501; Hill, *Puritanism and Revolution*, 1301; Purkiss, *The English Civil War*, 1849; Shagan, "Constructing Discord," 23.
100. Purkiss, *The English Civil War*, 1645.
101. Purkiss, *The English Civil War*, 1668, 2034.
102. Hibbard, *Charles I and the Popish Plot*, 3612, 3679.
103. Hibbard, *Charles I and the Popish Plot*, 4771.
104. Hyde, *The History of the Rebellion: A New Selection*, 83.
105. Raymond, P*amphlets and Pamphleteering in Early Modern Britain*, 91.
106. Susan Brigden, "Youth and the English Reformation," *Past & Present* 95, no. 1 (1 May 1982): 43, https://doi.org/10.1093/past/95.1.37.
107. Fox, "Rumours, News and Popular Political Opinion in Elizabethan and Early Stewart England," 604.
108. Purkiss, *The English Civil War*, 2089.

109. Purkiss, *The English Civil War*, 2086.
110. Raymond, *Pamphlets and Pamphleteering in Early Modern Britain*, 165.
111. Gods Late Mercy to England in Discovering of Three Damnable Plots by the Treacherous Papists and Iesuits in England and Wales (ProQuest, 1641), https://www.proquest.com/eebo/docview/2240855426?sourcetype=Books; The Truest Relation of the Discoverie of a Damnable Plot in Scotland (ProQuest, 1641), https://www.proquest.com/eebo/docview/2240900965?sourcetype=Books; A Happy Deliverance, or, a Wonderfull Preservation of Foure Worthy and Honourable Peeres of This Kingdome, Early English Books Online 2 (University of Michigan Library Digital Collections, 1641), https://name.umdl.umich.edu/A87074.0001.001; Anonymous, A Bloody Plot, Practised by Some Papists in Darbyshire, Early English Books Online (John Thomas, 1641), https://www.proquest.com/eebo/docview/2248580183?sourcetype=Books; Anonymous, No Pamphlet, Bvt a Detestation against All Such Pamphlets as Are Printed, Concerning the Irish Rebellion, Early English Books Online (ProQuest, 1642), https://www.proquest.com/eebo/docview/2240884002/99859018?sourcetype=Books; The Iesuites Plot Discovered Intended against the Parliament and City of London Very Lately (ProQuest, 1642), https://www.proquest.com/docview/2248534516?sourcetype=Books.
112. Shagan, "Constructing Discord," 23.
113. Hibbard, *Charles I and the Popish Plot*.
114. Prior, "Religion, Political Thought and the English Civil War," 25–6; Shagan, "Constructing Discord," 7; Hibbard, *Charles I and the Popish Plot*, 3212.
115. Purkiss, *The English Civil War*, 1891; Shagan, "Constructing Discord", 27.
116. Shagan, "Constructing Discord", 29, 39, 31.
117. Purkiss, *The English Civil War*; Hibbard, *Charles I and the Popish Plot*, 3717.
118. Purkiss, *The English Civil War*, 2086.
119. Purkiss, *The English Civil War*, 2177.
120. Godfrey Davies, *The Oxford History of England: The Early Stuarts*, 1603–1660 (Oxford University Press, 1959).
121. Thomson, *Zealots*, 81.

6. A TALE OF TWO COUNTRIES: AMERICAN CIVIL WAR

1. Charles Dickens, "To W. C. Macready, 1 April 1842 (01 April 1842)," in *The British Academy/The Pilgrim Edition of the Letters of Charles Dickens*,

Vol. 3: 1842–1843, ed. Madeline House, Graham Storey, and Kathleen Mary Tillotson (Oxford University Press, 1974), 175–6.
2. Charles Dickens, *American Notes for General Circulation* (Chapman and Hall, 1850), https://www.loc.gov/item/01026779/, Kindle, 86–7.
3. David M. Potter, *The Impending Crisis: America Before the Civil War 1848–1861* (New York: Harper Perennial, 1976), 12.
4. James McPherson, *Battle Cry of Freedom* (Oxford University Press, 1988), 35.
5. Potter, *The Impending Crisis*, 8.
6. "Historical Statistics of the United States: Colonial Times to 1970, Part 1" (U.S. Bureau of the Census, 1975), https://www.census.gov/history/pdf/histstats-colonial-1970.pdf, 8.
7. Colin Woodard, *American Nations: A History of the Eleven Rival Regional Cultures of North America* (Penguin, 2011).
8. Dickens, *American Notes for General Circulation, Kindle*, 71.
9. Woodard, *American Nations*.
10. Donald R. Wright, "African Americans," in *A Companion to 19th Century America*, ed. William L. Barney (Blackwell Publishers, 2001), 195.
11. Martin Robison Delany, *The Condition, Elevation, Emigration, and Destiny of the Colored People of the United States* (Project Gutenberg, 1852), https://www.gutenberg.org/files/17154/17154-h/17154-h.htm.
12. Wright, "African Americans," 199.
13. "Historical Statistics of the United States," 14.
14. McPherson, *Battle Cry of Freedom,* 54, footnote 17.
15. Claudia Goldin, "A Brief History of Education in the United States," NBER Working Paper Series on Historical Factors in Long Run Growth (United States National Bureau of Economic Research, August 1999), https://www.nber.org/system/files/working_papers/h0119/h0119.pdf, 3.
16. McPherson, *Battle Cry of Freedom*, 19–20.
17. McPherson, *Battle Cry of Freedom*, 40.
18. McPherson, *Battle Cry of Freedom*, 19.
19. George Frederick Holmes, "Universities and Colleges," *Southern Literary Messenger*, no. 20 (1854): 609; John McCardell, *The Idea of a Southern Nation* (W.W. Norton & Company, 1979), 213–4; Bertram Wyatt-Brown, *Southern Honor: Ethics and Behavior in the Old South* (Oxford University Press, 1982), 92.
20. McPherson, *Battle Cry of Freedom*, 94.
21. David Hochfelder, "The Communications Revolution and Popular Culture," in *A Companion to 19th Century America*, ed. William L. Barney (Malden, Massachusetts: Blackwell Publishers, 2001), 306.
22. James Fenimore Cooper, *The American Democrat* (H&E Phinney, 1838), 160.

23. Dickens, *American Notes for General Circulation*, Kindle, 21.
24. "When Charles Dickens Fell out with America," *BBC*, 14 February 2012, https://www.bbc.com/news/magazine-17017791.
25. National Park Service, "Longfellow's Poems on Slavery," *Longfellow House Washington's Headquarters*, February 2, 2022, https://www.nps.gov/long/learn/historyculture/longfellows-poems-on-slavery.htm.
26. McPherson, *Battle Cry of Freedom 12*; Hochfelder, "The Communications Revolution and Popular Culture," 304.
27. William F Channing, "Lecture III: The American Fire-Alarm Telegraph," in *Annual Report of the Board of Regents by the Smithsonian Institution* (A. O. P. Nicholson, 1855), 148.
28. McPherson, *Battle Cry of Freedom*, 12.
29. McPherson, *Battle Cry of Freedom*, 12; Donald E Reynolds, *Editors Make War: Southern Newspapers in the Secession Crisis* (SIU Press, 2006), xiii.
30. McCardell, *The Idea of a Southern Nation*, 12.
31. McPherson, *Battle Cry of Freedom*, 13.
32. James L. Crouthamel, "The Newspaper Revolution in New York 1830–1860," *New York History* 45, no. 2 (April 1964): 103.
33. Reynolds, *Editors Make War*, 5.
34. Dickens, *American Notes for General Circulation*, Kindle, 243.
35. McCardell, *The Idea of a Southern Nation*, 154.
36. McCardell, *The Idea of a Southern Nation*, 159.
37. McPherson, *Battle Cry of Freedom*.
38. McCardell, *The Idea of a Southern Nation*; Potter, *The Impending Crisis*; James W. Loewen and Edward H. Sebesta, *Confederate and Neo-Confederate Reader: The "Great Truth" about the "Lost Cause"* (University Press of Mississippi, 2010).
39. Gaddis, *On Grand Strategy*; Hochfelder, "The Communications Revolution and Popular Culture," 2001.
40. Eric Foner, *Free Soil, Free Labor, Free Men: The Ideology of the Republican Party Before the Civil War* (Oxford University Press USA, 1995).
41. Dickens, *American Notes for General Circulation*, Kindle, 132.
42. Dickens, *American Notes for General Circulation*, Kindle, 132–5.
43. John Hope Franklin, *The Militant South 1800–1861* (University of Illinois Press, 1956), 22.
44. Frederick Douglass, *Narrative of the Life of Frederick Douglass: 1838* (Enhanced Media, 2011), 11.
45. Potter, *The Impending Crisis: America Before the Civil War 1848–1861*, 451; McPherson, Battle Cry of Freedom, 11.
46. McPherson, *Battle Cry of Freedom*, 91.
47. Franklin, *The Militant South 1800–1861*, 22.
48. Franklin, *The Militant South 1800–1861*, 23.

49. McPherson, *Battle Cry of Freedom*, 92; Michael T. Bernath, *Confederate Minds: The Struggle for Intellectual Independence in the Civil War South* (University of North Carolina Press, 2010), 94.
50. Dickens, *American Notes for General Circulation*, Kindle, 121.
51. McPherson, *Battle Cry of Freedom*; Louis P. Masur, *The Civil War: A Concise History* (Oxford University Press USA, 2011); Ashworth, *The Republic in Crisis, 1848–1861*; David Dzurec, "'To Destroy Popery and Everything Appertinent Thereto': William Chaney, the Jesuit John Bapst and the Know-Nothings in Mid-Nineteenth-Century Maine," *The Catholic Historical Review* 103, no. 1 (Winter 2017): 73–98.
52. Holly Jackson, *American Radicals: How Nineteenth-Century Counterculture Shaped the Nation* (Crown, 2019), Audible, Chapter 5: Coming Out from the World, 03:30:02–03:30:32.
53. McPherson, *Battle Cry of Freedom*, 8.
54. Wyatt-Brown, *Southern Honor*, 76.
55. Jackson, *American Radicals*; Ashworth, *The Republic in Crisis, 1848–1861*.
56. Elizabeth R Varon, *Disunion: The Coming of the American Civil War, 1789–1859* (The University of North Carolina Press, 2008).
57. Varon, *Disunion: The Coming of the American Civil War, 1789–1859*, 73.
58. Douglass, *Narrative of the Life of Frederick Douglass: 1838*, 75.
59. Ashworth, *The Republic in Crisis, 1848–1861*; Jackson, *American Radicals*.
60. Varon, *Disunion*; Reynolds, *Editors Make War*.
61. Jackson, *American Radicals*.
62. Ashworth, *The Republic in Crisis, 1848–1861*, 19.
63. McCardell, *The Idea of a Southern Nation*, 46–7.
64. McCardell, *The Idea of a Southern Nation*, 44.
65. McCardell, *The Idea of a Southern Nation*, 171.
66. McCardell, *The Idea of a Southern Nation*, 172.
67. Reynolds, *Editors Make War*, 72.
68. William Alexander Caruthers, *Cavaliers of Virginia, or the Recluse of Jamestown. An Historical Romance of the Old Dominion*, vol. 1, 2 vols. (Harper & Brothers, 1834).
69. Potter, *The Impending Crisis*, 471.
70. Ashworth, *The Republic in Crisis, 1848–1861*; McCardell, *The Idea of a Southern Nation*; McPherson, *Battle Cry of Freedom*.
71. Franklin, *The Militant South 1800–1861*.
72. Dickens, *American Notes for General Circulation*, 126.
73. Randolph Roth, *American Homicide* (The Belknap Press of Harvard University Press, 2009), 213.
74. Roth, *American Homicide*, 213.

75. Wyatt-Brown, *Southern Honor*, 28.
76. "Treasures of Congress: Struggles over Slavery: The 'Gag' Rule" (U.S. National Archives and Records Administration, 2000), https://www.archives.gov/exhibits/treasures_of_congress/text/page10_text.html.
77. Ashworth, *The Republic in Crisis, 1848–1861*, 19.
78. Theodore Dwight Weld, Angelina Grimké, and Sarah Grimké, *American Slavery As It Is: Testimony of a Thousand Witnesses* (American Anti-Slavery Society, 1839).
79. McCardell, *The Idea of a Southern Nation*, 159.
80. Potter, *The Impending Crisis*.
81. Ashworth, *The Republic in Crisis, 1848–1861*, 28.
82. Potter, *The Impending Crisis*; McCardell, *The Idea of a Southern Nation*.
83. Potter, The Impending Crisis.
84. McCardell, *The Idea of a Southern Nation*, 111; Potter, *The Impending Crisis: America Before the Civil War 1848–1861*, 88.
85. Potter, *The Impending Crisis*, 66.
86. Potter, *The Impending Crisis*, 162.
87. Foner, *Free Soil, Free Labor, Free Men*, 104–5.
88. Potter, *The Impending Crisis*, 94.
89. McCardell, *The Idea of a Southern Nation*, 251; John M. Belohlavek, "American Expansion, 1800–1867," in *A Companion to 19th Century America*, ed. William L. Barney (Blackwell Publishers, 2001), 97.
90. McCardell, *The Idea of a Southern Nation*, 74–5.
91. Wyatt-Brown, *Southern Honor*; McPherson, *Battle Cry of Freedom*.
92. Muscoe Russell Hunter Garnett, *The Union, Past and Future: How It Works and How to Save It* (Ino T. Towers, 1850), 4–6, 13.
93. Garnett, *The Union, Past and Future: How It Works and How to Save It*.
94. Potter, *The Impending Crisis*, 132.
95. Masur, *The Civil War*, 14.
96. Potter, *The Impending Crisis*; Ashworth, *The Republic in Crisis, 1848–1861*.
97. Jared Brock, "The Story of Josiah Henson, the Real Inspiration for 'Uncle Tom's Cabin,'" *Smithsonian Magazine*, 16 May 2018, https://www.smithsonianmag.com/history/story-josiah-henson-real-inspiration-uncle-toms-cabin-180969094/.
98. McPherson, *Battle Cry of Freedom*, 88.
99. Josiah Henson, *The Life of Josiah Henson, Formerly a Slave, Now an Inhabitant of Canada, as Narrated by Himself* (Arthur D. Phelps, 1849).
100. McPherson, *Battle Cry of Freedom*, 90.
101. McPherson, *Battle Cry of Freedom*, 120; Jackson, *American Radicals*.
102. Robert K. Sutton, *Stark Mad Abolitionists: Lawrence, Kansas, and the Battle over Slavery in the Civil War Era* (Skyhorse, 2017).

103. McCardell, *The Idea of a Southern Nation*, 74–5.
104. Ashworth, *The Republic in Crisis, 1848–1861*, 50.
105. Ashworth, *The Republic in Crisis, 1848–1861*, 81; Reynolds, *Editors Make War*, 33.
106. Potter, *The Impending Crisis*, 167; McPherson, *Battle Cry of Freedom*, 65.
107. Masur, *The Civil War*, 9–10.
108. McPherson, *Battle Cry of Freedom*, 137.
109. Foner, *Free Soil, Free Labor, Free Men*, 94.
110. "Appeal of the Independent Democrats in Congress to the People of the United States" (United States Library of Congress, 19 January 1854), https://www.loc.gov/resource/mss15610.028_0602_0607/?sp=2.
111. McCardell, *The Idea of a Southern Nation*, 261.
112. Jackson, *American Radicals*.
113. Potter, *The Impending Crisis*, 206–8.
114. McPherson, *Battle Cry of Freedom*, 147–8.
115. McPherson, *Battle Cry of Freedom*, 149, 160–1.
116. McCardell, *The Idea of a Southern Nation*, 262–3.
117. McCardell, *The Idea of a Southern Nation*, 170–3.
118. McPherson, *Battle Cry of Freedom*, 147; Potter, *The Impending Crisis*, 302.
119. McPherson, *Battle Cry of Freedom*, 39.
120. Bernath, *Confederate Minds*, 18–19.
121. Hinton Rowan Helper, *The Impending Crisis of the South* (Outlook Verlag BmbH, 1857), 301.
122. Rowan Helper, *The Impending Crisis of the South*, xiii.
123. Foner, *Free Soil, Free Labor, Free Men*, 11.
124. Foner; Ashworth, *The Republic in Crisis, 1848–1861*.
125. Foner, *Free Soil, Free Labor, Free Men*, 40–1.
126. Ashworth, *The Republic in Crisis, 1848–1861*, 15.
127. George Fitzhugh, *Cannibals All!, Or, Slaves Without Masters* (A. Morris, 1857), 29.
128. McPherson, *Battle Cry of Freedom*, 56.
129. Loewen and Sebesta, *Confederate and Neo-Confederate Reader*, 31.
130. McPherson, *Battle Cry of Freedom*; Ashworth, *The Republic in Crisis, 1848–1861*.
131. Reynolds, *Editors Make War*, 3.
132. Reynolds, *Editors Make War*, 72.
133. Reynolds, *Editors Make War*, 14–15.
134. Reynolds, *Editors Make War*, 9–10.
135. Garnett, *The Union, Past and Future*, 28.
136. Fitzhugh, *Cannibals All*, xxvii.
137. McCardell, *The Idea of a Southern Nation*, 206.

138. McPherson, *Battle Cry of Freedom*, 197.
139. McPherson, *Battle Cry of Freedom*, 208.
140. Reynolds, *Editors Make War*, 134; Ashworth, *The Republic in Crisis, 1848–1861*, 11.
141. McPherson, *Battle Cry of Freedom*, 228.
142. Reynolds, *Editors Make War*, 97.
143. Charles B. Dew, *Apostles of Disunion: Southern Secession Commissioners and the Causes of the Civil War* (University of Virginia Press, 2017).
144. Reynolds, Editors Make War.
145. Mark E. Neely Jr., *The Abraham Lincoln Encyclopedia* (Da Capo Press, Inc, 1982); William Seward, "The Irrepressible Conflict: History of Slavery as a Political Issue. The Origin And Aim Of Modern Parties. Speech of Hon. William H. Seward in the Senate of the United States," *New York Times*, 1 March 1860, https://timesmachine.nytimes.com/timesmachine/1860/03/01/97941274.html?pageNumber=9.
146. Donald E. Reynolds, *Editors Make War: Southern Newspapers in the Secession Crisis* (SIU Press, 2006), 5–6.
147. Eric Foner, *Free Soil, Free Labor, Free Men: The Ideology of the Republican Party Before the Civil War* (Oxford University Press USA, 1995), 66.
148. Potter, *The Impending Crisis*.

7. ALPHABETS AND ALIENS: VIETNAMESE INDEPENDENCE

1. Lakshmi Gandhi, "How Two Vietnamese Sisters Led a Revolt Against Chinese Invaders—in the 1st Century," *History*, 27 March 2024, https://www.history.com/news/trung-sisters-vietnam-rebellion-han-dynasty.
2. Stanley Karnow, *Vietnam: A History* (Penguin Books, 1983), 112.
3. Keith Weller Taylor, *The Birth of Vietnam* (University of California Press, 1991), 334.
4. Ben Kiernan, *Việt Nam: A History from Earliest Time to the Present*. (Oxford University Press, 2019).
5. Frances FitzGerald, *Fire in the Lake* (Back Bay Books/Little, Brown and Company, 1972); Goscha, *The Penguin History of Modern Vietnam*; Lawrence, *The Vietnam War*.
6. Pierre Asselin, *Vietnam's American War* (Cambridge University Press, 2018), 18.
7. Asselin, *Vietnam's American War*, 19.
8. FitzGerald, *Fire in the Lake*; Karnow, *Vietnam: A History*; Asselin, *Vietnam's American War*.
9. Huỳnh Kim Khánh, *Vietnamese Communism, 1925–1945* (Cornell University Press, 1986), 277.

10. Goscha, *The Penguin History of Modern Vietnam*, 186.
11. Asselin, *Vietnam's American War*, 24; Tucker, *Vietnam*, 38.
12. Goscha, *The Penguin History of Modern Vietnam*, 169.
13. Kim Khánh Huỳnh, *Vietnamese Communism, 1925–1945* (Cornell University Press, 1986), 33, 3.
14. Logevall, *Embers of War*.
15. Jonathan D. London, "Contemporary Vietnam's Education System: Historical Roots, Current Trends," in *Education in Vietnam*, ed. Jonathan D. London (Institute of Southeast Asian Studies, 2011), 10.
16. Shaun Kingsley Malarney, "Literacy for the Masses: The Conduct and Consequences of the Literacy Campaign in Revolutionary Vietnam," *Literacy for Dialogue in Multilingual Societies*, no. 84 (2012): 83–91; George Dutton, "Lý Toét in the City: Coming to Terms with the Modern in 1930s Vietnam," *Journal of Vietnamese Studies* 2, no. 1 (February 2007): 80.
17. Pham Lan Huong and Gerald W. Fry, "Education and Economic, Political, and Social Change in Vietnam," *Educational Research for Policy and Practice* 3 (2004): 202.
18. Khoi, "Literacy Training and Revolution: The Vietnamese Experience," 29.
19. Goscha, *The Penguin History of Modern Vietnam*, 133–4.
20. Lawrence, *The Vietnam War*; FitzGerald, *Fire in the Lake*; Huong and Fry, "Education and Economic, Political, and Social Change in Vietnam"; Goscha, *The Penguin History of Modern Vietnam*; Mark Philip Bradley, *Imagining Vietnam and America: The Making of Postcolonial Vietnam, 1919–1950* (The University of North Carolina Press, 2000).
21. David Marr, "The 1920s Women's Rights Debates in Vietnam," *The Journal of Asian Studies* 35, no. 3 (1976): 371–89, https://doi.org/10.2307/2053270.
22. Goscha, *The Penguin History of Modern Vietnam*, 148.
23. Goscha, *The Penguin History of Modern Vietnam*, 109–10.
24. Lawrence, *The Vietnam War*, 18.
25. Bradley, *Imagining Vietnam and America*, 32; Logevall, *Embers of War*, 30.
26. Goscha, *The Penguin History of Modern Vietnam*, 111–13; Asselin, *Vietnam's American War*, 25, 36; Logevall, *Embers of War*, 30.
27. Logevall, *Embers of War*, 23.
28. Vladimir I. Lenin, "Draft Theses on National and Colonial Questions," in *Lenin's Collected Works*, trans. Julius Katzer, vol. 31 (Progress Publishers, 1965), 144–51.
29. Khánh, *Vietnamese Communism, 1925–1945*, 56; Hồ Chí Minh, "The Path Which Led Me to Leninism," in *Selected Works of Ho Chi Minh*, vol. 4 (Foreign Languages Publishing House, 1960); Chí Minh Hồ,

"Twelve Recommendations," 5 April 1948, https://www.marxists.org/reference/archive/ho-chi-minh/works/1948/04/05.htm; Chí Minh Hồ, "The Imperialist Aggressors Can Never Enslave The Heroic Vietnamese People," *Lasting Peace, For a People's Democracy*, 4 April 1952; Bradley, *Imagining Vietnam and America*, 115; Goscha, *The Penguin History of Modern Vietnam*, 208.

30. Khánh, *Vietnamese Communism, 1925–1945*, 212–3, 216; Logevall, *Embers of War*, 104; Goscha, *The Penguin History of Modern Vietnam*, 148–9, 332.
31. Goscha, *The Penguin History of Modern Vietnam*, 379.
32. Hervé Tenoux, "Des Nouvelles de l'empire. La Diffusion Intercoloniale d'informations Paris-Dakar-Saigon 1887–1954" (Ph.D. Dissertation, Paris Diderot University, 1996), https://theses.fr/1996PA070024.
33. Bradley, *Imagining Vietnam and America*, 27.
34. Karnow, *Vietnam: A History*, 125.
35. Logevall, *Embers of War*, 28.
36. Asselin, *Vietnam's American War*, 23.
37. Jonathan D. London, "Contemporary Vietnam's Education System: Historical Roots, Current Trends," in *Education in Vietnam*, ed. Jonathan D. London (Institute of Southeast Asian Studies, 2011), 1–56.
38. Goscha, *The Penguin History of Modern Vietnam*, 139–40.
39. FitzGerald, *Fire in the Lake*, 61.
40. Karnow, *Vietnam: A History*; Bradley, *Imagining Vietnam and America*; Asselin, *Vietnam's American War*.
41. Bradley, *Imagining Vietnam and America*, 25; Lawrence, *The Vietnam War*, 4; Khánh, *Vietnamese Communism, 1925–1945*, 23.
42. Goscha, *The Penguin History of Modern Vietnam*, 148; Bradley, *Imagining Vietnam and America*, 42.
43. Asselin, *Vietnam's American War*; Huỳnh, *Vietnamese Communism, 1925–1945*, 20.
44. Khánh, *Vietnamese Communism, 1925–1945*, 78–9.
45. Khánh, *Vietnamese Communism, 1925–1945*, 69.
46. Logevall, *Embers of War*, 181.
47. Karnow, *Vietnam: A History*, 154; Logevall, *Embers of War*, 181.
48. Logevall, *Embers of War*, 30.
49. Asselin, *Vietnam's American War*; Huỳnh, *Vietnamese Communism, 1925–1945*, 20.
50. Karnow, *Vietnam: A History*, 102.
51. Goscha, *The Penguin History of Modern Vietnam*, 180.
52. Goscha, *The Penguin History of Modern Vietnam*, 184.
53. Karnow, *Vietnam: A History*; Khánh, *Vietnamese Communism, 1925–1945*; Asselin, *Vietnam's American War*.

54. Khánh, *Vietnamese Communism, 1925–1945*, 214.
55. Bradley, *Imagining Vietnam and America*, 30, 112.
56. Khánh, *Vietnamese Communism, 1925–1945*, 297.
57. Karnow, *Vietnam: A History*; Khánh, *Vietnamese Communism, 1925–1945*.
58. Goscha, *The Penguin History of Modern Vietnam*, 186.
59. Khánh, *Vietnamese Communism, 1925–1945*, 242.
60. Logevall, *Embers of War*, 60.
61. Khánh, Vietnamese Communism, 1925–1945, 245–7.
62. Logevall, *Embers of War*; 59; Huỳnh, *Vietnamese Communism, 1925–1945*, 248–9.
63. Logevall, *Embers of War*, 58–60.
64. Khánh, *Vietnamese Communism, 1925–1945*, 310; Asselin, Vietnam's American War, 40.
65. Khánh, *Vietnamese Communism, 1925–1945*, 275–6.
66. Khánh, *Vietnamese Communism, 1925–1945*, 320.
67. Asselin, *Vietnam's American War*, 40.
68. Khánh, *Vietnamese Communism, 1925–1945*, 167; Lawrence, *The Vietnam War*, 187; Logevall, *Embers of War*, 106–9.
69. FitzGerald, *Fire in the Lake*, 178.
70. Tucker, *Vietnam*, 38; Lawrence, *The Vietnam War*, 13–14; Logevall, *Embers of War*, 40,60; Goscha, *The Penguin History of Modern Vietnam*, 241.
71. Lawrence, *The Vietnam War*, 14–15; Asselin, *Vietnam's American War*, 29.
72. FitzGerald, *Fire in the Lake*, 143; Khánh, *Vietnamese Communism, 1925–1945*, 30.
73. Khánh, *Vietnamese Communism, 1925–1945*, 103.
74. Goscha, *The Penguin History of Modern Vietnam*, 236–48.
75. Karnow, *Vietnam: A History*, 122.
76. Khánh, *Vietnamese Communism, 1925–1945*.
77. Karnow, *Vietnam: A History*, 166–7; Logevall, *Embers of War*, 157.
78. Hồ, "The Path Which Led Me to Leninism."
79. Logevall, *Embers of War*, 385.
80. Khánh, *Vietnamese Communism, 1925–1945*, 257; Asselin, *Vietnam's American War*, 33.
81. FitzGerald, *Fire in the Lake*, 28.
82. Goscha, *The Penguin History of Modern Vietnam*, 273.
83. Lonán Ó Briain, *Voices of Vietnam: A Century of Radio, Red Music, and Revolution* (Oxford University Press, 2022).
84. Erich DeWald, "Taking to the Waves: Vietnamese Society around the

Radio in the 1930s," *Modern Asian Studies* 46, no. 1 (January 2012): 146–7.
85. Logevall, *Embers of War*, 270.
86. Bradley, *Imagining Vietnam and America*, 122.
87. FitzGerald, *Fire in the Lake*; Karnow, *Vietnam: A History*; Bradley, *Imagining Vietnam and America*; Lawrence, *The Vietnam War*; Goscha, *The Penguin History of Modern Vietnam*; Asselin, *Vietnam's American War*.
88. Fox Butterfield, "The Truman and Eisenhower Years: 1945–1960," in *The Pentagon Papers: The Secret History of the Vietnam War*, ed. Neil Sheehan et al. (Racehorse Publishing, 2017), 5.
89. Mark Philip Bradley, *Imagining Vietnam and America: The Making of Postcolonial Vietnam, 1919–1950* (The University of North Carolina Press, 2000), 143.
90. Bradley, *Imagining Vietnam and America*, 143.
91. Logevall, *Embers of War*, 188; Goscha, *The Penguin History of Modern Vietnam*, 236.
92. Goscha, *The Penguin History of Modern Vietnam*, 295–6.
93. Lawrence, *The Vietnam War*, 34–5; McMaster, *Dereliction of Duty*, 33–4.
94. Asselin, *Vietnam's American War*, 41.
95. Wendy Wall, "Anti-Communism in the 1950s," *The Guilder Lehrman Institute of American History*, 2015, https://www.gilderlehrman.org/ap-us-history/period-8?modal=/history-resources/essays/anti-communism-1950s; Lydia Saad, "Gallup Vault: Americans' Views of Socialism, 1949–1965," *Gallup*, 10 August 2018, https://news.gallup.com/vault/240749/gallup-vault-americans-views-socialism-1949-1965.aspx.
96. Lawrence, *The Vietnam War*, 42–3.
97. Michael J. Heale, *American Anti-Communism: Combating the Enemy Within, 1830–1970* (JHU Press, 1990); Logevall, *Embers of War*.
98. Nancy Bernhard, *US Television News and Cold War Propaganda, 1947–1960* (Cambridge University Press, 2003); "Red Channels: The Report of Communist Influence in Radio and Television," *Counterattack*, 1950.
99. Edwin R. Bayley, *Joe McCarthy and the Press* (University of Wisconsin Press, 1981), 176–7.
100. "The 1950s," *History*, 17 June 2010, https://www.history.com/topics/cold-war/1950s.
101. "Timeline of Polling History: People That Shaped the United States, and the World," *Gallup*, 30 January 2001, https://news.gallup.com/poll/9964/timeline-polling-history-people-shaped-united-states-world.aspx.
102. "The 1950s."

103. Lawrence, *The Vietnam War*; Goscha, *The Penguin History of Modern Vietnam*; Asselin, *Vietnam's American War*.
104. Logevall, *Embers of War*, 309, 331.
105. McMaster, *Dereliction of Duty*, 33; Lawrence, *The Vietnam War*, 30–1; Logevall, *Embers of War*, 137.
106. Karnow, *Vietnam: A History*, 184–5.
107. Logevall, *Embers of War*, 254, 343.
108. Karnow, *Vietnam: A History*, 184; Tucker, *Vietnam*, 57; Bradley, *Imagining Vietnam and America*, 177; Lawrence, *The Vietnam War*, 38–9; Logevall, *Embers of War*, 265; Asselin, *Vietnam's American War*, 56.
109. Tucker, *Vietnam*, 57; Bradley, *Imagining Vietnam and America*, 177; Lawrence, *The Vietnam War*, 39.
110. Karnow, *Vietnam: A History*, 24; McMaster, *Dereliction of Duty*, 34.
111. Logevall, *Embers of War*, 187; Heale, *American Anti-Communism*, 166.
112. Karnow, *Vietnam: A History*, 267.
113. "1960 Census of the Population: Supplementary Reports: Race of the Population of the United States, by States: 1960" (U.S. Department of Commerce, 7 September 1961), https://www.census.gov/library/publications/1961/dec/pc-s1-10.html; Richard A. Easterlin, "The American Baby Boom in Historical Perspective," in *Population, Labor Force, and Long Swings in Economic Growth: The American Experience*, ed. Richard A. Easterlin (National Bureau of Economic Research, 1968), 77–110.
114. Young and Young, *The 1950s*.
115. Thomas D. Snyder, "120 Years of American Education: A Statistical Portrait" (National Center for Education Statistics, January 1993).
116. Daniel S. Lucks, *Selma to Saigon: The Civil Rights Movement and the Vietnam War* (University Press of Kentucky, 2014).
117. "Section 31: 20th Century Statistics," U.S. Census Bureau, Statistical Abstract of the United States (U.S. Census Bureau, 1999), 31, https://www2.census.gov/library/publications/1999/compendia/statab/119ed/tables/sec31.pdf.
118. "Section 31: 20th Century Statistics," 31.
119. Young and Young, *The 1950s*, 20.
120. Brock J. Vaughan, "War, Media, and Memory: American Television News Coverage of the Vietnam War," *Bridges: An Undergraduate Journal of Contemporary Connections* 4, no. 1 (2020): 1–9.
121. FitzGerald, *Fire in the Lake*; Karnow, *Vietnam: A History*; Tucker, *Vietnam*; Asselin, *Vietnam's American War*.
122. FitzGerald, *Fire in the Lake*; Karnow, *Vietnam: A History*; Tucker, *Vietnam*.
123. Goscha, *The Penguin History of Modern Vietnam*, 298.

124. Lawrence, *The Vietnam War*, 55; Asselin, *Vietnam's American War*, 40.
125. David Halberstam, *The Coldest Winter* (Hachette Books, 2007), 489.
126. Logevall, *Embers of War*, 527.
127. Asselin, *Vietnam's American War*, 75.
128. FitzGerald, *Fire in the Lake*, 93; Lawrence, *The Vietnam War*, 60.
129. Asselin, *Vietnam's American War*, 73.
130. Tucker, *Vietnam*, 95.
131. McMaster, *Dereliction of Duty*, 35–6.
132. Lawrence, *The Vietnam War*, 57.
133. Goscha, *The Penguin History of Modern Vietnam*, 325.
134. FitzGerald, *Fire in the Lake*, 89.
135. Karnow, *Vietnam: A History*; McMaster, *Dereliction of Duty*; Lawrence, *The Vietnam War*.
136. FitzGerald, *Fire in the Lake*, 105; Lawrence, *The Vietnam War*, 61; Goscha, *The Penguin History of Modern Vietnam*, 332–43.
137. FitzGerald, *Fire in the Lake*, 96.
138. McMaster, *Dereliction of Duty*, 36.
139. Lawrence, *The Vietnam War*, 55; Asselin, *Vietnam's American War*, 59.
140. Chí Minh, "The Imperialist Aggressors Can Never Enslave The Heroic Vietnamese People."
141. Hồ Chí Minh, "Instructions Given at The Conference Reviewing The Mass Education In The First Half Of 1956," trans. Christian Liebl, July 16, 1956, https://www.marxists.org/reference/archive/ho-chi-minh/works/1956/07/16.htm.
142. Chí Minh, "Instructions Given at The Conference Reviewing The Mass Education In The First Half Of 1956".
143. Kim Khánh Huỳnh, *Vietnamese Communism*, 216.
144. Khoi, "Literacy Training and Revolution: The Vietnamese Experience," 30.
145. Goscha, *The Penguin History of Modern Vietnam*, 221.
146. Lawrence, *The Vietnam War*, 55.
147. Asselin, *Vietnam's American War*, 87.
148. Lawrence, *The Vietnam War*, 65.
149. Asselin, *Vietnam's American War*, 104.
150. FitzGerald, *Fire in the Lake*, 155.
151. Tucker, *Vietnam*, 50.
152. FitzGerald, *Fire in the Lake*, 20.
153. FitzGerald, *Fire in the Lake*, 158.
154. Butterfield, "Origins of the Insurgency in South Vietnam," 81.
155. Goscha, *The Penguin History of Modern Vietnam*, 335.
156. Karnow, *Vietnam: A History*, 197.
157. FitzGerald, *Fire in the Lake*, 203.

158. FitzGerald, *Fire in the Lake*, 183–200.
159. Karnow, *Vietnam: A History*, 265.
160. FitzGerald, *Fire in the Lake*, 83–4.
161. Karnow, *Vietnam: A History*, 270.
162. Karnow, *Vietnam: A History*, 275–6.
163. FitzGerald, *Fire in the Lake*, 86.
164. Karnow, *Vietnam: A History*, 275–6.
165. Karnow, *Vietnam: A History*, 279, 312.
166. Karnow, *Vietnam: A History*, 312–13.
167. FitzGerald, *Fire in the Lake*, 131–3.
168. FitzGerald, *Fire in the Lake*, 73–4.
169. Karnow, *Vietnam: A History*, 112.

8. THE UKRAINIAN CURSE OF NONEXISTENCE

1. Oksana Zabuzhko, *Fieldwork in Ukrainian Sex*, trans. Halyna Hryn (Amazon Crossing, 1996), 34.
2. Anna Reid, Borderland: *A Journey Through the History of Ukraine* (Basic Books, 2015), 143.
3. Reid, *Borderland*, 14; Serhii Plokhy, *The Gates of Europe: A History of Ukraine* (Basic Books, 2021), 1056.
4. Plokhy, *The Gates of Europe*, 1990.
5. Rajan Menon, Eugene B. Rumer, and Deborah Chasman, *Conflict in Ukraine: The Unwinding of the Post-Cold War Order* (London: MIT Press, 2015); Andrew Wilson, *The Ukrainians: Unexpected Nation* (Yale University Press, 2015); Paul D'Anieri, *Ukraine and Russia: From Civilized Divorce to Uncivil War* (Cambridge University Press, 2019); Olexander Scherba, *Ukraine vs. Darkness: Undiplomatic Thoughts*, Ukrainian Voices, Book 7 (Ibidem, 2021).
6. Reid, *Borderland*; D'Anieri, *Ukraine and Russia*.
7. Gerard Toal, *Near Abroad: Putin, the West and the Contest over Ukraine and the Caucasus* (Oxford University Press, 2017), 199–201.
8. Wilson, *The Ukrainians*, 105; Reid, *Borderland*, 2; Plokhy, *The Gates of Europe*, 1215.
9. Reid, *Borderland*, 91.
10. Wilson, *The Ukrainians*, 113.
11. Wilson, 111; Taras Kuzio, *Ukraine—Crimea—Russia: Triangle of Conflict*, ed. Andreas Umland (Ibidem-Verlag, 2012), 55.
12. Plokhy, *The Gates of Europe*, 4263; Wilson, *The Ukrainians*, 115.
13. Reid, *Borderland*, 143.
14. Plokhy, *The Gates of Europe*, 1986

15. Plokhy, *The Gates of Europe*, 2634.
16. Reid, *Borderland*.
17. "Nobody Wants Us: The Alienated Civilians of Eastern Ukraine, Brussels: Europe Report" (International Crisis Group, 1 October 2018).
18. Andrew Wilson, *Ukraine Crisis: What It Means for the West*. (Yale University Press, 2014), 119; Wilson, *The Ukrainians*, 81; Kateryna Ivaschenko-Stadnik, "What's Wrong with the Donbas? The Challenges of Integration Before, During and After the War," in *Ukraine in Transformation*, ed. Alberto Veira-Ramos, Tetiana Liubyva, and Evgenii Golovakha (Palgrave Macmillan, 2020), 264.
19. Kuzio, *Ukraine—Crimea—Russia*, 35, 59; Wilson, *The Ukrainians*, 148; Wilson, *Ukraine Crisis*, 123.
20. Reid, *Borderland*, 91; Menon, Rumer, and Chasman, *Conflict in Ukraine*, 7–8; Wilson, *The Ukrainians*, 81; Lawrence Freedman, *Ukraine and the Art of Strategy* (Oxford University Press, 2019), 61; Plokhy, *The Gates of Europe*, 223.
21. Scherba, *Ukraine vs. Darkness*, 11.
22. Bernd Pompino-Marschall, Elena Steriopolo, and Zygis Marzena, "Ukrainian," *Journal of the International Phonetic Association* 47, no. 3 (2017): 349, https://doi.org/10.1017/S0025100316000372.
23. Laada Bilaniuk, "A Typology of Surzhyk: Mixed Ukrainian-Russian Language," *International Journal of Bilingualism* 8, no. 4 (2004): 412.
24. Plokhy, *The Gates of Europe*, 2684.
25. Reid, *Borderland*, 77; Wilson, *The Ukrainians*, 51.
26. Reid, *Borderland*, 209; Wilson, *The Ukrainians*, 102.
27. Wilson, *The Ukrainians*, 118.
28. Frances A. Swyripa, Maude-Emmanuelle Lambert, Jessica Poulin and Clayton Ma, "Ukrainian Canadians," *The Canadian Encyclopedia*, last modified July 30, 2024, https://www.thecanadianencyclopedia.ca/en/article/ukrainian-canadians.
29. Orest Subtelny, *Ukraine: A History* (University of Toronto Press, 2009).
30. Freedman, *Ukraine and the Art of Strategy*, 62; Marvin Kalb, *Imperial Gamble: Putin, Ukraine, and the New Cold War* (The Brookings Institution, 2015), 78.
31. Reid, *Borderland*, 147–8; Plokhy, *The Gates of Europe*, 4557; Freedman, *Ukraine and the Art of Strategy*, 63.
32. Reid, *Borderland*, 147–8; Plokhy, *The Gates of Europe*, 4557.
33. Plokhy, *The Gates of Europe*, 4734.
34. Kalb, *Imperial Gamble*, 83; Wilson, *The Ukrainians*, 149; Plokhy, *The Gates of Europe*, 4597, 4600; Wilson, *Ukraine Crisis*, 104.
35. Freedman, *Ukraine and the Art of Strategy*, 63.
36. Reid, *Borderland*, 148–9; Plokhy, *The Gates of Europe*, 4928.

37. Kalb, *Imperial Gamble*, 85; Plokhy, *The Gates of Europe*, 4809.
38. Wilson, *The Ukrainians*; Wilson, *Ukraine Crisis*; Reid, *Borderland*; Plokhy, *The Gates of Europe*.
39. Plokhy, *The Gates of Europe*, 4936.
40. Reid, *Borderland*, 148–9.
41. Reid, *Borderland*, 148; Plokhy, *The Gates of Europe*, 4943, 4961.
42. Plokhy, *The Gates of Europe*, 4056.
43. Plokhy, *The Gates of Europe*, 5013.
44. Toal, *Near Abroad,* 201–2
45. Kalb, *Imperial Gamble*; Plokhy, *The Gates of Europe*.
46. Wilson, *The Ukrainians*, 216.
47. Plokhy, *The Gates of Europe*, 1331.
48. Bilaniuk, "A Typology of Surzhyk," 409.
49. Vladimir Fesenko, "Ukraine: Between Europe and Eurasia," in *Eurasian Integration: The View from Within*, ed. Piotr Dutkiewicz and Richard Sakwa (Routledge, 2014), 127; Mychailo Wynnyckyj, *Ukraine's Maidan, Russia's War: A Chronicle and Analysis of the Revolution of Dignity* (Ibidem, 2019), 54.
50. Bilaniuk, "A Typology of Surzhyk," 413.
51. Plokhy, *The Gates of Europe*, 5312.
52. Reid, *Borderland*, 205; Plokhy, *The Gates of Europe*, 5478.
53. Kuzio, *Ukraine—Crimea—Russia*; Kalb, *Imperial Gamble*; Scherba, *Ukraine vs. Darkness*.
54. Plokhy, *The Gates of Europe*, 4832.
55. Tetyana Nikitina, "The Ukrainian Media Landscape," in *Ukraine in Transformation*, ed. Alberto Veira-Ramos, Tetiana Liubyva, and Evgenii Golovakha (Palgrave Macmillan, 2020), 198.
56. Nikitina, "The Ukrainian Media Landscape," 198–9.
57. Tymofii Brik and Stanislav Korlkov, "Religious Markets in Ukraine: Post-Communist Revivals and New Directions," in *Ukraine in Transformation*, ed. Alberto Veira-Ramos, Tetiana Liubyva, and Evgenii Golovakha (Palgrave Macmillan, 2020), 172; Nikitina, "The Ukrainian Media Landscape," 150.
58. Menon, Rumer, and Chasman, *Conflict in Ukraine*; Reid, *Borderland*; Kalb, *Imperial Gamble*; Plokhy, *The Gates of Europe*.
59. Menon, Rumer, and Chasman, *Conflict in Ukraine*; Samuel Charap and Timothy J. Colton, *Everyone Loses: The Ukraine Crisis and the Ruinous Contest for Post-Soviet Eurasia* (Routledge, 2017).
60. Toal, *Near Abroad*, 203.
61. Wilson, *Ukraine Crisis*, 41; Kalb, *Imperial Gamble*, 109; D'Anieri, *Ukraine and Russia*, 34; Freedman, *Ukraine and the Art of Strategy*, 63; Plokhy, *The Gates of Europe*, 5599.

62. Menon, Rumer, and Chasman, *Conflict in Ukraine*; Reid, *Borderland*; Wilson, *The Ukrainians*; Plokhy, *The Gates of Europe*.
63. Plokhy, *The Gates of Europe*, 5568.
64. Wynnyckyj, *Ukraine's Maidan, Russia's War*, 56–7; Reid, *Borderland*, 87.
65. Zenon E. Kohut, "The Development of a Little Russian Identity and Ukrainian Nationbuilding," *Harvard Ukrainian Studies* 10, no. 3–4 (December 1986): 560; Kalb, *Imperial Gamble*, 119.
66. Nikitina, "The Ukrainian Media Landscape," 201–2.
67. "Five Years of Development of Ukrainian Television," *Media Detector*, 17 October 2006, https://detector.media/production/article/7643/2006-10-17-pyat-let-razvytyya-ukraynskogo-televydenyya/; Nikitina, "The Ukrainian Media Landscape."
68. Wilson, *Ukraine Crisis*, 220.
69. Vladimir Fesenko, "Ukraine: Between Europe and Eurasia," in *Eurasian Integration: The View from Within*, ed. Piotr Dutkiewicz and Richard Sakwa (Routledge, 2014), 127.
70. Wilson, *Ukraine Crisis*, 104.
71. Reid, *Borderland*; Wilson, *Ukraine Crisis*; Kalb, *Imperial Gamble*; Menon, Rumer, and Chasman, *Conflict in Ukraine*; Wilson, *The Ukrainians*; Veronika Melkozerova, "Donbas In The 1990s: How It Defined Ukraine's Future," *Kyiv Post*, 2 April 2021, https://www.kyivpost.com/ukraine-politics/decade-that-shaped-ukraine-how-1990s-made-donbas-what-it-is-today.html?fbclid=IwAR03WNp4uNsUQ5N_j0n_Fc46NiSobxknpcGgxiGgC-U2nTFs7SVq05-LjxQ.
72. Wilson, *Ukraine Crisis*, 120.
73. Fesenko, "Ukraine," 132; Reid, *Borderland*, 238.
74. Reid, *Borderland*, 48; Kuzio, *Ukraine—Crimea—Russia*, 58; Melkozerova, "Donbas In The 1990s."
75. Kuzio, *Ukraine—Crimea—Russia*, 33.
76. D'Anieri, *Ukraine and Russia*, 21
77. Wilson, *Ukraine Crisis*, 163.
78. Nikitina, "The Ukrainian Media Landscape," 217; "Contemporary Media Use in Ukraine" (Broadcasting Board of Governors and Gallup, June 2014), https://www.usagm.gov/wp-content/media/2014/06/Ukraine-research-brief.pdf?_ga=2.196786412.179723463.1605739064-1610282411.1605039205#:~:text=Television%20is%20the%20dominant%20news,for%20news%20at%20least%20weekly.
79. Nikitina, "The Ukrainian Media Landscape," 220.
80. "Media Ownership Monitor: Ukraine" (Institute of Mass Information, 2016), https://ukraine.mom-gmr.org/en/owners/.
81. "Five Years of Development of Ukrainian Television," *Media Detector*.
82. Alla Nedashkivska, "Symbolic Bilingualism in Contemporary Ukrainian

Media," *Canadian Slavonic Papers* 52, no. 3–4 (2010): 357, https://doi.org/10.1080/00085006.2010.11092653.
83. Marta Dyczok, *Ukraine's Euromaidan: Broadcasting through Information Wars with Hromadske Radio* (E-International Relations, 2016).
84. Tetyana Nikitina, "The Ukrainian Media Landscape," in *Ukraine in Transformation*, ed. Alberto Veira-Ramos, Tetiana Liubyva, and Evgenii Golovakha (Palgrave Macmillan, 2020), 195–233.
85. Nikitina, "The Ukrainian Media Landscape," 221, https://ukraine.mom-gmr.org/en/findings/oligarchy/.
86. "Media Ownership Monitor: Ukraine " (Institute of Mass Information, 2016), https://ukraine.mom-gmr.org/en/findings/oligarchy/ Nikitina, "The Ukrainian Media Landscape," 221.
87. "Media Ownership Monitor Ukraine," https://ukraine.mom-gmr.org/en/media/detail/outlet/5-channel/.
88. "Media Ownership Monitor Ukraine," https://ukraine.mom-rsf.org/en/findings/oligarchy/.
89. Nikitina, "The Ukrainian Media Landscape," 203–4
90. Wilson, *Ukraine Crisis*, 201.
91. Menon, Rumer, and Chasman, *Conflict in Ukraine*, 30–1.
92. Wilson, *Ukraine Crisis*, 43; Kalb, *Imperial Gamble,* 128; Menon, Rumer, and Chasman, *Conflict in Ukraine*, 32; Reid, *Borderland*, 243; Wilson, *The Ukrainians*, 311; Nikitina, "The Ukrainian Media Landscape," 205; Plokhy, *The Gates of Europe*, 5784.
93. D'Anieri, *Ukraine and Russia*; Reid, *Borderland*; Wilson, *The Ukrainians*; Menon, Rumer, and Chasman, *Conflict in Ukraine*.
94. D'Anieri, *Ukraine and Russia*, 110–11.
95. Reid, *Borderland*; D'Anieri, *Ukraine and Russia*; Wynnyckyj, *Ukraine's Maidan, Russia's War*; Plokhy, *The Gates of Europe*.
96. D'Anieri, *Ukraine and Russia*, 104–5
97. Nikitina, "The Ukrainian Media Landscape," 210.
98. Nikitina, "The Ukrainian Media Landscape," 210–11.
99. Nedashkivska, "Symbolic Bilingualism in Contemporary Ukrainian Media," 353.
100. Office for Democratic Institutions and Human Rights. "Ukraine: Parliamentary Elections 28 October 2012, OSCE/ODIHR Election Observation Mission Final Report," Warsaw, Poland: OSCE (3 January 2013),19.
101. "Media Ownership Monitor Ukraine," https://ukraine.mom-gmr.org/en/media/.
102. Nikitina, "The Ukrainian Media Landscape," 206.
103. Nikitina, "The Ukrainian Media Landscape," 207; Wilson, *The Ukrainians*, 198.

104. "Ukraine: Parliamentary Elections 28 October 2012," OSCE/ODIHR Election Observation Mission Final Report (Warsaw: Office for Democratic Institutions and Human Rights, 3 January 2013), 19; Nikitina, "The Ukrainian Media Landscape," 211–12.
105. Ivan Verstyuk, "Ukraine's Deep-Rooted Media Problem," *Columbia Journalism Review*, 4 December 2013, https://archives.cjr.org/behind_the_news/ukraines_deep-rooted_media_pro.php.
106. Nikitina, "The Ukrainian Media Landscape," 209–10.
107. Ivanna Gorina, "Yanukovych's Convictions Have Not Been Expunged," *Rossiyskaya Gazeta*, 13 July 2005, https://www.rg.ru/2005/07/13/yanukovich.html; Kalb, *Imperial Gamble*.
108. Nedashkivska, "Symbolic Bilingualism in Contemporary Ukrainian Media," 353–4.
109. Wilson, *The Ukrainians*, 252.
110. Wilson, *Ukraine Crisis*, 19; Wynnyckyj, *Ukraine's Maidan, Russia's War*, 58; Toal, *Near Abroad*, 209; Kalb, *Imperial Gamble*, 130.
111. Wilson, *Ukraine Crisis*, 107.
112. Menon, Rumer, and Chasman, *Conflict in Ukraine*; Reid, *Borderland*.
113. Reid, *Borderland*, 245.
114. Wilson, *Ukraine Crisis*, 125; Reid, *Borderland*, 245–6.
115. Wilson, *Ukraine Crisis*, 60, 90.
116. Wynnyckyj, *Ukraine's Maidan, Russia's War*, 58.
117. Wilson, *The Ukrainians*, 317.
118. Elisabeth Rosenthal, "Liberal Leader From Ukraine Was Poisoned," *The New York Times*, 12 December 2004, https://www.nytimes.com/2004/12/12/world/europe/liberal-leader-from-ukraine-was-poisoned.html.
119. Reid, *Borderland*; Kalb, *Imperial Gamble*; Wynnyckyj, *Ukraine's Maidan, Russia's War*; Plokhy, *The Gates of Europe*.
120. Plokhy, *The Gates of Europe*, 5826; Reid, *Borderland*, 247; Wilson, *The Ukrainians*, 318.
121. Reid, *Borderland*; Wynnyckyj, *Ukraine's Maidan, Russia's War*; Maxim Gatskov and Ksenia Gatskova, "Civil Society in Ukraine," in *Ukraine in Transformation*, ed. Alberto Veira-Ramos, Tetiana Liubyva, and Evgenii Golovakha (Palgrave Macmillan, 2020), 148–70; Kalb, *Imperial Gamble*.
122. D'Anieri, *Ukraine and Russia*, 120; Plokhy, *The Gates of Europe*, 5826.
123. Reid, *Borderland*, 248.
124. Kalb, *Imperial Gamble*, 131.
125. Charap and Colton, *Everyone Loses*; Menon, Rumer, and Chasman, *Conflict in Ukraine*.
126. Menon, Rumer, and Chasman, *Conflict in Ukraine*; Freedman, *Ukraine and the Art of Strategy*.

127. D'Anieri, *Ukraine and Russia*, 131.
128. Charap and Colton, *Everyone Loses*, 1697.
129. Kuzio, *Ukraine—Crimea—Russia*; Toal, *Near Abroad*; Plokhy, *The Gates of Europe*; Wilson, *The Ukrainians*; D'Anieri, *Ukraine and Russia*; Melkozerova, "Donbas In The 1990s."
130. Wilson, *The Ukrainians*, 187, 190.
131. Fesenko, "Ukraine," 134; Wilson, *The Ukrainians*, 60, 330; D'Anieri, *Ukraine and Russia*, 106.
132. Charap and Colton, *Everyone Loses*, 1732.
133. Vladimir Vladimirovich Putin, "Address by President of the Russian Federation" (The Kremlin, 18 March 2014), http://en.kremlin.ru/events/president/news/20603; D'Anieri, *Ukraine and Russia*, 127, 131; Kalb, *Imperial Gamble*, 134; Charap and Colton, *Everyone Loses*, 1257; Freedman, *Ukraine and the Art of Strategy*, 55, 89.
134. Oleg Noginsky, "Ukraine: Between Europe and Eurasia," in *Eurasian Integration: The View from Within*, ed. Piotr Dutkiewicz and Richard Sakwa (Routledge, 2014), 150–60; Zabuzhko, *Fieldwork in Ukrainian Sex*; Charap and Colton, *Everyone Loses*.
135. Charap and Colton, *Everyone Loses*, 1726, 1770; Kalb, *Imperial Gamble*, 21; D'Anieri, *Ukraine and Russia*, 139; Freedman, *Ukraine and the Art of Strategy*, 101.
136. Nikitina, "The Ukrainian Media Landscape," 211
137. "Five Years of Development of Ukrainian Television." *Media Detector*.
138. "Five Years of Development of Ukrainian Television" *Media Detector*.;
139. Svitlana Oksamytna, "Education in Transition: Structure, Expansion and Inequality," in *Ukraine in Transformation*, ed. Alberto Veira-Ramos, Tetiana Liubyva, and Evgenii Golovakha (Palgrave Macmillan, 2020), 133.
140. "Mobile Cellular Subscriptions (per 100 People)—Ukraine," International Telecommunication Union (ITU) World Telecommunication/ICT Indicators Database (The World Bank, 2019), https://data.worldbank.org/indicator/IT.CEL.SETS.P2?locations=UA.
141. Wilson, *The Ukrainians*, 314.
142. Reid, *Borderland*; Wilson, *Ukraine Crisis*; Menon, Rumer, and Chasman, *Conflict in Ukraine*; D'Anieri, *Ukraine and Russia*; Freedman, *Ukraine and the Art of Strategy*; Wynnyckyj, *Ukraine's Maidan, Russia's War*; Plokhy, *The Gates of Europe*.
143. Kalb, *Imperial Gamble*; Menon, Rumer, and Chasman, *Conflict in Ukraine*; Reid, *Borderland*; Wilson, *The Ukrainians*; Charap and Colton, *Everyone Loses*; D'Anieri, *Ukraine and Russia*.
144. D'Anieri, *Ukraine and Russia*, 142.

145. Roman Kupchinsky, "Russia's New Ukrainian Disinformation Campaign," *Eurasia Daily Monitor* 6, no. 176 (25 September 2009), https://jamestown.org/program/russias-new-ukrainian-disinformation-campaign/; "Ukrainian President's Poisoning Was Falsified," *RT*, 28 September 2009, https://www.rt.com/usa/ukrainian-president-poisoning-falsified/; "Segodnya: The Prosecutor General's Office Announced the Falsification of the Poisoning of Yushchenko," *Korrespondent*, 19 September 2009, https://korrespondent.net/ukraine/politics/972167-segodnya-v-genprokurature-zayavili-o-falsifikacii-otravleniya-yushchenko.
146. "Media Ownership Monitor Ukraine"; "Pro-Yanukovich Ukrainian Businessman Buys Local Media Group," *Reuters*, 21 June 2013, https://www.reuters.com/article/us-ukraine-media-kurchenko-idUSBRE95K0P520130621.
147. Interfax-Ukraine, "Stepan Bandera Becomes Ukrainian Hero," *Kyiv Post*, 22 January 2010, https://www.kyivpost.com/post/7790.
148. Plokhy, *The Gates of Europe*, 5857.
149. D'Anieri, *Ukraine and Russia*, 129.
150. Wilson, *Ukraine Crisis*, 38.
151. D'Anieri, *Ukraine and Russia*, 132.
152. D'Anieri, *Ukraine and Russia*, 202.
153. D'Anieri, *Ukraine and Russia*, 142; Reid, *Borderland*, 251; Wilson, *The Ukrainians*, 333.
154. Wilson, *The Ukrainians*, 342.
155. "Ukraine Ex-PM Yulia Tymoshenko Jailed over Gas Deal," *BBC*, 11 October 2011, https://www.bbc.com/news/world-europe-15250742.
156. John McCain, "Dear Vlad, The #ArabSpring Is Coming to a Neighborhood near You," *Twitter*, 5 December 2011, https://twitter.com/senjohnmccain/status/143689929975799809?lang=en.
157. D'Anieri, *Ukraine and Russia*, 189.
158. Menon, Rumer, and Chasman, *Conflict in Ukraine*, 74–5.
159. Nikitina, "The Ukrainian Media Landscape," 212–13.
160. Wilson, *Ukraine Crisis*, 148.
161. Nikitina, "The Ukrainian Media Landscape"; Danilo Khomutovskii, New Ukrainian Cinema: Flash: The Fifth Series, Interview, 10 March 2021, https://www.youtube.com/watch?v=mUCDNBXXOpw.
162. Nedashkivska, "Symbolic Bilingualism in Contemporary Ukrainian Media," 358.
163. Nedashkivska, "Symbolic Bilingualism in Contemporary Ukrainian Media," 362.
164. Wynnyckyj, *Ukraine's Maidan, Russia's War*, 56–7.
165. Kalb, *Imperial Gamble*, 139; Wilson, *The Ukrainians*, 347; Charap and Colton, *Everyone Loses*, 2553; D'Anieri, *Ukraine and Russia*, 195.

166. Wilson, *Ukraine Crisis*, 64; D'Anieri, *Ukraine and Russia*, 202; Menon, Rumer, and Chasman, *Conflict in Ukraine*, 61; Wynnyckyj, *Ukraine's Maidan, Russia's War*, 78.
167. Charap and Colton, *Everyone Loses*, 916.
168. Fesenko, "Ukraine," 136; D'Anieri, *Ukraine and Russia*, 95.
169. Wynnyckyj, *Ukraine's Maidan, Russia's War*; Igor Guzhva, Olesya Medvedeva, and Maxim Minin, "Euro 2012, the Law on the Russian Language, 'Svoboda' Got into the Rada. What Was 2012 for Ukraine," *Strana*, 16 August 2021, https://strana.news/news/348310-2012-hod-v-istorii-ukrainy-evrokubok-v-kieve-i-timoshenko-v-tjurme.html.
170. Menon, Rumer, and Chasman, *Conflict in Ukraine*, 45–6.
171. Menon, Rumer, and Chasman, *Conflict in Ukraine*; Wilson, *Ukraine Crisis*; Wynnyckyj, *Ukraine's Maidan, Russia's War*.
172. D'Anieri, *Ukraine and Russia*, 186.
173. "All Key Political Forces Use 'Jeans'" (Institute of Mass Media, 7 August 2012), https://imi.org.ua/monitorings/vsi-klyuchovi-politichni-sili-vikoristovuyut-djinsu-i28586.
174. Institute of Mass Media, "IMI: In September, 11% Of The Materials In The Press Are Political 'Jeans", (9 September 2012), https://imi.org.ua/monitorings/imi-u-veresni-11-materialiv-v-presi-tse-politichna-djinsa-i28581.
175. "Ukraine: Parliamentary Elections 28 October 2012.", 20.
176. Verstyuk, "Ukraine's Deep-Rooted Media Problem."
177. "OSCE/ODIHR Election Observation Mission Final Report," Office for Democratic Institutions and Human Rights 21–2.
178. Reid, *Borderland*; Kalb, *Imperial Gamble*; Menon, Rumer, and Chasman, *Conflict in Ukraine*; Wilson, *The Ukrainians*; Wynnyckyj, *Ukraine's Maidan, Russia's War*.
179. Toal, *Near Abroad,* 245, 249.
180. D'Anieri, *Ukraine and Russia*, 200; Wilson, *Ukraine Crisis*, 64; Charap and Colton, *Everyone Loses*, 2532.
181. Wilson, *Ukraine Crisis*, 64.
182. Gatskov and Gatskova, "What's Wrong with the Donbas?," 157.
183. Reid, *Borderland*, 253; Wilson, *The Ukrainians*, 345; D'Anieri, *Ukraine and Russia*, 208; Wynnyckyj, *Ukraine's Maidan, Russia's War*, 62; Plokhy, *The Gates of Europe*, 5891.
184. Wynnyckyj, *Ukraine's Maidan, Russia's War*, 69.
185. "Ukraine 2013 Public Opinion Poll Shows Dissastisfaction With Socio-Political Conditions" (International Foundation for Electoral Systems, 5 December 2013), https://www.ifes.org/news/ukraine-2013-public-opinion-poll-shows-dissastisfaction-socio-political-conditions.
186. Alberto Veira-Ramos and Evgenii Golovakha, "Empirical Evidence of

Persistent Institutional Duality in Ukraine," in *Ukraine in Transformation*, ed. Alberto Veira-Ramos, Tetiana Liubyva, and Evgenii Golovakha (Palgrave Macmillan, 2020), 44.
187. "World Press Freedom Index 2021: Ukraine" (Reporters without Borders, 2021), https://rsf.org/en/ukraine.
188. "Ukraine: Parliamentary Elections 28 October 2012," Office for Democratic Institutions and Human Rights.
189. Menon, Rumer, and Chasman, *Conflict in Ukraine*; Nikitina, "The Ukrainian Media Landscape."
190. "Pro-Yanukovich Ukrainian Businessman Buys Local Media Group."
191. "Individuals Using the Internet (% of Population)—Ukraine," International Telecommunication Union (ITU) World Telecommunication/ICT Indicators Database (The World Bank, 2018), https://data.worldbank.org/indicator/IT.NET.USER.ZS?locations=UA.
192. Nikitina, "The Ukrainian Media Landscape," 218; "Contemporary Media Use in Ukraine."
193. Nikitina, "The Ukrainian Media Landscape," 225.
194. "Ukraine: Parliamentary Elections 28 October 201" Office for Democratic Institutions and Human Rights; "Jeans Monitoring Report: November 2013" (Institute of Mass Media, 11 December 2013), https://imi.org.ua/monitorings/zvit-z-monitoringu-djinsi-listopad-2013-roku-i28529.
195. "Jeans Monitoring Report: October 2013" (Institute of Mass Media, 4 November 2013), https://imi.org.ua/monitorings/golovni-djinsovikijovtnya-simonenko-medvedchuk-katerinchuk-ta-kostusev-monitoringimi-i28535.
196. Veira-Ramos and Golovakha, "Empirical Evidence of Persistent Institutional Duality in Ukraine," 42.
197. Fesenko, "Ukraine"; Noginsky, "Ukraine"; Kalb, *Imperial Gamble*; Menon, Rumer, and Chasman, *Conflict in Ukraine*; Charap and Colton, *Everyone Loses*; Toal, *Near Abroad*; Wynnyckyj, *Ukraine's Maidan, Russia's War*.
198. Toal, *Near Abroad*, 212; Wilson, *Ukraine Crisis*, 66.
199. Wynnyckyj, *Ukraine's Maidan, Russia's War*, 74.
200. Kalb, *Imperial Gamble*, 141; Menon, Rumer, and Chasman, *Conflict in Ukraine*, 79; Wynnyckyj, *Ukraine's Maidan, Russia's War*, 108.
201. Wynnyckyj, *Ukraine's Maidan, Russia's War*, 103; Menon, Rumer, and Chasman, *Conflict in Ukraine*, 9; Wilson, *Ukraine Crisis*, 75.
202. Wynnyckyj, *Ukraine's Maidan, Russia's War*, 127.
203. Wilson, *Ukraine Crisis*; "Maidan-2013" (Ilko Kucheriv Democratic Initiatives Foundation and Kyiv International Institute of Sociology, 10 December 2013), https://www.kiis.com.ua/?lang= eng&cat=reports&id=216&page=1&y=2013.

204. Toal, *Near Abroad*, 252.
205. "Which Way Ukraine Should Go—Which Union Should Join?," Population Preferences For Two Weeks Before The Vilnius Summit (Kyiv International Institute of Sociology, 26 November 2013), https://www.kiis.com.ua/?lang=eng&cat=reports&id=204&page=2&y=2013.
206. "Which Way Ukraine Should Go—Which Union Should Join?."
207. Wilson, *Ukraine Crisis*, 74.
208. Olga Onuch, "Social Networks and Social Media in Ukrainian 'Euromaidan' Protests," *The Washington Post*, 2 January 2014, https://www.washingtonpost.com/news/monkey-cage/wp/2014/01/02/social-networks-and-social-media-in-ukrainian-euromaidan-protests-2/.
209. Onuch, "Social Networks and Social Media in Ukrainian 'Euromaidan' Protests".
210. Onuch, "Social Networks and Social Media in Ukrainian 'Euromaidan' Protests"; "Ukrainians' Thoughts on the Foreign Policy and Language Issue" (Kyiv International Institute of Sociology, 13 June 2013), https://www.kiis.com.ua/?lang=eng&cat=reports&id=175&page=4&y=2013.
211. Onuch, "Social Networks and Social Media in Ukrainian 'Euromaidan' Protests".
212. Wilson, *Ukraine Crisis*, 76; Menon, Rumer, and Chasman, *Conflict in Ukraine*, 9.
213. Noginsky, "Ukraine," 151–2; Freedman, *Ukraine and the Art of Strategy*, 66; Wynnyckyj, *Ukraine's Maidan, Russia's War*, 30; D'Anieri, *Ukraine and Russia*, 95.
214. Alyona Getmanchuk, "Tracing the Origins of the Ukraine Crisis: Should the EU Share the Blame?," *Europe's World*, Summer (2014): 78–82.
215. D'Anieri, *Ukraine and Russia*, 211; Tetyana Bohdanova, "Unexpected Revolution: The Role of Social Media in Ukraine's Euromaidan Uprising," *European View* 13 (2014): 135; Wynnyckyj, *Ukraine's Maidan, Russia's War*, 71; Nikitina, "The Ukrainian Media Landscape," 214–15; Kalb, *Imperial Gamble*, 141.
216. Kalb, *Imperial Gamble*, 141.
217. Reid, *Borderland*, 259.
218. Wynnyckyj, *Ukraine's Maidan, Russia's War*, 100; Kalb, *Imperial Gamble*, 141; Reid, *Borderland*, 260; Charap and Colton, *Everyone Loses*, 2588; D'Anieri, *Ukraine and Russia*, 213; Freedman, *Ukraine and the Art of Strategy*, 76; Plokhy, *The Gates of Europe*, 5905.
219. "Maidan-2013."
220. Wynnyckyj, *Ukraine's Maidan, Russia's War*, 107.
221. Wilson, *Ukraine Crisis*, 75.
222. Onuch, "Social Networks and Social Media in Ukrainian 'Euromaidan' Protests."

223. Kalb, *Imperial Gamble*, 143; Wynnyckyj, *Ukraine's Maidan, Russia's War*, 107.
224. Kalb, *Imperial Gamble*, 143; Charap and Colton, *Everyone Loses*, 2576; D'Anieri, *Ukraine and Russia*, 215; Wilson, *Ukraine Crisis*, 79.
225. D'Anieri, *Ukraine and Russia*, 184.
226. Kalb, *Imperial Gamble*, 144.
227. "Jeans Monitoring Report: November 2013."
228. "Euromaidan Participants Can Deliver Terrible Infections throughout Ukraine," *Obozrevatel*, 8 December 2013, https://news.obozrevatel.com/politics/81523-uchastniki-evromajdana-mogut-razvezti-po-vsej-ukraine-strashnyie-infektsii-ekspert.htm; "Maidanists End up in Hospitals with Mental Disorders, Pneumonia and Intoxication," *Obozrevatel*, 10 December 2013, https://news.obozrevatel.com/kiyany/life/15734-evromajdanovtsyi-popadayut-v-bolnitsyi-s-rasstrojstvami-psihiki-pnevmoniej-i-opyaneniem.htm; "The Fate of a Multimillion-Strong Country Cannot and Should Not Be Decided on the Maidans—Medvedchuk," *Obozrevatel*, 13 December 2013, https://news.obozrevatel.com/politics/61307-sudba-mnogomillionnoj-stranyi-ne-mozhet-i-ne-dolzhna-reshatsya-na-majdanah-medvedchuk.htm.
229. Lilia Ragutskaya, "Symonenko Urged to Replace Gay Ministers from Europe," *Obozrevatel*, 10 December 2013, https://news.obozrevatel.com/politics/27063-simonenko-prizval-postavit-na-mesto-ministrov-geev-iz-evropyi.htm.
230. Reporters without Borders and Institute of Mass Information. "Media Ownership Monitor: Ukraine".
231. Wilson, *The Ukrainians*, 348
232. Kalb, *Imperial Gamble*, 154; D'Anieri, *Ukraine and Russia*, 224.
233. Wilson, *Ukraine Crisis*, 146.
234. Wilson, *Ukraine Crisis*, 69.
235. Wilson, *The Ukrainians*, 353; D'Anieri, *Ukraine and Russia*, 214.
236. Menon, Rumer, and Chasman, *Conflict in Ukraine*, 9.
237. Sektor. "Українці! Нам потрібна така "європа"? Чи може краще відродити справжню Європу у себе вдома і збудувати сильну національну державу, котра буде вільною не лише від московських імперіалістів, але й від західних ліберастів?!" ("Ukrainians! Do we need such a 'Europe'? Could it be better to revive a real Europe at home and build a strong nation-state that would be free not only from the Moscow imperialists, but also from the Western Liberals?!"), *Facebook* (11 May 2014). https://www.facebook.com/photo.php?fbid=1425535021040528
238. Anton Shekhovtsov, "Look Far Right, and Look Right Again," *OpenDemocracy*, 11 July 2014, https://www.opendemocracy.net/en/

odr/look-far-right-and-look-right-again-avaz-batalion-neo-pagan-neo-nazi/.
239. Wynnyckyj, *Ukraine's Maidan, Russia's War*, 132.
240. Reid, *Borderland*; Wilson, *The Ukrainians*; Toal, *Near Abroad*; Wynnyckyj, *Ukraine's Maidan, Russia's War*; D'Anieri, *Ukraine and Russia*; Plokhy, *The Gates of Europe*.
241. Kalb, *Imperial Gamble*, 142.
242. D'Anieri, *Ukraine and Russia*, 223.
243. D'Anieri, *Ukraine and Russia*, 223; Wynnyckyj, *Ukraine's Maidan, Russia's War*, 112–13.
244. Wynnyckyj, *Ukraine's Maidan, Russia's War*, 110.
245. "Ukraine Crisis: Transcript of Leaked Nuland-Pyatt Call," *BBC*, 7 February 2014, https://www.bbc.com/news/world-europe-26079957.
246. Wynnyckyj, *Ukraine's Maidan, Russia's War*, 113.
247. Kalb, *Imperial Gamble*, 152.
248. Toal, *Near Abroad*, 44.
249. Simon Hegelich and Dietmar Janetzko, "Are Social Bots on Twitter Political Actors? Empirical Evidence from a Ukrainian Social Bot," in *Tenth International AAAI Conference on Web and Social Media* (2016): 579–82; Anastasia Karimov, "Kremlin Bloghouse," *Kommersant*, [13 February 2012, https://www.kommersant.ru/doc/1868022; Peter Tanchak, "The Invisible Front: Russia, Trolls, and the Information War against Ukraine," in *Revolution and War in Contemporary Ukraine*, ed. Olga Bertelsen (Columbia University Press, 2017), 253–82; Chris Elliott, "The Readers' Editor On... pro-Russia Trolling below the Lineon Ukraine Stories," *The Guardian*, 4 May 2014, https://www.theguardian.com/commentisfree/2014/may/04/pro-russia-trolls-ukraine-guardian-online; Max Seddon, "New Leaked Documents Show Russian Trolls Targeting Obama, Harry Potter Fans," *Buzzfeed News*, 3 June 2014.
250. Menon, Rumer, and Chasman, *Conflict in Ukraine*; Wynnyckyj, *Ukraine's Maidan, Russia's War*.
251. Reid, *Borderland*; Wilson, *Ukraine Crisis*; Menon, Rumer, and Chasman, *Conflict in Ukraine*; Freedman, *Ukraine and the Art of Strategy*; Wynnyckyj, *Ukraine's Maidan, Russia's War*; Plokhy, *The Gates of Europe*.

9. ALL HAIL FINLAND?

1. Nicholas Reece, "More than 4 Billion People Are Eligible to Vote in an Election in 2024. Is This Democracy's Biggest Test?," The Conversation, 14 January 2024, https://theconversation.com/more-than-4-billion-people-are-eligible-to-vote-in-an-election-in-2024-is-this-democracys-biggest-test-220837.

2. Paul M. Barrett, Cecely Richard-Carvajal, and Justin Hendrix, "Digital Risks to the 2024 Elections: Safeguarding Democracy in the Era of Disinformation," February 2024, New York University Center for Business and Human Rights, https://bhr.stern.nyu.edu/publication/digital-risks-to-the-2024-elections-safeguarding-democracy-in-the-era-of-disinformation/.
3. "Cooperation between the Authorities Ensures Secure Elections" (Finnish Transport and Communications Agency National Cyber Security Centre, 1 January 2024), https://www.kyberturvallisuuskeskus.fi/en/news/cooperation-between-authorities-ensures-secure-elections.
4. Panu Moilanen, Miriam Hautala, and Dominic Saari, "Disinformation Landscape in Finland," *EU Disinfo Lab*, May 2023, https://www.disinfo.eu/wp-content/uploads/2023/05/Finland_DisinfoFactsheet.pdf.
5. "Skills Matter: Additional Results from the Survey of Adult Skills," OECD Skills Studies (OECD, 2019), https://doi.org/10.1787/1f029d8f-en.
6. "Adults With Inadequate Literacy Skills" (Conference Board of Canada, 2012), https://www.conferenceboard.ca/hcp/adlt-lowlit-aspx.
7. Jonathan Rothwell, "Assessing the Economic Gains of Eradicating Illiteracy Nationally and Regionally in the United States" (Barbara Bush Foundation for Family Literacy, 8 September 2020), https://www.barbarabush.org/wp-content/uploads/2020/09/BBFoundation_GainsFromEradicatingIlliteracy_9_8.pdf.
8. Marin Lessenski, "Media Literacy Index 2021—Double Trouble: Resilience to Fake News at the Time of Covid-19 Infodemic" (Open Society Institute, March 2021), https://osis.bg/wp-content/uploads/2021/03/MediaLiteracyIndex2021_ENG.pdf; Marin Lessenski, "How It Started, How It Is Going: Media Literacy Index 2022" (Open Society Institute, 6 December 2022), https://osis.bg/wp-content/uploads/2022/10/HowItStarted_MediaLiteracyIndex2022_ENG_.pdf; Marin Lessenski, "Media Literacy Index 2023—Bye, Bye, Birdie": Meeting the Challenges of Disinformation" (Open Society Institute, 2023), https://osis.bg/wp-content/uploads/2023/06/MLI-report-in-English-22.06.pdf.
9. Jon Bateman and Dean Jackson, "Countering Disinformation Effectively: An Evidence-Based Policy Guide" (Carnegie Endowment for International Peace, 31 January 2024), https://carnegieendowment.org/research/2024/01/countering-disinformation-effectively-an-evidence-based-policy-guide?lang=en&center=global.
10. Moilanen, Hautala, and Saari, "Disinformation Landscape in Finland."
11. Brin and Charlton, "Canada."
12. Jenkins and Graves, "United States."
13. Reunanen, "Finland."

14. "What Are Finns Like?" *Visit Finland*, 2024, https://www.visitfinland.com/en/articles/what-are-finns-like/.
15. Varpu Rusila, "Re: Questions about Finland for a Book," 31 August 2023.
16. "Finns Prioritize Travel Frequency over International Travel Expenses, Survey Reveals," *Helsinki Times*, 11 October 2023, https://www.helsinkitimes.fi/themes/themes/travel/24302-finns-prioritize-travel-frequency-over-international-travel-expenses-survey-reveals.html.
17. Richard Wike et al., "Attitudes on an Interconnected World," 6 December 2023, https://www.pewresearch.org/global/2023/12/06/attitudes-on-an-interconnected-world/.
18. Sandy Dietrich and Erik Hernandez, "Language Use in the United States: 2019" (United States Census Bureau, August 2022), https://www.census.gov/content/dam/Census/library/publications/2022/acs/acs-50.pdf.
19. "Mother Tongue by Knowledge of Official Languages, Language Spoken Most Often at Home and Other Language(s) Spoken Regularly at Home: Canada, Provinces and Territories, Census Metropolitan Areas and Census Agglomerations with Parts" (Ottawa: Statistics Canada, 17 August 2022), https://www150.statcan.gc.ca/t1/tbl1/en/tv.action?pid=9810017101& pickMembers%5B0%5D=1.1&pickMembers%5B1%5D=2.1&pickMembers%5B2%5D=3.1&pickMembers%5B3%5D=4.1&pickMembers%5B4%5D=5.1.
20. Richard Wike et al., "Attitudes on an Interconnected World," 6 December 2023, https://www.pewresearch.org/global/2023/12/06/attitudes-on-an-interconnected-world/.
21. "Population, Total - Canada, Finland, Slovak Republic" (World Bank Group, n.d.), https://data.worldbank.org/indicator/SP.POP.TOTL?locations=CA-FI-SK.
22. "Finland," The World Factbook (United States Central Intelligence Agency, 8 July 2024), https://www.cia.gov/the-world-factbook/countries/finland/#people-and-society.
23. Jukka U. Palo et al., "Genetic Markers and Population History: Finland Revisited," *European Journal of Human Genetics* 17 (2009): 1336–46, https://doi.org/10.1038/ejhg.2009.53.
24. "Foreign-Born Population," (OECD, 2019), https://www.oecd.org/en/data/indicators/foreign-born-population.html?oecdcontrol-38c744bfa4-var1=CAN%7CFIN%7CSVK%7CUSA.
25. John Last, "Bitter Disappointment as Finland's Attempt to Reform Indigenous Law Fails—Again," *CBC News*, 28 February 2023, https://www.cbc.ca/news/world/finland-law-indigenous-1.6761845.
26. "Gini Index—Finland, Canada, United States," World Bank, Poverty and

Inequality Platform (World Bank Group, 2023), https://data.worldbank.org/indicator/SI.POV.GINI?locations=FI-CA-US.
27. Eric Jensen et al., "The Chance That Two People Chosen at Random Are of Different Race or Ethnicity Groups Has Increased Since 2010" (U.S. Census Bureau, 12 August 2021), https://www.census.gov/library/stories/2021/08/2020-united-states-population-more-racially-ethnically-diverse-than-2010.html.
28. Mike Schneider, "U.S. Census Changes How It Identifies People by Race and Ethnicity, Creates Middle Eastern Category for First Time," *PBS News*, 28 March 2024, https://www.pbs.org/newshour/politics/u-s-census-changes-how-it-identifies-people-by-race-and-ethnicity-creates-middle-eastern-and-north-african-category-for-first-time.
29. Philip Oltermann and Jon Henley, "France and Germany Urged to Rethink Reluctance to Gather Ethnicity Data," *The Guardian*, 16 June 2020, https://www.theguardian.com/world/2020/jun/16/france-and-germany-urged-to-rethink-reluctance-to-gather-ethnicity-data.
30. "Canada's Population Estimates: Strong Population Growth in 2023" (Ottawa: Statistics Canada, 27 March 2024), https://www150.statcan.gc.ca/n1/daily-quotidien/240327/dq240327c-eng.htm.
31. Donald J. Savoie, *Canada: Beyond Grudges, Grievances, and Disunity* (Montreal & Kingston, CA: McGill-Queen's University Press, 2023); "Confederational Fairness: As Premiers Meet, Which Provinces Say They Get More, or Less, out of Federation?" (Angus Reid Institute, 15 July 2024), https://angusreid.org/confederational-fairness-premiers-meeting/.
32. "Canada's Demographic Estimates for July 1, 2023: Record-High Population Growth since 1957" (Statistics Canada, 27 September 2023), https://www150.statcan.gc.ca/n1/daily-quotidien/230927/dq230927a-eng.htm; "The Canadian Census: A Rich Portrait of the Country's Religious and Ethnocultural Diversity" (Statistics Canada, 26 October 2022), https://www150.statcan.gc.ca/n1/daily-quotidien/221026/dq221026b-eng.htm.
33. "Profile of Interest: Ethnic or Cultural Origin," Special Interest Profile, 2021 Census of Population (Statistics Canada, 2021), https://www12.statcan.gc.ca/census-recensement/2021/dp-pd/sip/details/page.cfm?Lang=E&PoiId=2&Dguid=2021A000011124.
34. "Profile of Interest: Ethnic or Cultural Origin."
35. "Immigrants Make up the Largest Share of the Population in over 150 Years and Continue to Shape Who We Are as Canadians" (Ottawa: Statistics Canada, 26 October 2022), https://www150.statcan.gc.ca/n1/daily-quotidien/221026/dq221026a-eng.htm.
36. "Canada's Population Estimates: Strong Population Growth in 2023."
37. "Profile of Interest: Ethnic or Cultural Origin"; John Paul Tasker, "Emigration from Canada to the U.S. Hits a 10-Year High as Tens of

Thousands Head South," *CBC News*, 30 May 2024, https://www.cbc.ca/news/politics/canadians-moving-to-the-us-hits-10-year-high-1.7218479.
38. Frances A. Swyripa, "Ukrainian Canadians."
39. "Canada-Ukraine Relations" (Global Affairs Canada, 2022), https://www.international.gc.ca/country-pays/ukraine/relations.aspx?lang=eng.
40. Marie-Josée Hogue, "Public Inquiry into Foreign Interference in Federal Electoral Processes and Democratic Institutions" (Ottawa: Public Inquiry into Foreign Interference in Federal Electoral Processes and Democratic Institutions, 3 May 2024), https://foreigninterferencecommission.ca/fileadmin/user_upload/Foreign_Interference_Commission_-_Initial_Report__May_2024__-_Digital.pdf.
41. Essi Lehto, "Finland Passes Law to Block Migrants Crossing from Russia," *Reuters*, 12 July 2024, https://www.reuters.com/world/europe/finland-vote-turning-back-migrants-crossing-russia-2024-07-12.
42. Adrian Humphreys, "Could Canada Really Become the 51st U.S. State? How Trump's Joke Could Become Reality," *National Post*, 12 December 2024, https://nationalpost.com/news/could-one-way-to-make-america-great-again-be-a-transfusion-of-canadians.
43. "Individuals Using the Internet (% of Population)—Canada, Finland, United States" (World Bank Group, n.d.), https://data.worldbank.org/indicator/IT.NET.USER.ZS?locations=CA-FI-SK-US&skipRedirection=true&view=map.
44. Esa Reunanen, "Finland," Digital News Report 2024 (Reuters Institute, 17 June 2024), https://reutersinstitute.politics.ox.ac.uk/digital-news-report/2024/finland; Colette Brin and Sébastien Charlton, "Canada," Digital News Report 2024 (Reuters Institute, 17 June 2024), https://reutersinstitute.politics.ox.ac.uk/digital-news-report/2024/canada; Joy Jenkins and Lucas Graves, "United States," Digital News Report 2024 (Reuters Institute, 17 June 2024), https://reutersinstitute.politics.ox.ac.uk/digital-news-report/2024/united-states.
45. Esa Reunanen, "Finland," Digital News Report 2024; Emily Tomasik, "More Americans Want the Journalists They Get News from to Share Their Politics than Any Other Personal Trait" (Pew Research Center, 16 May 2024), https://www.pewresearch.org/short-reads/2024/05/16/more-americans-want-the-journalists-they-get-news-from-to-share-their-politics-than-any-other-personal-trait/.
46. Reunanen, "Finland."
47. "2024 World Press Freedom Index—Journalism under Political Pressure" (Reporters Without Borders, 2024), https://rsf.org/en/2024-world-press-freedom-index-journalism-under-political-pressure?year=2024&data_type=general.
48. Brin and Charlton, "Canada."

49. Brin and Charlton; Colette Brin, "Canada," 2021 Digital News Report (Reporters without Borders and Institute of Mass Information, 23 June 2021), https://reutersinstitute.politics.ox.ac.uk/digital-news-report/2021/canada.
50. "Snapshot 2022 Canada's Newspapers" (News Media Canada, 2022), https://nmc-mic.ca/wp-content/uploads/2023/02/Snapshot-2022-FACT-SHEET_Final-02.02.2023.pdf.
51. Joy Jenkins and Lucas Graves, "United States," Digital News Report 2023 (Reuters Institute, 14 June 2023), https://reutersinstitute.politics.ox.ac.uk/digital-news-report/2023/united-states; David Folkenflik, "NPR Quits Twitter after Being Falsely Labeled as 'State-Affiliated Media,'" *NPR*, 12 April 2023, https://www.npr.org/2023/04/12/1169269161/npr-leaves-twitter-government-funded-media-label.
52. Jenkins and Graves, "United States."
53. Megan Brenan, "Media Confidence in U.S. Matches 2016 Record Low" (Gallup, 19 October 2023), https://news.gallup.com/poll/512861/media-confidence-matches-2016-record-low.aspx.
54. John F. Helliwell et al., "Happiness of the Younger, the Older, and Those in Between," World Happiness Report, 20 March 2024, http://doi.org/10.18724/whr-f1p2-qj33.
55. "OECD Better Life Index" (OECD, 2023), https://www.oecdbetterlifeindex.org/#/11111111111.
56. Kiley Hurst, "About 1 in 4 U.S. Teachers Say Their School Went into a Gun-Related Lockdown in the Last School Year" (Pew Research Center, 11 April 2024), https://www.pewresearch.org/short-reads/2024/04/11/about-1-in-4-us-teachers-say-their-school-went-into-a-gun-related-lockdown-in-the-last-school-year/.
57. "Corruption Perceptions Index" (Transparency International, 2023), https://www.transparency.org/en/cpi/2023.
58. "OECD Survey on Drivers of Trust in Public Institutions—2024 Results: Building Trust in a Complex Policy Environment" (OECD, 2024), https://doi.org/10.1787/9a20554b-en.
59. "Public Trust in Government: 1958-2024" (Pew Research Center, 24 June 2024), https://www.pewresearch.org/politics/2024/06/24/public-trust-in-government-1958-2024.
60. Jenn Hatfield, "More than 80% of Americans Believe Elected Officials Don't Care What People like Them Think" (Pew Research Center, 30 April 2024), https://www.pewresearch.org/short-reads/2024/04/30/more-than-80-of-americans-believe-elected-officials-dont-care-what-people-like-them-think/; Janell Fetterolf and Sofia Hernandez Ramones, "72% of Americans Say the U.S. Used to Be a Good Example of Democracy, but Isn't Anymore" (Pew Research Center, 10 July

2024), https://www.pewresearch.org/short-reads/2024/07/10/72-of-americans-say-the-us-used-to-be-a-good-example-of-democracy-but-isnt-anymore/; "Americans' Dismal Views of the Nation's Politics" (Pew Research Center, 19 September 2023), https://www.pewresearch.org/politics/2023/09/19/americans-dismal-views-of-the-nations-politics/.
61. Hays, "Oklahoma Governor Vetoes State PBS Funding, Accuses Network of Using 'Tax Dollars to Indoctrinate Kids.'"
62. Eric Merkley, "Polarization Eh? Ideological Divergence and Partisan Sorting in the Canadian Mass Public," *Public Opinion Quarterly* 86, no. 4 (31 January 2023): 932–43; Justin Ling, "Far and Widening: The Rise of Polarization in Canada" (Public Policy Forum, August 2023), https://ppforum.ca/wp-content/uploads/2023/08/TheRiseOfPolarizationInCanada-PPF-AUG2023-EN2.pdf.
63. "As Newsrooms Grapple with Shifting Media Landscape, Most Canadians Oppose Government Intervention" (Angus Reid Institute, 13 July 2023), https://angusreid.org/canada-media-consolidation-torstar-postmedia-government-funding-cbc/.

10. THE FUTURE OF THE INFORMATION ANIMAL

1. Matt Egan, "AI Could Pose 'Extinction-Level' Threat to Humans and the US Must Intervene, State Dept.-Commissioned Report Warns," *CNN Business*, 12 March 2024, https://www.cnn.com/2024/03/12/business/artificial-intelligence-ai-report-extinction/index.html.
2. Michael Lawrence, Scott Janzwood, and Thomas Homer-Dixon, "What Is a Global Polycrisis? And How Is It Different from a Systemic Risk?" (Cascade Institute, September 2022), https://cascadeinstitute.org/wp-content/uploads/2022/04/What-is-a-global-polycrisis-v2.pdf.

INDEX

Advertising, 1, 12, 189, 193, 197, 199, 207
Alphabet, 3, 47, 60, 61, 97
   Greek, 71, 73, 90
   Quôc nhu, 12, 148
   Ukraine, 177
Apocalypse, 112
Aristocracy, 79, 95, 108, 117, 121
Aristocrat, 104, 108, 129
Aristophanes, 75, 80, 81, 88, 91
Artificial intelligence, 3, 15, 18, 48, 52, 60, 63, 69
   Finnish election, 209
   Research and artificial intelligence, 30, 227, 230
Associated Press, 11, 124

Bible, 98-100, 105, 106, 135, 137, 179
Biome, 37, 107
   Anglo, 107
   European, 104, 212
   Hellenic, 88–89
Books, 40, 58, 135, 139, 142
   As propaganda, 11, 139, 156
   Book of Common Prayer, 101, 105, 109, 113
   Complaints about, 10
   Increase in volume of books in:
      England, 96-97, 113
      United States, 124, 130, 140
      Vietnam, 150
Broadcast, 195, 220, 221, 223
   Control over broadcast, 187, 188, 189, 193, 195,
   News anchoring, 163
   Of strikes in Ukraine, 183
   Of United States Congressional hearings, 161
   Public broadcast, 220, 221, 223, 224
   Radio in Vietnam, 11, 157-158

Calvin, John, 98, 100, 102
Calvinist, 102
Catholic:
   England, 47, 98, 100–117

INDEX

United States, 134, 163
Vietnam, 147, 156, 160, 163, 165
Cavalier, 110, 121, 129
Caxton, William, 95, 97
CBC, 220, 221, 224
Censor-ship, 26, 58
   United States, 11, 130, 139, 141
   Vietnam, 150, 152, 154, 156
Computer, 20, 23, 41, 64
Computer science, 27, 40, 42
Communist:
   China, 160
   South Korea, 162
   Ukraine, 182, 183, 186, 199, 202
   United States, 160–161
      Bay of Pigs in Cuba, 169
   Vietnam, 149, 151–153, 155–157, 164, 165–168, 170, 171, 172
Confucian, 146, 147, 149, 168
Control of:
   Flow of information, 7, 110, 116, 142
   Information ecosystem, 12, 48, 63, 64, 65, 111, 117, 154, 167, 170, 171, 182, 183, 185, 198, 199, 206, 230, 233
   Intellectual property, 124
   Mail, 11, 141–142
   Media, 156, 176, 187, 189, 193, 195
   Petitions, 11, 130
   Print, 10, 47, 97–98, 150

Radio, 11, 158
Spartan information ecosystem, 74–75, 77, 91
Convention-s, 125, 131, 163
Corruption, 150, 165, 185, 191, 194, 197, 198, 201, 222
Courantos, 10, 103, 111
Covenanter, 112
Culture, 44, 75, 89, 91, 92, 94, 125, 128, 136, 177, 179, 186, 205, 213, 218
Cuneiform, 54–55, 61, 64, 91

Darwin, Charles, 7, 66
Dickens, Charles, 119, 120–121, 122, 123, 124, 125, 126, 129, 130, 141, 142
Debates, 102, 112, 119, 125, 143
Democracy, 26, 65, 132, 225, 230, 231, 233
   Bourgeois democracy, 150
   Capitalist democracy, 132
   In Athens, 9, 57, 72, 79, 80, 81, 83, 84, 85, 88, 89
   In England, 48
   In relation to the information environment, 4, 34, 231
   In Ukraine, 193, 207
   In the United States, 162, 222
   In Vietnam, 152, 165
Digital, 6, 51, 53, 64, 69, 124, 171, 199, 202, 220, 236
Douglass, Frederick, 126, 127
Drone, 201

Economy, 4, 13, 57, 65, 68, 95,

INDEX

99, 115, 128, 162, 198, 232, 233
Business model, 115, 138, 207, 230, 231
Commerce, 96, 126
Debt, 155, 188, 193
Economic interests/ties, 91, 97, 129, 211, 215, 217, 233
  Athens, 65, 72, 81, 84
  England, 107, 115
  Sparta, 77
  Ukraine, 176, 185, 188, 191, 193, 194, 197, 200
  United States, 120, 126, 129, 134, 136
  Vietnam–US Friendship Association, 159
  Vietnam, 167, 172
Funding, 223, 224, 231
  For research, 22, 32, 227, 228
  In Athens:
    Citizen fundraising, 83
    Tributes, 84
  In England, parliament's function, 110, 111
  In United States, 119, 135, 137,
  In Vietnam, 154, 164,
  In Ukraine, 184, 188,
Labour, 76, 83, 97, 107, 125, 135, 136, 137, 141, 165, 180
Profiteers, 66, 231, 237
  Media including newspapers, 58, 119, 142, 227
  Sophists, 89
  Printers, 103, 142
  Innovators, 60, 229, 230
  Revenue, 103, 110, 207, 220
  Tax, 80, 111, 128–129, 155, 201
  Trade, 10, 72, 76, 77, 81, 84, 88, 89, 91, 97, 104, 105, 106, 107, 108, 112, 115, 125, 131, 141, 177, 185, 198
Editors of news, 128, 134, 140, 142, 201
  Interference with, 189, 201
  Relationship between editor and audience, 127, 138
  Violence against, 128
Education, 4, 13, 54, 65, 67, 68, 211, 233
  Area of research, 21
  In England, 10, 94, 99, 105, 106 115
  In Finland, 210, 221
  In Sparta, 75
  In Vietnam, 11, 12, 146, 147, 148, 149, 151, 154, 163, 166-167, 172
  In Ukraine, 201
    University education rates, 193
  In United States, 120, 121, 122, 124, 125, 126, 136
  School, 55, 105–106, 122, 127, 148, 151, 154, 165, 166, 169, 182, 184, 189, 213, 222
Email, 8, 201, 213

INDEX

Ethnicity, 74, 181, 182, 215, 216
Exile, 80, 100, 102, 149, 184
Exiling, 11, 65, 116

Film, 52, 159, 184, 192, 195, 196
   Movie, 58, 154, 192, 194, 196
Flow, of information, 7, 26, 40, 47, 53, 63, 101, 104, 107, 108, 110, 111, 130, 142, 149, 170, 171, 218, 235
   Disruption to, 168
   in letters, 96
   in ideas, 98
Free speech, 130, 136, 231

Geography, 18, 68, 88, 91, 218, 223
Godly, 10, 11, 93, 100, 102-107, 109, 110, 112, 113, 117, 120
Gutenberg, Johann, 61, 95

Hate Speech, 27, 209
Hieroglyphs, 61
Herodotus, 72, 81, 82, 91
Hồ Chí Minh, 11, 65, 154, 155, 156, 157, 158–159, 160, 164, 166, 167, 172
   Nguyễn Sinh Cung, 149
   Nguyễn Ái Quốc, 149, 150, 152, 154
Honour, 72, 73, 79, 85, 86, 87, 128, 129, 130, 132, 145, 203
   Dishonour, 76
Humboldt, Alexander, 7, 23, 24, 36

Immigration, 104, 217

Imperial Free City, 95, 99, 100
Information Competition, 2, 3, 7, 8, 14, 31, 32, 36, 66, 235
   In England, 10, 48, 99, 103, 117
   In Greece, 9, 79, 84, 85
   In the United States, 11, 119, 130, 131, 135, 137,
   In Ukraine, 13, 191, 192, 193, 204,
   In Vietnam, 12, 172-173
Information Flood, 7, 8, 236
   In Athens, 83, 88
   In England, 11, 97, 113
   In the United States, 130, 133, 137, 141, 142
   In Vietnam, 150, 155, 171
Information Pollution, 8, 9, 37, 88, 161, 189, 197, 202, 206, 236
   Disinformation, 2, 4, 5, 6, 14, 15, 27, 29, 30, 32, 35, 37, 47, 48, 60, 207, 209, 210, 211, 218, 219, 222, 227, 231
   Jeansa, 12, 189, 193, 197, 199, 202
   Rumour, 9, 10, 47, 87, 88, 110, 112, 114, 124, 139, 183, 202
Internet, 4, 12, 21, 64, 123, 199, 201, 206, 219, 220, 221,

Journal, 123, 136, 139, 140, 142, 152, 179

Language, 47, 53, 55, 60, 62, 63, 216, 219, 226, 236

INDEX

English language, 94, 115, 212, 214
Finnish language, 212, 213
Foreign language speaking, 214
Language laws and reforms in Ukraine, 190, 192, 193, 197
Language Skills, 54, 55, 212
Language use in Ukraine, 176, 181–183, 184–185, 187, 188, 196, 201, 205
Russian language, 182, 183, 184–185, 188, 190, 195, 197
Shared language, 20, 88
Surzhyk, 182,
Ukrainian language, 177, 178, 179
Vernacular, 98, 99, 100, 179
Vietnamese language, 154
Lecture, 125, 126, 164
Letters, 62, 116, 133, 138, 159–160
   Censorship of, 111
   Complaints about, 10
   Creating networks, 61, 116
   Fabricated letters, 114
   Increase in volume, 96–97
Library, 57, 159
   Libraries, 126, 167
Literacy rates, 211, 233
   In Athens, 80
   In Canada, 210
   In England, 48, 105, 106
      Growing literacy rates, 112, 115, 117
   In Finland, 210
   In Ukraine, 184
   In United States, 11, 122, 210
   In Vietnam, 12, 146
   Literacy for political mobilization, 166–167, 172
Luther, Martin, 98, 99, 100
Lutheran, 102, 215

Magazine, 162
Manifest Destiny, 132, 162, 179, 186
McLuhan, Marshall, 61
Media literacy, 14, 210, 211
Music, 138, 184, 200

Network, 62, 82, 86, 96, 97, 104, 107, 112, 152, 169, 172, 201
Newspapers:
   In Canada, 221
   In England, 10, 103,
   In Ukraine, 187, 194
      In Russian, 195
      Political advertising, 197
   In the United States, 11, 124–125, 136, 142, 170
      Attacks on, 135, 141
      Atrocity stories, 139–140
      Circulation, 129, 137–138, 163
      Impact of cheaper printing costs, 123–124, 40
      Impact of postage rates, 63, 123, 140
   Liberator, 127, 128

INDEX

In Vietnam, 150, 153, 154, 155, 160
   Censorship of, 154, 156
   Circulation, 150
News media, 11, 21, 124, 125, 137, 161, 170, 189, 199, 206–207, 210, 213, 220, 221, 223, 230–231, 233
   News outlet, 124, 170, 202, 221
Novel, 96, 129, 132, 133, 175

Organisation for Economic Development, 210, 221
Oligarchy, 83, 84, 85
   Oligarch-ic, -ies, 12, 74, 84–85, 86, 185, 186, 187, 188, 189, 190, 193, 195, 198, 199, 202, 204
Online, 2, 58, 197, 199, 202, 206, 213
Opening, of information ecosystems, 9, 12, 65, 146, 148, 165, 176, 183
Oral, 6, 61, 73, 79, 82

Painting, 56, 61, 82, 104
Pamphlet, 57, 99, 102, 102-103, 104, 112, 113, 114, 125, 150, 151, 155
Paper, 10, 47, 52, 57, 60, 61, 81, 94, 96, 97, 103, 115, 123
Papyrus, 72, 81
Pericles, 80, 82, 83, 88, 89
   Periclean, 57, 83
Periodical, 63, 123, 129, 136, 150, 184

Petition, 10, 11, 104-105, 108, 113, 117, 130-131, 149
Play, 9, 57, 72, 75, 81, 82, 88, 89, 90, 103, 112, 149
Plato, 9, 46, 88, 90
Poetry, 75, 90, 110, 123
Poem, 73, 179
Population:
   In Athens, 87
   In Canada, 216
      Finns in Canada, 21
      Ukrainians in Canada, 218
   In England:
      Impact of Black Plague, 94–95
      Growth, 105
      Size, 100
   In Finland, 215
   In Ukraine:
      Impact of Second World War, 181
      Jewish, 180
      Tatars, 184
   In the United States:
      Canadians in the United States, 217
      Growth, 120
      African Americans, 121
      Size, 215-216
   In Vietnam:
      French settlers, 147
      Kinh, 147
Population ecology, 36
Postal service, 10, 11, 62, 94, 96, 115, 154
Printing, 9, 10, 12, 47, 53, 57, 60,

INDEX

61, 95–97, 99, 113, 123, 124, 126, 136, 137, 140, 171, 236
Proselytise, 66, 85, 89, 99, 117, 142, 152, 152, 155, 237
Protest:
  In England, 106, 112, 117, 206
  In Russia, 195
  In Ukraine: 183, 196–197, 198
    Maidan Square, 11, 200–203
    Orange Revolution, 191
    Over making Russian an official language, 197
    Ukraine without Kuchma, 188
  In Vietnam: 151, 153, 159,
    Suicides, 159, 170
Protestant:
  In England: 10, 98, 99–100, 101–102, 104, 105, 106, 107, 110, 111, 112, 116, 166
  In the United States, 120, 121, 127
Pulpit, 99, 110, 132
Puritan, 102, 107, 121
Pym, John, 111, 112, 113, 115, 117

Radio, 11, 60, 158, 160, 163, 171, 172, 183, 187, 193, 199, 220
Religion, 99, 101, 103, 104, 109, 111, 115, 120, 150, 173, 177, 215, 216
Roads (as a means for moving information),
  In Athens, 9, 62

  In United States, the South, 125–126

Social media, 2, 3, 12, 13, 21, 26, 30, 48, 52, 57, 58, 60, 103, 201, 202, 206, 207, 211, 213, 220, 227, 233
  Facebook, 201, 202, 220
  Twitter/X, 195, 212
  VKontakte, 202
  YouTube, 220
Socrates, 9, 88, 90
Sophist, 80-81, 89
Speeches:
  American political speeches, 125
  Gag Rule, 130
  Lincoln, Abraham, "House Divided", 140
  Seward, William, "The Irrepressible Conflict", 140
  Blinken, Antony J, 17
  English Parliamentarians, 112
  Pericles' Funeral Oration, 88
  Thucydides, 90
  Vietnamese Revolutionary Youth Association, 152
  Putin, Vladimir V, 193
Strike, 151, 153, 183, 189, 197
Sumerian, 54
Sumner, Charles, 123, 134, 142

Telegraph, 11, 61, 65, 123, 140, 150
Telephone, 60, 221
  Mobile, 53, 62, 193, 221

INDEX

Cell, 13, 191, 193, 206
Television, 51, 163, 170, 171, 172, 182, 183, 184, 186-187, 193, 195, 196, 197, 199, 201, 213
TV, 163, 184, 193
Thucydides, 75, 78, 80, 82, 87, 90, 91
Troy, 73, 96
Trưng sisters, 145, 146, 149, 151, 153, 156, 173
Truth, 11, 42–45, 130, 170
Tyranny, 79, 80
Tyrant, 86, 93

Water (travel), 48, 65, 104, 107, 123
Boat, 9, 123
Canal, 10, 11, 65, 123, 126, 148
Naval, 72, 78, 186, 204
Steam, 130
Website, 197, 201, 213
Wilson, Edward Osborne, 22
Writing, 9, 10, 61, 72, 73, 81, 82, 90, 96, 106, 116, 146, 148

Yle, 220, 221